LAURAGAIS

STEEPED IN HISTORY, SOAKED IN BLOOD

LAURAGAIS

STEEPED IN HISTORY, SOAKED IN BLOOD

COLIN DUNCAN TAYLOR

Matador
9 Priory Business Park,
Wistow Road, Kibworth Beauchamp,
Leicestershire. LE8 0RX
Tel: 0116 279 2299
Email: books@troubador.co.uk
Web: www.troubador.co.uk/matador
Twitter: @matadorbooks

ISBN 978 1789015 836

British Library Cataloguing in Publication Data.
A catalogue record for this book is available from the British Library.

Printed by Printed and bound in Great Britain by 4edge Limited
Typeset in 11pt Adobe Garamond Pro by Troubador Publishing Ltd, Leicester, UK

Matador is an imprint of Troubador Publishing Ltd

I dedicate this book to the memory of Lucette Colombié and Claude Combes, both of whom helped me enormously with my research, both of whom sadly passed away while I was in the midst of writing.

Contents

IV. A Hundred Years of Misery

V. In Search of *Pastel*

VI. A Question of Religion

VII. From the Bottom of a Lake

VIII. The English Cemetery

IX. A Deadly Occupation

INTRODUCING THE LAURAGAIS

To find the Lauragais, head for south-west France. Pronounced *'lo-ra-gay',* it lies in the middle of the Midi, at the heart of Occitania, astride the ancient route from Carcassonne to Toulouse. Perhaps these words make the Lauragais sound important, but they merely describe its geography. Today, the Lauragais has no particular economic or strategic significance. Industrialisation and many other aspects of modern life seem to have passed it by. Most travellers do the same, including the vast majority of the two million who squeeze inside the medieval walls of Carcassonne every year and the five million who stroll through the streets of Toulouse. Lost in the middle between these two giants of tourism, the Lauragais attracts only a few per cent of such overwhelming numbers.

So why write a book about an area which so few take the time to explore? More importantly, why read one? The answer is this: if you scrape below the surface of the Lauragais you will discover a land steeped in history and soaked in blood, a place where century after century the people have suffered and sometimes prospered, been told what faith to follow or what language to speak. For over two thousand years, the Lauragais and its inhabitants were often at the centre of movements and events – commercial, cultural, military, political and religious. In times gone by, the Lauragais rarely escaped the attentions of the great and the good, or the ambitious and the avaricious. Its geographic position and fertile soil made it too important to ignore.

In the Lauragais, the reminders of these vibrant and often violent times have not been consigned to the museums, the history books and the gift shops. This is a land where the past is a part of everyday life. You can stumble across it during a country stroll, hear it spoken during a sortie to an ancient market, pull it over your head in the shape of a *pastel*-dyed garment, or drink it down with a glass of the world's oldest sparkling wine. And then there are the people who have shaped this land, the living and the dead, families that have lived in the same house or village for hundreds of years. In a setting like this, the concept of folk memory becomes both credible and comprehensible.

I have been exploring and living in the Lauragais for twenty years, gradually discovering its past and absorbing its present, and most importantly making friends. One day I called in on one of them, and quite by accident what should have been an innocuous social visit transported me back in time by several centuries. My friend showed me the deepest parts of his home, and what I saw prompted me to start writing this book, the story of an extraordinary land and its people.

At the outset I made an important discovery: there is nothing like trying to write about a subject to realise how little you truly know about it. So I resumed my travels in and around the Lauragais, and naturally I asked other friends to help me tell its story, even if at times this made the experience an intoxicating time-trip back and forth across the ages. *Where* I was at any particular moment was rarely in doubt; it was the *when* that was sometimes problematic. On other occasions I had the sense I was exploring places no one had visited for centuries, and this solitude reminded me that the Lauragais provides the perfect antidote to its more popular and crowded neighbours.

For long periods during its early history the Lauragais found itself in frontier land as empires and kingdoms struggled for supremacy: the Romans, the Visigoths, the Franks and the Moors; then the counts of Toulouse and the kings of Aragon, England and France; and it was the setting for some of the last military action to take place during Napoleon's first reign as emperor.

The Lauragais was also plagued by religious conflict. In the thirteenth century it was ravaged by armies from the north during the Albigensian Crusade and its population terrorised by the Inquisition. In the sixteenth century it tore itself apart for forty years during the religious wars between Catholics and Protestants.

More peacefully, the Lauragais lies on a natural axis of communication. From the gates of Toulouse, a wide corridor of flat land arcs its way southwards and eastwards, cutting the Lauragais neatly in two before continuing its journey to Carcassonne and then onwards to the Mediterranean. As well as armies on the march, this route has been used by merchants and other travellers for at least three thousand years. Among the earliest were the Phoenicians, transporting Cornish tin via Bordeaux to the Mediterranean. A century before the birth of Christ, the Romans built a road through here, the Via Aquitania, to connect Narbonne, Toulouse and Bordeaux. A thousand years later, the first pilgrims trudged through the Lauragais on their way to Saint-Jacques de Compostelle. Since then, each successive form of transport has used this same axis. Today, the Roman road, the Canal du Midi, the railway and the *autoroute* keep one another close company all the way through the Lauragais.

Agriculture has long dominated the landscape. The Lauragais has been a land of cereal production since Roman times, and for centuries the countryside was dotted with windmills grinding the grain into flour. In 1355 the Black Prince's men set fire to twenty of them in one small town alone. A century later this same rich earth nourished a new crop: *pastel*, or woad, the source of the blue dye that was exported all over Europe and brought fame and fortune to Toulouse.

The flat central corridor of the Lauragais is flanked by rolling countryside, and both the hills and the plains are today planted with a range of crops that has diversified to include wheat and barley, soya beans and sorghum, oilseed rape and maize, and in summer the countryside is ablaze with sunflowers. Dotted among these fields are patches of woodland, the last remnants of the vast oak forests that once covered much of the Lauragais.

Towards the east, the land rises abruptly to become the Montagne Noire. During times of religious troubles, this mountain was a refuge for the persecuted. At others, it served as a hideout for fearsome brigands who plundered the Lauragais, and a secret base for the Resistance during the second world war.

To the south lie mightier mountains. If you find yourself in the southern part of the Lauragais on a clear day, the Pyrenees seem so close you could almost reach out and touch them.

Amid these rural landscapes stand the timeless buildings, the physical reminders of a magnificent history: walled towns and villages, forts, castles, palatial mansions, churches, abbeys, monasteries, and windmills shorn of their sails.

The first written record of the name 'Lauragais' dates from the twelfth century and the word probably derives from what was once its main town – the fortified village of Laurac. In the fourteenth century the Lauragais became a diocese, then a county, and at the start of the sixteenth century a young Catherine de Medici – not yet Queen of France – inherited the title Countess of the Lauragais from her mother. During the Revolution, the administrative map of France was torn up. The Lauragais was dismembered and its parts incorporated into four newly-created departments: Ariège, Aude, Haute-Garonne and the Tarn. But the old name was never forgotten by its inhabitants, and in the 1920s many communes added 'Lauragais' to their names.

Although its geographic limits have fluctuated over the centuries, the Lauragais has always lain within an area bounded by Castres to the north, Carcassonne to the east, Pamiers to the south, and Toulouse to the west. Today the Lauragais is home to around 175,000 people living in 2,200 square kilometres, making it comparable in size and population to Herefordshire in England.

On the *autoroute*, a journey through the heart of the Lauragais will take you three-quarters of an hour, but all you will see are tantalising glimpses of gorgeous countryside and distant signs of human habitation. This book will take you on a more leisurely trip through time in a land that is endearingly modest about its illustrious past. But this is not a history book, even if it does follow a path that is broadly chronological. Instead, it is a tale of exploration, the discovery of people, places and events in the present as well as the past.

Knowledge may be power, but it can also be a source of pleasure. Without knowledge, if you visit a ruined château all you will see is a pile of old stones, a pleasant stroll through a field of sunflowers will reveal nothing more than a mass of bright petals, and a cruise along a shady canal on a hot day will cause the eyes to close and the ears to fill with the song of the cicadas. But if you know the story of those who built or lived in the château, or those who reside there now, or the battle that took place in the bright yellow field, or the harsh lives of the men and women who dug the canal, these reminders of the past take on a new potency. They certainly did for me one beautiful spring morning when I called in on a friend from the tennis club.

Prologue

'If you are interested in history,' says Jean-Pierre, 'you should see my *cave*.'

I shuffle in my seat and consider the words of my host: is he offering to show me his basement, or is he referring to the hiding place above or below ground where he keeps his wine? Either way, what could be so interesting about his cellar? Monsieur Bonnet is the *président*, or chairman, of Puylaurens tennis club. Perhaps he wants to show me a redundant racket press from the age of wooden frames and catgut strings, or a tube of deflated tennis balls that were once white, or even a signed poster of Henri Leconte. I have always been fascinated by history, but even my enthusiasm has its limits.

I hear the scrape of a chair; Jean-Pierre rises to his feet.

'Come on! I'll show you!'

He trots downstairs in his old tennis shoes and I follow him out of politeness. He leads me into an empty room on the ground floor and vanishes into the shadows at the far end. I cross the room and peer through an open doorway. A rickety staircase descends towards a blank wall, makes a quarter turn and disappears into the gloom.

A voice rises from below. 'Be careful near the bottom. There's a tread missing.'

I place one hand against the crumbling mortar of the wall for moral support and take the first step. A handrail would be reassuring.

After a couple of shaky moves, I pause and strain my eyes. Where is the missing tread? From somewhere beyond my field of vision a low-wattage bulb diffuses an eerie glow, but all I can see below me is a large rectangular object, ghostly pale in the half-light.

'Don't forget the missing step!'

My fingers clutch at the wall and I look down at my feet. Now I see it, the treacherous black hole of the missing tread. I hop over it safely and jump down onto an earth floor. My eyes adjust and I glance around me expectantly.

The cellar is empty apart from the pale rectangle which I now see is a refrigerator. Its door hangs open and dusty bottles of wine lie forgotten on the wire shelves. Has he brought me down here for this?

'There's nothing here apart from your old fridge!'

'At first sight, perhaps not, but we have stepped back in time to the Middle Ages.'

I look around me unconvinced.

'What you see of my house above ground is mainly seventeenth century, but this part is much older. It was designed to withstand a siege.'

I try to guess how an empty room with a beaten earth floor and a defunct refrigerator would help anyone resist a besieging army. The wine wouldn't last long, and thirsty men soon surrender. No, Jean-Pierre's cellar is more like a dungeon than a place of refuge.

'They would never run out of water.' He points towards a hatchway cut into the side of a squat stone construction leaning against the south wall. 'Look in there!'

He hands me a torch, and I pop my head through the opening. I shine the lamp down a cylindrical stone-lined shaft and see its reflection a long way below me. How can there be water up here? Puylaurens is perched on a hilltop at 350 metres above sea level, or 1,100 feet if you prefer, and the land drops away in all directions.

I straighten up and nearly bang my head on a rusty iron pulley. I examine a long length of chain hanging beside me. 'It must be a very deep well.'

'Not really. The water table is close to the surface in Puylaurens and there are dozens of houses with wells. It's ten metres to the bottom of this one, and it always holds a good three metres of water, even in summer. Now, let me show you the grain silo.'

He draws my attention to a circular patch of floor where the earth is a slightly different shade of brown.

'That's the silo?'

'It was, but it's been filled in for safety. You can still see the outline though.'

I scrape at the earth with my heel. Thanks to a more striking example I have seen nearby, I can easily picture what was once hollowed out in the floor of my friend's cellar. Down the road on the western edge of town, the moats of Puylaurens used to widen into a lake where the washerwomen did their laundry. Today, the area has been transformed into a dusty car park and the cliff on the east side has been cut back flush with the ramparts which rise above it. By chance, this demolition has chopped vertically through the centre of a silo. At first sight you may mistake it for a natural cavity in the rock, but on closer inspection you can make out the profile of a carefully shaped vessel with a flat bottom and half a stone stopper. Before it was sliced in two, the stopper hermetically sealed the silo, and as long as it remained unopened, the grain could be stored for several years. In an idle moment, I once calculated that the silo in the car park would have held one-and-a-half cubic metres of grain, enough to make 4,000 baguettes. There were numerous other silos in Puylaurens, and the town had enough bread and water to withstand a very long siege.

Jean-Pierre coughs and points out another feature of his subterranean domain. An archway in his north wall has been sealed up, fairly recently judging by the style of brick and the type of mortar. In former times many of the *caves* were interconnected, so people could pass unseen from house to house and escape their enemies.

I take a long look around me and try to imagine taking refuge in this cellar during a siege. I know Puylaurens was attacked several times over the centuries, and next door above the Patisserie Perié a cannonball has remained embedded in Madame Colombié's front wall since the Catholic bombardment of 1568. On that occasion, the town's defences held firm and the body count was six for the besieged and six hundred for the assailants, a score which I have always found disturbingly one-sided, even allowing for a degree of exaggeration by the defenders who did the counting.

I take some photographs of the water well and the grain silo and the escape route, and then I follow Jean-Pierre back to the comparative modernity of his seventeenth century ground floor. We shake hands and I step outside. The sudden transition to bright sunlight is dazzling and I reach for my sunglasses. I head downhill through the remnants of the Porte Neuve, built in the eighteenth century to replace an older fortified gate in the town walls, and I turn a corner and glance up at the façade above me. Madame Colombié's front wall has been re-pointed with a pale yellow mortar that perfectly matches the colour of the ancient stone, and the Catholic cannonball protrudes from the smooth surface like a nasty black boil.

Monsieur Perié's window display drags me irresistibly back to the present and I recall the name of one of his specialities. Surely my visit to Jean-Pierre's cellar justifies a moment of self-indulgence? Moments later I walk out of the patisserie holding a fancy cardboard box. Inside is a creation Monsieur Perié calls a

Pavé Mediéval, or a Medieval Cobblestone, but even in Puylaurens I won't find a street paved with anything this good. I march across the road onto the advanced fortifications of Les Ravelins and ignore the troop of men playing *pétanque* near the war memorial. Instead, I make straight for the railings along the southern edge of the square. I am impatient to consume my cake and take in one of my favourite panoramas.

I tear open my cardboard treasure chest and take a bite. Monsieur Perié uses almonds *and* hazelnuts in his praline, and I try to decide if I prefer the crunchy base of a Medieval Cobblestone or its creamy chocolate topping. Before I can reach a conclusion all the ingredients have blended into one and are sliding towards my stomach. I run my tongue around the inside of my mouth and resist the temptation to take another bite, at least for a few moments. Instead, I admire the landscape before me.

I shall never tire of this view. To my left is a long mountain. It looks almost green in the sunlight, but its name is the Montagne Noire, the Black Mountain. Before me, the plain of Revel stretches south towards the Pyrenees and the Spanish border. To my right, gentle ridges rise from the plain, and the land of a thousand hills rolls westwards towards the city of Toulouse.

This is the Lauragais, a land which lies at the heart of the swathe of southern France where everyone once spoke Occitan, the language of the troubadours. On this magnificent morning, spring has painted the countryside in shades of green, from the delicate tones of new growth and fresh leaves to the darker colours of evergreens and hardy crops that have grown through the winter.

It is a tranquil scene, as tranquil as Jean-Pierre's cellar, but each time I study this view I see more than a single rusty cannonball. I see a thousand years of history embedded in the stone walls of the châteaux or fortified towns and villages of Durfort, Garrevaques, Montgey, Revel, Saint-Félix-Lauragais, Sorèze and countless others.

I see the Cathars slaughtering Simon de Montfort's crusaders below the first ridge to my south (yes, it was usually the other way around). I see smoke stretching across the southern sky as the Black Prince and his men burn and loot their way through the Lauragais. I see thousands of Catholics gathering on the plain below me while their leaders decide which Protestant stronghold to attack next. I see Marshal Soult leading his army deeper into the Lauragais to escape the Duke of Wellington and the end of an empire. And high in the Montagne Noire I see German aircraft bombing and strafing the camps of the Resistance.

I take another bite of Pavé Mediéval and glance behind me. Having a medieval water well and grain silo in your home, or a cannonball lodged in your front wall, may seem like minor historical details compared with such legendary figures and momentous events as these, but my impromptu visit to Jean-Pierre's cellar reminds me this is a land where the past is a part of everyday life. You can bump into history at any moment, even when you call in on a friend to discuss a tennis tournament. Perhaps this explains why so much has been discovered or re-discovered during the last forty years or so by people who are not professional historians. Some are outsiders who have settled here, others belong to families that have lived here for centuries, but they all share an insatiable curiosity about the origins of the world around them – the ruins outside their village, the time-worn château they have inherited or acquired, the unintelligible language spoken by their grandparents, or even the colour of the paint on their shutters.

When people like these cannot find the answers, their curiosity becomes an obsession and they labour away for years to discover the explanation for themselves, and then they share their passion with others like me. The history of the Lauragais is in their blood, and after two decades in this enchanted land, it is in mine too.

There is something else in my blood this morning, thanks to Monsieur Perié's Medieval Cobblestone. I don't know if it is because of this sugar rush, or my visit to Jean-Pierre's *cave*, or my view of the Lauragais, but I am struck by a sudden and overwhelming desire to share the story of this land through the pages of a book. After all, I tell myself, I am blessed with good fortune. I simply need to call up a few more friends and acquaintances, drop in for a cup of coffee or a glass of wine, and ask them to give me the inside story. They have already done the hard work and they will be delighted to share their enthusiasm because such is the nature of the enthusiast.

Momentarily, a doubt casts its shadow over my own enthusiasm. Am I oversimplifying the task ahead of me? Almost certainly, but when the last corner of Medieval Cobblestone disappears from view, another rush of excitement makes my hands tingle. My eyes dart over the landscape, impatient to start, but where, and in which century or millennium? I glance at the Montagne Noire. Maybe I should start over there with a visit to the rocky outcrop of the Berniquaut and its Iron Age fortifications and traces of Neolithic man. Or perhaps I should ask Madame Colombié to explain that one-sided siege and let me take a closer look at her cannonball. Local legend maintains that he or she who touches it will henceforth enjoy good luck, and anyone embarking on a project such as mine would welcome some of that.

My eyes swivel south in the direction of my own home. It is hidden behind the nearest rise, but on the ridge beyond, the silhouette of a château stands black against a backdrop of snowy mountain peaks. Right there! The perfect point of departure! It's practically on my doorstep, and the tragedy that took place in the fields of Montgey unfolded in the spring of 1211, only a few decades after the first written record of the name 'Lauragais'.

Today the Château de Montgey is a private dwelling, but I already know much of its history from Roman times to the present day. It is a tale which I could describe with a single word in French: *rocambolesque*. In English, I would need several: fantastic, extravagant, and so full of unexpected twists and turns that someone must have made it up.

Montgey is the only Cathar castle still occupied by the living, but the owners once told me they also share it with the dead. Were they being serious? When I pay Pierre and Sophie Bouyssou another visit I shall try to establish the truth about their ghost. Like most places with a long history, the Lauragais is also a land of legends. One of my challenges in writing this book will be to differentiate between the two.

Part I

Those Murderous Cathars

1

An Air of Malevolence

I drive up a brutal hill and my wheels spin on loose gravel. The sombre mass of the château dominates the ridge above me. I turn right at the abandoned church of Saint-Barthélemy, deconsecrated but not yet deconstructed, and I take a tiny lane that skirts around the hillside. The ridge between the lane and the foot of the château is overgrown, and through the foliage I see broken houses. Their roofs lie fallen and buried in the undergrowth, and I glimpse blue sky through empty windows in a crumbling wall. I imagine a village sacked by the enemy and abandoned by the survivors.

I pass through an open gateway and find myself below a canopy of trees so thick it seems as if dusk has fallen. Massive sections of moss-covered stone wall hide behind thick bushes. I turn a corner and peer at a stone griffin, a proud and courageous beast that seems to warn me to keep my distance. I draw closer and see the griffin has been beheaded. I cannot escape the air of malevolence that surrounds me.

I park on the grass and look up at a blank expanse of grey stone. I already know from a previous visit that this is one of the oldest parts of the medieval defences. The walls are three metres thick, and I trace the outline of a breach made centuries ago by less peaceful visitors and subsequently patched up with considerable care. I make a quick calculation: to create this breach, the attackers would have torn down more than fifty tonnes of stone and mortar.

In the twenty-first century, there are easier ways to gain entry to a château, and I walk towards the iron gates in search of a doorbell, but my arrival is announced by two oversized and ferocious-looking dogs. I remove my hand from the gate latch and the dogs lose interest. They amble off and begin to gnaw on bones the size of my knee.

I remind myself that I am not an invader. I have an appointment. Take courage! I turn the handle and the gate swings open silently. I slip inside and keep a wary eye on the dogs. They show no reaction and I tip-toe across a wide terrace towards an inner gateway. In the curtain wall beyond the dogs, the grey roof of a watchtower points at the sky like a raised hand ordering me to halt. Who goes there? I am sure the sentry inside is eyeing me suspiciously and fidgeting with the trigger of his crossbow. I creep into a cavernous passageway and penetrate deeper inside the château's defences. I could gallop through this gateway on horseback without having to duck.

The inner courtyard is paved with large pebbles tinged with green lichen from the winter rains. In one corner, three metal chairs lounge around a table by a water well. On all four sides of the courtyard massive walls rise to the sky, and somewhere above my head appears a patch of blue. There is no sign of modernity and I feel lost in an unknown age. A stone sundial hangs on the south-facing wall and its traditional inscription reminds me in Latin that every hour wounds and the last one will kill me. How reassuring!

'*Allo!*' I shout. The echo of my voice dies away and there is total silence. I haven't been here for a few years and I cannot remember which door I should take. I think I hear a noise behind me and I sidle towards an open archway below the sundial and peer inside. '*Allo?*' No reply. I turn and cross the courtyard and climb a flight of stone steps towards a more imposing entrance. The door is ajar and I glimpse a staircase, a tapestry and a sense of timelessness. '*Allo?*' I call for a third time. No audible sound comes from inside, but the silence is not true silence. It is filled with echoes from a past that stretches back so far and so violently, it gives me vertigo.

I stumble back down the steps into the courtyard and call the château's number on my mobile phone. Through the doorway above me comes the sound of distant ringing, but it is not the irritating synthesised tune of a modern handset. The telephone at the Château de Montgey announces a caller with the resplendent sound of an old-fashioned bell. I wait and listen, and a scene from a black-and-white film flickers in my memory, a scene where a telephone rings hopelessly and incessantly in a desolate house where everyone has been murdered.

Something brushes against my hand and I jump. The larger beast – which I later learn is a Bernese mountain dog – has licked my fingers. The telephone falls silent and I hear a voice in my ear.

'*Pierre Bouyssou à l'appareil.*'

'It's Colin. I'm in the courtyard with the dogs.'

'Don't worry about them, they're not vicious. Come on in!'

2

SOLDIERS OF CHRIST, TRAVELLERS OF GOD

An hour later, and I am alone in *la grande salle*, the great hall. In medieval times, this was the centre of life in any castle, and at the Château de Montgey it still is. I look around me. I am standing by a monumental fireplace and its hearth is screened by a simple tapestry. A larger tapestry showing a classical scene decorates the wall at the opposite end of the room, and below it is a piano which Pierre's mother bought from Debussy's mistress. The north wall is covered by a collection of portraits, landscapes and still-lifes. I have learned from Pierre that this is the oldest wall in the château; its lower section was built by the Romans two thousand years ago.

I drift towards one of the windows in the south wall and turn my thoughts to the more recent past, to something that happened here eight centuries ago. From this spot, a young man peered out one evening in April 1211 and saw an unusual and alarming sight. His name was Jourdain de Roquefort, and he was wondering what on earth the men pitching camp below his walls thought they were doing. He was the lord of Montgey, but their tents were spreading across his fields like a plague of locusts and the smoke of their camp fires was already obscuring his view of the Montagne Noire. Before long, Jourdain's informants told him the uninvited guests were pilgrims from Germany, and they planned to stay the night before completing their journey to Lavaur.

I try to imagine what must have passed through Jourdain's mind as he stood here towards sunset, what inspired him to hatch his murderous plan. Maybe it was the memory of the massacre of 20,000 Cathars at Béziers a couple of years earlier, or perhaps it was the sight of a long line of mountain peaks cutting into the evening sky.

I too gaze into the distance. It is a perfect spring day and the Pyrenees rise black above the hazy plain. From where I am standing, the twin peaks of Soularac and Saint-Barthélemy dominate the horizon – not because they are the highest but because they are the closest. No doubt Jourdain searched with his eyes for the Château de Montségur – the 'safe mountain' – perched on its rocky outcrop below those twin peaks. Seventy-five kilometres as the crow flies was too far to be able to see it with the naked eye, but he knew exactly where it was. Montségur had been rebuilt a few years earlier and it was a centre of resistance for the heretical Cathars.

Even though we are separated by eight centuries, my view of the mountains will be much the same as Jourdain's, but the land around Montgey has undoubtedly altered. Below me, I see green fields of winter wheat and the brown earth of ploughed fields waiting to be sown with summer crops. In one of them down towards the cemetery, aerial photographs have revealed the foundations of a palatial Roman villa, but in Jourdain's day much of this land was covered by forest and he would have been able to trace the route of the old road to Lavaur where it passed through the dense trees below him. It was an ideal spot for an ambush, the perfect place to butcher the pilgrims as soon as they set off after breakfast the next morning. There was only one difficulty: Jourdain and his men would need help if they were going to kill all 6,000 of their enemies.

One particular aspect of this story had always intrigued me. Jourdain de Roquefort was a Cathar. Most things I had read about this period of history presented the Cathars as the victims, an enlightened people who put up a heroic and ultimately tragic resistance against the northern hordes unleashed upon them by the pope. Their priests were called the perfect ones – *parfaits* or *parfaites* depending on their gender – and around a quarter of them were women.[1] These holy men and women abstained from pleasures of the flesh – no meat and no sex – and they led humble lives. They lived in the community from the proceeds of their own labour, and this kept them in close contact with the general population and helped them attract followers from all levels of society, people who were reacting against what they perceived as the moral, spiritual and political corruption of the Catholic Church.

So why, I had always wondered, would a nice Cathar lord like Jourdain de Roquefort be preparing to slaughter thousands of pilgrims below the walls of his château? I have discovered the answer today during my conversation with Pierre Bouyssou in his study.

Modern pilgrims still travel across the plain below Montgey following the Chemin d'Arles towards Saint-Jacques de Compostelle. They march in peace and leave little behind them apart from footprints and a scattering of euros to help the local economy. In contrast, Jourdain's visitors had descended on this part of France to impose their own brand of Christianity through

1 The terms *parfait* and *parfaite* derive from the Latin *perfectus, perfecta*, but they were always combined with *hereticus* or *heretica* when used by the Catholic Church. The phrase *hereticus perfectus* signified a confirmed heretic or one of the Cathar clergy. It had nothing to do with the concept of perfection or purity.

force of arms. They were soldiers of Christ and travellers of God at one and the same time. They were crusaders *and* pilgrims, and they were here on what the Catholic Church described as an affair of peace and faith.

During the twelfth century, the Catholic Church crushed the heresies that had spread across other parts of Europe by capturing and executing the leaders, but divergent beliefs persisted in two main areas: Lombardy in northern Italy, and the area of southern France which would later become known as the Languedoc and has the Lauragais at its heart. The term 'Cathar' first appeared around 1160,[2] but the heretics never referred to themselves as such, preferring instead to call themselves good Christians, or more simply, good men or good women. But their beliefs diverged from the teachings of the Catholic Church when it came to the question of why, if God is all-powerful, does he allow bad things to happen? The Cathars' answer was a dualism in which a good god ruled the spiritual world and an evil god ruled the material world.

What proportion of the population adhered to this alternative faith? It is impossible to say, but they were always in the minority. Some historians have focused on specific villages and come up with figures ranging from five to twenty-five per cent. This wide variation probably had something to do with the inclination of the local lord. There were also those who hedged their bets and maintained links with both religions, including Jourdain de Roquefort and some of his family, as we shall discover later.

When Pope Innocent III was elected in 1198, he resolved to restore the authority of his church and bring the heretics to heel. In the feudal hierarchy of medieval Christendom the Supreme

2 The origin of the term 'Cathar' has been disputed for eight centuries. The polite explanation is that it comes from the Greek *katharoi* meaning 'pure'. Another origin was proposed by Alain de Lille sometime between 1185 and 1200 in his *De Fide Catholica*: 'Cathar' comes from the Latin *cattus* and, according to Alain, signified someone who sodomised felines, because a cat was the form in which Lucifer appeared to the heretic.

Being was God and his representative on earth was the pope, but without an army of his own the pope depended on his vassals to impose his authority. Innocent III spent the next ten years trying to persuade the French king and his nobles to take up arms against the Cathar heretics. It was only after the murder of a papal legate in 1208 that he made any progress. The crime was blamed on Count Raymond VI of Toulouse, and the pope promptly declared a crusade, later named the Albigensian Crusade after the city of Albi sixty kilometres to the north of Montgey. Next, he needed to recruit some crusaders.

What was it that attracted young men like the German pilgrims camping out in Jourdain de Roquefort's fields to travel all the way to the south of France to wage war on the pope's behalf? First, the religious aspect. The pope awarded this expedition the same level of spiritual significance as the earlier crusades to the Holy Land where the enemies had been infidels rather than heretics. All those who joined the new crusade for forty days would, through this single act, have completed their penance for all the sins to which they had confessed. This type of forgiveness was called an indulgence. In addition, Innocent III proclaimed that if you were unable or unwilling to become a crusader yourself, you could pay someone else to go in your place and still receive the indulgences for your own sins.

Another attraction was the prospect of material gain. Before the Albigensian Crusade, religious law prescribed burning at the stake for unrepentant heretics, and excommunication for anyone who aided or protected them. This time the pope decreed an extra punishment for the aiders and abettors: their titles and possessions would be confiscated and given to the crusaders. So the nobility could look forward to picking up a title or two, and the lowly knight or man-at-arms who completed his forty days of crusading would be able to return home with a purified soul and saddlebags bulging with plunder.

In 1209 the crusaders marched south. According to one contemporary source they numbered 20,000 knights and 200,000 men. Like many estimates of its day, this was probably an exaggeration, but there is no doubt that the army was large and powerful. In July 1209, the crusaders achieved an early and unexpectedly-easy victory at Béziers and massacred the inhabitants, Cathars and Catholics alike. The next month they captured Carcassonne and its lord, Viscount Trencavel. True to the pope's promise, the crusade's religious leader offered Trencavel's titles and possessions to the three most powerful barons of the crusade, but one after the other they all declined. They already owned plenty of lands in the north, their forty days were nearly up, and they preferred to return home in one piece with all their sins forgiven. In the end, one of the minor barons had to be ordered to accept the titles and estates of Viscount Trencavel. His name was Simon de Montfort.[3]

Simon quickly discovered it was one thing to be awarded Viscount Trencavel's possessions by the pope's representative, and quite another to take control of them. Geographically, they stretched east-west from Béziers to Carcassonne and northwards to Albi. For the next nine years, he would spend most of his life on the back of a horse in an endless attempt to impose his authority on his new vassals and to root out the Cathars who sheltered among them.

By the time Jourdain de Roquefort was planning his massacre, the crusaders had begun burning the *parfaits* and *parfaites* en masse, and many of their protectors had become dispossessed fugitives. At the start of 1211, Simon was trying to clear out the remaining Cathar strongholds in the Montagne Noire north of Carcassonne. Once he had seized the Château de Cabaret near Lastours, he marched on Lavaur and mounted a siege towards the end of March.

---

3 This was the fourth Simon de Montfort. It was his youngest son, Simon de Montfort V, Earl of Leicester, who led the rebellion against England's Henry III in 1264.

There were two people inside the town who were of particular interest to Simon. First was the lord of Lavaur, who was in fact a lady: Guiraude had assumed the title following the death of her husband. She was an ardent Cathar and had given shelter to hundreds of *parfaits* inside her walls. And then there was her brother, Aimery de Montréal. He was the lord of Laurac and the Lauragais, and before the crusade he had been Viscount Trencavel's richest vassal. When Carcassonne fell in 1209 he swiftly swore allegiance to its new lord, Simon de Montfort, but soon changed his mind. Now he was holed up in Lavaur with eighty of his knights.

Simon de Montfort wanted the pair of them – brother and sister, traitor and heretic – dead or alive.

The siege dragged on for over a month. When a fresh contingent of German crusaders arrived in Carcassonne they were dispatched immediately to join the army at Lavaur. They broke their journey below the walls of Montgey.

3

A Ghostly Acquisition

I am still staring out of a window in the great hall. A noise makes me turn. Pierre shuffles towards me with a glass of red wine on a silver tray. He is over eighty years old and not quite so steady on his feet. A pool of red liquid spreads around the base of the glass like blood from an artery.

'I am clumsy,' he mutters. He fetches a yellow paper napkin from a dresser against the Roman wall and fastidiously cleans the bottom of my glass. He offered me whisky, but a glass of bordeaux seemed more appropriate for an Englishman who is immersing himself in medieval history. In the days of Jourdain de Roquefort, Bordeaux belonged to England, and the English bought its wines in huge quantities. A few years before the Albigensian Crusade, King John had placed a single order for 120 tonnes. My tastes are more modest and I am happy to take a sip from a single glass, but it reminds me that I am more knowledgeable about what happened eight centuries ago than I am about Montgey's more recent past.

'Pierre, how did you come to be the owner of Montgey?'

We make ourselves comfortable at a table near the fireplace and he pours himself a measure of Glenlivet. 'My family has lived in this area for centuries,' he begins. 'I've traced my own genealogy back to 1565 and it probably goes back much further. My great-grandfather was mayor of Montgey, but I grew up in a neighbouring village – Nogaret.'

I had spotted Nogaret a couple of kilometres to the south when I was looking out of Pierre's windows at the Pyrenees. One summer's day when he was ten years old Pierre decided to take a country walk to Montgey with some of his cousins.

'Back then the fields were still divided into tiny parcels and we passed along sunken roads in the shade of the trees. I was the oldest and I was carrying my shotgun in case we met a wild boar. Somehow, we ended up at the Château de Montgey and we played in the abandoned park. It was completely overgrown, the château was falling into ruin and there was no one there. It was like being in a fairy tale, and I imagined that one day I would become the lord of Montgey.

'My family farmed the land around the château, and over the next few years when I was helping with the harvest I often used to push open the gate and step inside. The place held a strange attraction for me, a human version of tropism perhaps. I sensed so much history in here, as if these ancient walls had absorbed the past.'

I take another mouthful of bordeaux and scribble a few notes while Pierre tells me that, in 1948, the château was bought by a lady called Mademoiselle Delamy. She had grand plans for the château, but was unable to slow its decay. The village rumour mill had long maintained that the man she employed as her gardener was the last wizard in the Tarn, and most people kept well away. Pierre was an exception: by now he was a successful and well-respected young lawyer, but he was unable to resist the peculiar pull the château had exerted on him since boyhood. At one point he offered to buy it and allow Mademoiselle Delamy to continue living there until her dying breath, but she declined.

'I came to be on good terms with her,' says Pierre, 'and for my work I sometimes organised receptions here in the château for a couple of hundred people. She was an eccentric woman and full of grand airs, but she could be quite charming. When she died, her relatives naturally expected to inherit Montgey. They were furious when they discovered the terms of her will.'

I put two-and-two together and jump to a conclusion. 'She left the château to you?'

He laughs. 'No. She bequeathed it to the Department of the Tarn to be turned into a museum.'

It is not that easy to give away a château, particularly one with an unknown history. The architect for historic buildings took one look at its ruinous state and declared the Château de Montgey was of insufficient public interest to justify the 300 million old francs that would be required to save it. The Department said '*non, merci*' and gave it back to Mademoiselle Delamy's estate. At this point Pierre made another offer to buy the château and her heirs accepted it, presumably with some relief.

'I remember coming here with my children two or three days after Montgey became mine. It was a beautiful Sunday morning in July and we stood outside the walls. I looked at the locked gates leading into the courtyard knowing I held the key in my hand. The walls of the château and the alleys of the park were a part of my childhood, and now my dream had come true. I unlocked the gates and we all trooped in here, into the great hall. My children rushed around in excitement and I was thrilled, but suddenly we all fell silent and listened.'

Pierre pauses and points to the ceiling above my head. Suddenly the room feels colder.

'We all heard them: slow footsteps above our heads moving diagonally towards the east tower. My children whispered, "Father, do you hear? There's someone up there!" I reassured them, I told them it was nothing, but I knew it was no living person. Even today, if the gates are locked no one can get in. Another thing struck me: it was ten in the morning, not the traditional hour for ghosts.'

I glance up at the ceiling and suppress a shiver. Strips of aquamarine paint glow between the dark wood of exposed beams and joists. I hold my breath and listen, but there are no footsteps. 'Were you frightened?'

'No, I have never seen the ghost during the hours of darkness, and he's not alarming in daylight.'

Pierre notes my look of incredulity. 'You can believe or disbelieve me as you wish. By nature, I have a Cartesian mind, I am a lawyer, but Sophie and I have both seen the ghost during the day, and at night we hear strange noises. Usually it's the sound of footsteps, but once we were woken by the noise of a heavy trunk being dragged down the spiral staircase: *toc-toc-toc*. It was a devilish sound.'

He looks at me with what I can only think of as the ghost of a smile. 'Maybe you think I was dreaming, but it's my impression the past has been concentrated and stored inside these ancient walls. This is a home with at least two thousand years of history. We don't know enough about life and death; we don't know what may resurge from the past. But what is certain is that Sophie and I have both seen the ghost many times in two different parts of the château. We only see his top half and he is always grey, but he isn't disagreeable.'

We exchange a look and Pierre's expression becomes apologetic.

'I'm not making fun of you, I assure you. My daughter always used to laugh at me until a month ago when she finally saw the ghost for the first time. I was so pleased because I haven't seen him myself for ten years. And then, last Sunday, the lady who helps us look after the château rushed into the kitchen with a look of terror on her face. She had seen him on the first floor, but he merely gave her a glance and disappeared. As I said, he never does anything unpleasant.'

Although I share Pierre's disinclination to believe in phantoms, my body temperature has dropped by several degrees. Before today, I had always assumed he had conjured up the ghost to amuse or frighten his visitors, but now I have heard the full story, I am not so sure. I take another sip of bordeaux and remember all the blood spilt below these walls in 1211.

4

THE MASSACRE

The crusader army surrounding Lavaur was the largest they had assembled since the massacre at Béziers in 1209. Jourdain de Roquefort knew that if Lavaur fell, Toulouse would undoubtedly be the next target, and Dame Guiraude and Aimery de Montréal would suffer a grisly end. It was obvious that the 6,000 reinforcements camped out in the fields of Montgey would only hasten the end of the siege. Jourdain dispatched a messenger post-haste to Toulouse to warn Count Raymond of the new danger. In response, the Count of Foix and his son, Roger-Bernard, set out from the city with a band of soldiers and mercenaries. On their way to Montgey their ranks were swollen by thousands of local peasants who joined them once they understood what was afoot. After nearly two years of war, the people of the Lauragais had good reason to hate the crusaders, and even some of the local Catholics had concluded that the men wearing the cross were more motivated by greed than religion.

The Count of Foix and his ragtag army reached Montgey under cover of darkness. With Jourdain's help, they chose a site for an ambush in the woods below the château somewhere between the cemetery of Montgey and the modern-day village of Auvezines. Then they waited.

Next morning the crusaders prepared for the last stage of their journey. They had walked or ridden fifteen hundred kilometres across Europe to take part in this crusade, and soon the waiting would be over. By nightfall they would reach Lavaur and the heart of the action. Over breakfast, some may have reflected on the service they would render the pope by slaughtering the heretics, while others were more preoccupied with thoughts of the riches they would plunder from the vanquished. Maybe some of them were nervous about the forthcoming action, little suspecting that they would find themselves in a bloody fight rather sooner than they had expected.

The crusaders struck camp and soon they were marching through the gloom of the forest. Suddenly they were attacked from all sides with horrifying savagery. Those who survived the first moments of the ambush tried to scatter but they were pursued by their attackers. Nearly all of them were butchered or left for dead, and many were killed by the peasants using nothing more sophisticated than farm tools, pikes or stones.

A few years later, a Cistercian monk and close companion of Simon de Montfort wrote a history of the Albigensian Crusade. In his account, Pierre des Vaux-de-Cernay includes an anecdote to illustrate the cruelty of the Cathar heretics: *'While [the Cathars] were massacring the crusaders...a crusader-priest sought asylum in a nearby church so that, if he were to die for the church, he would also die in a church. That wicked traitor, Roger-Bernard, son of the Count of Foix...pursued the priest, dared to enter the church and marched up to him. "Who are you?" he asked. "I am a crusader and a priest." "Prove to me you are a priest," said the executioner. The other man immediately pushed back his hood and showed his tonsure. The cruel Roger-Bernard, with no regard for the sanctity of the priest or the place, raised his sharpened axe which he held in his hand and brought it down in the middle of the shaven head and beat this servant of the church to death in a church'.*[4]

Even allowing for the partisanship of Pierre des Vaux-de-Cernay, it was certainly a violent battle. Four years later, the Count of Toulouse and the Count of Foix found themselves in Rome trying to argue against the threatened confiscation of their lands by the pope. On the first day, Bishop Foulque of Toulouse brought up the subject of Montgey and accused the Count of Foix of killing, mutilating, crippling or disembowelling so many of the pilgrims that the land of Montgey was covered in blood and none of the survivors could walk without help.

One young squire managed to flee with his life and limbs intact. He carried the news of the massacre to Simon de Montfort at the gates of Lavaur.

None of the historical texts comment on the size of the Cathar contingent, and it is unclear how they were able to inflict such a crushing defeat on such a large army. Jourdain de Roquefort and his allies certainly enjoyed an element of surprise, and the crusaders would have been marching in column, not line of battle. Another point to bear in mind is that not all of the crusaders were fighting men; included in their ranks were priests, servants and numerous other camp-followers.

Pierre des Vaux-de-Cernay offers another explanation: the victims were unarmed, even though they knew they were marching through enemy territory and were on their way to take part in a siege. No doubt he wanted to portray his fellow-crusaders as innocent victims, but his suggestion may not be as ridiculous as it seems. To understand why, ask yourself a question: have you

4 Translated from : Vaux-de-Cernay, Pierre des. *Histoire de l'hérésie des Albigeois et de la sainte guerre contre eux (de l'an 1203 à l'an 1218).* Translated into French by François Guizot. Paris: J-L-J Brière Libraire, 1824 (page 139).

ever tried marching or riding a horse for twenty-five kilometres wearing a suit of armour and carrying your weapons, shield and other accoutrements necessary for a battle? It is not easy, as Pierre Bouyssou witnessed in April 2011 when he organised a re-enactment to mark the 800th anniversary of the Battle of Montgey. He was astonished by the number of spectators who turned up, and by the army of men who came to 'fight' the battle dressed in surprisingly authentic armour and chain mail. While he was briefing them on the terrace outside the main gate with the help of a flip chart and marker pen, these unaccustomed knights began to topple over one by one, struck down by nothing more dangerous than the April sun, and this was simply from the effort of standing still. His daughter soon found herself with an unforeseen job: offering carafes of water to the overheated knights.

In medieval times, unless an army expected to be attacked, heavy arms and armour were carried by cart when on the march. The crusaders may have assumed they were too large a force to be threatened by the local population, or the small garrison of a château like Montgey. Perhaps Pierre des Vaux-de-Cernay was right and they were dressed for a journey, not a battle.

Whatever the explanation, Jourdain de Roquefort and his allies knew retribution would fall swiftly. After the slaughter, they looted as much as they could carry and fled by a circuitous south-westerly route to the safety of Toulouse.

As soon as he heard about the massacre from the escaped squire, Simon de Montfort set out on horseback with a large force to search for his enemies in the hills of the Lauragais. He spent the night at Lanta and then gave up the chase, reluctant to split his army for too long. On the way back to Lavaur he passed through Montgey to survey the carnage.

5

Retribution

Sophie joins us in the great hall and sips a glass of champagne. We chat about mutual friends, and then I thank my hosts for their hospitality and prepare to leave. Outside in the courtyard the dogs are still gnawing at their bones, and I am grateful when Sophie escorts me as far as the gates. I step back into the present and climb into my car.

I take a different route home and head south towards the cypress trees that surround the cemetery of Montgey a kilometre away. The road soon flattens out and I am crossing the battlefield. Through the trees to my left I can see where the crusaders made their camp.

The cemetery of Montgey is a triangular piece of ground enclosed by a stone wall in the middle of a field. It strikes me as an appropriate place from which to survey the site of a massacre, and Simon de Montfort would have caught his first sight of the battlefield from somewhere nearby.

The cemetery is at peace and the wind blows softly through the cypress trees. Through the gaps between them I glimpse the majesty of the Pyrenees to the south and the brooding mass of the Château de Montgey to the north. I try to imagine the sight that would have met Simon de Montfort when he came here after his fruitless pursuit of the assassins in the hills of the Lauragais. I picture a battlefield covered in the bodies of the dead and the dying. The cries of the wounded float in the breeze, but up on the ridge, the château and the village and the surrounding countryside are deathly silent. Everyone has fled to Toulouse or is cowering in the woods, terrified of retribution.

The Cathars' pre-emptive strike may have delayed the fall of Lavaur, but not for long. Simon de Montfort buried his dead at Montgey and transported the injured to safety, and then he renewed his siege with greater ferocity. The town fell within a few weeks, and on 3 May 1211 the crusaders avenged the massacre of the German 'pilgrims'. Dame Guiraude was thrown screaming and sobbing into a well and stones were piled on top of her for good measure. Her brother Aimery and his knights were due to be hanged as traitors, but the gallows collapsed and they were put to the sword instead. Then the victors lit the most murderous bonfire of the crusade and threw four hundred *parfaits* and *parfaites* into the flames.

The following day, a large number of crusaders promptly packed their bags and left. They had finished their forty days with a victory, but Simon de Montfort had no intention of going home. Instead, he returned to Montgey in the second half of May. The village was still deserted, and this time he razed it to the ground and set fire to the château.

Pierre Bouyssou told me that during his renovations he uncovered sections of foundation blackened by fire. He also blames the crusaders for that fifty-tonne breach in his north wall. During more recent works on the land to the north of the château, he has discovered the charred remains of bricks, tiles and pottery, and a layer of blackened earth between fifteen and twenty centimetres thick. This was the site of the old village of Montgey, and it was never rebuilt after it was sacked by Simon de Montfort.

As for the château itself, Jourdain de Roquefort was back at home within a few years, and he managed to keep control of his possessions for the next three decades until he died sometime between 1246 and 1248. In contrast, the Count of Toulouse and the Count of Foix spent the rest of their lives in conflict with the church. They lost their argument with the pope in Rome in 1215; Count Raymond was stripped of all his lands apart from Provence, and Count Roger-Raymond had already lost the Château de Foix to Simon de Montfort.

Jourdain's immunity from the wrath of the crusaders is even more surprising when one considers some of his relatives. Three paternal uncles and an aunt were Cathar priests, and as for his father, Guillaume de Roquefort, he was described by Pierre des Vaux-de-Cernay as one of the worst enemies of the Church. Guillaume was accused of murdering the Abbot of Eaunes and another monk near Carcassonne in 1209, and the following year he fought against the crusaders at the siege of the Château de Termes. He escaped on that occasion, but a couple of months after the massacre at Montgey he was killed while defending the city of Toulouse.

During the years that followed the Albigensian Crusade, several members of Jourdain's family and entourage were called before the Inquisition. This organisation was set up in Toulouse in 1229 and, as a means of eradicating the Cathar heresy, it proved much more effective than military action and violent repression. The work of the Inquisition was slow, patient and relentless, and in the space of a few decades the remaining *parfaits* and *parfaites* were forced into a precarious and often nomadic existence that obliged them to depend entirely on charity. Contact with their faithful became a risky, clandestine affair.

For its time, the procedures of the Inquisition were exemplary. It did not use torture; the accused appeared before an inquisitor and two assessors; and evidence was taken down in writing. Ironically, these inquisitorial registers are our main source of information about the Cathar faithful – who they were, how they operated and what they believed. Without them, for example, we would not know what Jourdain de Roquefort's mother told the Inquisition on 24 August 1243. Marquèse Isarn was the daughter of a *parfaite*, and during her interrogation she admitted that both she and Jourdain had been instructed in the Cathar faith by a well-known heretic priest. In mitigation she claimed to have worked as a spy for another inquisitor, perhaps mindful of the fate of her brother, Pierre Isarn, who had been the Cathar bishop of Carcassonne until he was burned at the stake.

At around the same time, Jourdain's wife, Béatrix, was called before the Inquisition in Toulouse and sentenced to life imprisonment. His two children and their wives were known heretics. More modest inhabitants of his domains were interrogated as well; some saw their possessions confiscated and others were imprisoned.

There is no indication that Jourdain himself appeared before the Inquisition. Somehow, he succeeded in following his faith and remaining on good terms with the Catholic Church. No doubt it helped that he gave away some of his feudal rights on the other side of the Montagne Noire to the Abbey of Saint-Papoul, and he had several relatives in the Catholic camp. One of his cousins was Abbot of Sorèze; the eldest of his father's siblings served as Bishop of Carcassonne on two occasions during the crusade; and another cousin, Bernard de Roquefort, was a member of the Inquisition, although he perished in 1242 when the Cathars from Montségur rode into Avignonet-Lauragais in the dead of night and hacked Bernard and ten of his colleagues to death in their beds.

During this period, some inquisitors were so zealous they dug up the graves of supposed heretics and burned their decomposing bodies. Would a few donations and some family ties have been enough to appease such fanatics and stop them pursuing one of the main instigators of the massacre of Montgey?

Jourdain de Roquefort remains an enigmatic figure.

I lean my elbows on the wall of the cemetery and study the silhouette of the château. What the Romans built up there 2,000 years ago is uncertain: probably a watchtower, or maybe a small temple because the name Montgey is believed to derive from Mons Jovis, the Latin for Mount Jupiter.

I lower my gaze to the field where the immense, highly organised Roman villa once stood, and where pieces of mosaic are still turned up by the plough. The centuries that followed the fall of Rome were chaotic and terrifying for the common people, and in this part of the world early Christians often huddled together for physical and spiritual protection inside an enclosure built around their church. Aerial photography has revealed that the cemetery where I am standing, and the ruined apse of a chapel that stands in one corner, were once part of such a community. Fragments of pottery suggest the site was occupied until the eleventh century, and then, just as a more orderly and cultured society was taking root in the Lauragais under the protection of powerful lords such as the Roquefort family, the crusaders arrived. In the fields around me, the men wearing the cross were the ones to be cut to pieces on that cruel day in 1211, but it was usually the other way around.

Pierre and Sophie Bouyssou knew little of this in 1970 when they bought Montgey. The château was in a sorry state, and they inherited no archives, no written accounts, no traces of the past apart from the ancient walls. If they had not saved the physical structure, it is possible someone else may have done so, but few other people would have devoted so much time and energy to the painstaking and detailed research that has enabled Pierre and Sophie to rediscover the history of their home.

Pierre told me he has the nose of a hunter when it comes to sniffing out the truth, and it is an invaluable attribute both for a lawyer and an amateur historian. In 2008, he published the results of over thirty years of research in his book, *'Histoire de Montgey, Tome 1'*. It is a serious academic study which contains no mention of ghostly manifestations, and it only covers the period up to 1500. I can't help wondering what he may one day reveal in Volume 2 which, he told me, is a work in progress.

During my visit, Pierre reminded me several times that Montgey is the only Cathar castle still occupied by the living. Before I left the great hall, I told him how pleased I was to learn that it was once again home to a knight: he was made a Chevalier de la Légion d'Honneur on New Year's Day 2016. He seemed mildly embarrassed by my observation.

'I was a barrister for fifty-one years. It's normal to receive the Légion d'Honneur, particularly if you know the right people. Yes, it's also partly in recognition of what we have achieved at Montgey, but what is more unusual is that both Sophie and I have received the same decoration. She was made a Chevalière de la Légion d'Honneur eighteen months before me.'

Dusk is falling and I squint at the outline of the château for one last time and grapple with a linguistic problem: how shall I translate *le chevalier* and *la chevalière*? The British honours system suggests knight and dame, but I much prefer the more literal knight and knightess.

6

UNEARTHING THE DEAD

Over the next few days, I study my notes and listen to the recordings I made during my visit to Pierre and Sophie's home, and I can't help thinking that the story of Montgey with its childhood fantasies, its ghosts and its massacre, not to mention its stinging riposte to the Black Prince which I shall save for a later chapter, may be far too *rocambolesque* for anyone to believe. If there can be no murder without a body, surely there can be no massacre without industrial quantities of skeletons?

This morning, in search of more macabre evidence I am making a sortie dressed in the modern equivalent of lightweight travelling armour: black padded shorts, a lurid lycra shirt, and a helmet that makes my head resemble a mushroom. A bicycle is the best means of transport for this type of expedition: I can absorb the scents, sights and sounds of the countryside at a speed not dissimilar to that of an errant knight's steed.

Like the German pilgrims eight centuries earlier, I break my journey at Auvezines. The village lies a couple of kilometres down the road from Montgey, and through a long avenue of plane trees

I can just make out the shape of the château and its abandoned church on the hill. Behind me, the two houses on the crossroads in the centre of the village show no signs of life and their shuttered windows stare at me like the dead eyes of corpses. I can sense their gaze and it makes me uneasy, but they are not the reason for my visit. I have come here to see a memorial, a rough stone stele with a simple metal plaque bearing an inscription:

'Ici et aux environs reposent 6000 croisés surpris en embuscade fin d'avril 1211' ('In this place and nearby rest 6,000 crusaders ambushed towards the end of April 1211').

I run my fingers over the cold lump of rock and rub the golden letters of the inscription. One contemporary source put the number of dead at 5,000, already an exaggeration perhaps, and the plaque in front of me inflates that figure still further, but there is no doubt that the savagery and scale of the massacre at Montgey fired the imaginations of both the crusaders and the Cathars. It also lodged itself deep in the folk memory of the villagers, and towards the end of the eighteenth century the story resurfaced in a disturbingly literal fashion. Archaeological excavations around Montgey turned up skeletons and ancient arms in quantities that could only indicate the site of a battle, and the locals said, ah yes, that's why we call it the *cami dal sanc*, the field of blood.

Then, in 1817 the priest of Auvezines decided to transform his modest chapel into a proper church to compete with the one on the hill. Naturally his workmen started with the foundations, and they soon unearthed more armour, coins and piles of human bones. Of course, said the locals, our chapel was built on the graves of the crusaders using stones taken from an older chapel on the battlefield (this, presumably, was where Roger-Bernard buried his axe in the head of the crusader-priest). More trenches were dug and more bones were uncovered, and some of the skeletons were intact, including one belonging to a giant of a man two metres ten high, or six feet ten inches if you prefer.

During the years that followed, bones continued to appear in the surrounding fields and alongside the road to Puylaurens. Disturbed by the scale of these osseous discoveries, a new priest, Abbé Crozes, launched an appeal among the neighbouring parishes. He was determined to give the dead crusaders a proper burial and to prevent their bones being dug up and played with by children and dogs. As a result, in the second half of the nineteenth century the human remains were gathered together and buried under a mound, a calvary was erected on top of it, the stele was shaped and its plaque was cast, and a wall was built around the site so that no more bones could escape.

The calvary lies immediately behind the memorial stele. I climb a flight of stone steps in the shade of two enormous cedars and reach the top of the mound where tarnished bronze figures stand guard over the remains of the dead. I sit down in the shade and look up at Christ on his cross, the cross that the crusaders took as their symbol. There is no doubt a bloody battle took place around this spot, and Montgey was the only significant loss suffered by the crusaders during the nine years of Simon de Montfort's leadership. But is the ghost of Montgey linked to this massacre, or is it an echo from another violent event in the château's long history?

Stop it! I tell myself, I have a scientific background. In theory that should keep my imagination in check, and it is true that when I am reading and writing about Montgey in the comfort of my own study, I find it easy to mock Pierre with his stories of ghoulies and ghosties and things that go bump in the night. But my scepticism was far less pronounced when I was in the great hall where Jourdain de Roquefort planned his massacre. If the ghost is simply a figment of Pierre's imagination, then the same fantasy has also taken hold of his wife, his daughter and his housekeeper. If I sit here much longer with the bones of a thousand dead crusaders beneath me, it may take hold of me too.

Part II

On the Trail of a Troubadour

7

The Heart of Occitania

Sometimes I sit and listen to ancient country folk when they are deep in conversation, and I cannot understand a thing they say. Their words – particularly those including an 'r' – roll off the tongue with the lyricism of a medieval troubadour and they appear to be pronouncing all their consonants. To my ears, their speech sounds vaguely French with an undertone of Catalan and an unfamiliar syllabic stress.

'Are you speaking Occitan?' I ask, pronouncing it '*ock-see-tun*'.

Usually they say, 'no,' which is embarrassing because I really should recognise French by now, even when spoken with the pronounced accent of the south-west, but sometimes they say, 'Yes; could you follow what we were saying?'

I tell them I cannot speak a word of the thousand-year-old language spoken by the Cathars and most other people in this part of the world until well into the twentieth century. In justification, I add that although I know Occitan is an important part of the cultural heritage of the Lauragais, it is already hard enough trying to learn the only official language of the French Republic. Why struggle with Occitan as well? No one in my village below the age of sixty speaks it. Some know a few words learned from their parents, but none can converse in the language, let alone read or write it.

Despite this oral decline, during the years I have been living here I have detected visible signs of a renewed interest in the language of the troubadours, particularly in the tourist industry where today it is almost impossible to find a publication that fails to mention Occitan, or is unadorned by the outline of a gold cross gleaming from a red background. All four arms of the Occitan cross are equal and there are three blobs of gold at the end of each arm. Confusingly, it is also known as the cross of Languedoc, Provence, Toulouse or the Cathars.

This ancient red and gold symbol has also been seized upon by communities of all sizes as a means of promoting their Occitan heritage. Recently I have been struck – and sometimes amused – by the growing number of places that have erected bilingual road signs. To make life easier for the uninitiated, the Occitan name usually has the Occitan cross beside it. For example, we have Toulouse and *Tolosa*, Puylaurens and *Pueglaurenç*. Even tiny villages are at it: Belleserre, *Bèlasèrra,* and Lagardiolle, *La Gardiòla*. In the case of Bertre, *Bèrtre*, I am still trying to decide if the accent on the first vowel alters the pronunciation sufficiently to justify the cost of two extra signs on the roads leading into the village.

One summer's morning I discovered that this affection for Occitan rebranding was about to take a giant leap forward.

Friday 24 June 2016 is a day of high political drama due to the results of two popular votes. Over breakfast I discover my days are numbered as a citizen of the European Union. I barely have time to digest my buttered croissant before I experience another shock, or perhaps in comparison with Brexit I should call it a minor aftershock. The name of my region is changing to Occitanie, and when I study a map I discover I am living at its geographic heart.

At the beginning of 2016, France reduced its number of administrative regions from twenty-two to thirteen, and I found myself living in Languedoc-Roussillon-Midi-Pyrénées. Everyone agreed this was at least two hyphens too many, and the new regional council launched a project to find a new name. This was far too important a matter to leave entirely to the whims of an unpredictable electorate, and after initial consultation the project committee wisely put together a short-list of five names for the public to rank in a non-binding referendum: Languedoc, Occitanie, Languedoc-Pyrénées, Occitanie-Pays Catalan and Pyrénées-Méditerranée.

I voted for Languedoc because its spelling remains unchanged in English, it contains no accents or hyphens, and from a historical perspective it provides the best geographic fit with our new region. But over a late lunch I conclude I am not too disappointed by the choice of Occitanie, or Occitania as it was once called in Latin and Occitan. The name sounds as if it were invented for a work of fantasy fiction, and it fires my imagination to such an extent, my afternoon siesta is filled with dreams of an enchanted medieval land where troubadours and knights wandered freely from court to court and serenaded ladies whose virtue was always irreproachable.

When I wake up, my fantasy world is soon sullied by local politics. Within hours of the referendum result, the new name of Occitanie is being condemned from all sides. A group in the part of France between Perpignan and the Spanish border takes umbrage at the absence of the word 'Catalan' and launches a website with the opportunistic headline, 'Catexit: let's leave this region that doesn't recognise us!' Ironically, a representative of the far-right Front National calls 'Occitanie' a divisive and militant expression and he deplores the demise of 'Languedoc'.

The president of our neighbouring region, Aquitaine Limousin Poitou-Charentes, is not amused, although he will cheer up in three days' time when his own region adopts the far catchier name of Nouvelle Aquitaine. Meanwhile he mutters darkly about a takeover because, he asserts, in medieval times the term Occitania covered a much larger geography including significant parts of his own region. Occitania was the land where people once spoke Occitan, and that included nearly everywhere in France south of a line passing from Bordeaux through Limoges, Clermont-Ferrand and Grenoble down to Nice.

All this passion and anger over a change of name leaves me bemused. It is not as if the public has voted to tear up forty years of treaties and leave the European Union, but it does make me pause for thought during my evening aperitif. If the Languedoc is not the same as Occitania, what about the languages? I have never been sure of the difference between *la langue d'oc* and Occitan, or patois come to that. Local people seem to use the words interchangeably, and where do Catalan, Gascon or Provençal fit in? Suddenly I am aware of my ignorance about the languages spoken by Jourdain de Roquefort and his friends, my more elderly neighbours, and the troubadours I was dreaming about during my siesta.

After much searching I find two succinct, authoritative and almost identical responses to my first question, '*Ôc qu'es aquô?*' What is Occitan? Both the Department of Occitan Studies at the University of Montpellier and the Institute of Occitan Studies in Toulouse tell me the Occitan language evolved from Latin a little over a thousand years ago. One of the first written instances of the term *langue d'oc* appeared in an essay written by the Italian poet Dante Alighieri sometime between 1302 and 1305. The equivalent Latin word, *Occitan*, dates from around the same time, although it was rarely used until the twentieth century. Today, Occitan consists of six main dialects: Languedocian, Provençal, Gascon, Limousin, Auvergnat and Vivaro Alpin.

Dante's role in popularising the term *langue d'oc* boils down to a simple but memorable idea: he grouped the European languages of his day according to their word for 'yes'. In his essay, '*De vulgari eloquentia*' or '*On eloquence in the vernacular*', he tells us that at the end of the thirteenth century nearly all the English, Hungarian, Saxon, Slav and Teuton nations said *iô* when they answered in the affirmative. Yo! But as for the rest, '*...some now say* oc, *some* oil *and some* si.' For Dante, the land of *si* roughly corresponded to modern-day Italy, *oil* covered the northern two-thirds of France where Simon de Montfort and most of his crusaders came from, and the land of *oc* embraced the rest of France and much of northern Spain.

While I am browsing through the information offered by the University of Montpellier, I stumble across the name of a friend of mine. He is on the teaching staff but his roots are in the Lauragais. His father and grandfather were born in my village, and a long time ago his great-grandfather was our mayor. Dr Laurent Alibert has a rare gift for languages. Not only does he speak, in alphabetical order. English, French, Italian, Ossetian, Russian and Spanish, but more importantly for my purposes, he speaks Occitan. He reads and writes it as well, something which none of my older neighbours can do, and his doctorate is in Occitan Studies from the University of Montpellier where today he teaches the language to a new generation. Laurent, I realise with a rush of excitement, is the perfect person to tell me more about the past, present and future of Occitan. Fortune is smiling on my project already, and I still haven't touched Madame Colombié's cannonball. Even better, I am sure he will be able to recommend a good troubadour.

I send him an email and invite him to call in for coffee next time he comes to the village. He replies with some proposed dates and, unable to resist the habits of his profession, he includes a suggested reading list. I had imagined I would be the one asking the questions, but now it seems I have some studying to do before my Occitan tutorial.

8

Troubadours and Trobairitz

Dr Alibert's first recommendation lands in my postbox with a thump so loud it would terrify even the most dedicated of students. '*Grains of Gold*' is a heavyweight anthology of Occitan literature spanning the period between the year 950 and the present day. Even though the original texts are accompanied by English translations, I soon realise I shall have time to read only a tiny fraction of them before Laurent comes over for coffee. I need to focus my efforts. After a few days of turning pages in a darkened room, I conclude that if the troubadours were at the heart of the golden age of Occitan literature, I need to track one down, ideally from the Lauragais.

The word 'troubadour' comes from the Occitan verb '*trobar*', meaning 'to compose or discover'. We know of around 450 male troubadours, and twenty trobairitz as the women were called. They were kings and princes, nobles and knights, and aristocratic ladies. Richard the Lionheart is credited with two works, written in the Occitan he had learned from his mother, Eleanor of Aquitaine. For him, it was something of a family tradition; his great-grandfather, Guillaume IX Duke of Aquitaine, started composing in the early twelfth century and is generally regarded as the first known troubadour. When I glance through one of Guillaume's works, I am startled to discover it describes in rather crude terms a threesome with Lady Agnes and Lady Ermessen, both of whom were married to other members of the nobility. We have to wait until the middle of the twelfth century to find songs of *fin'amor*, (literally 'pure love', but more often translated as 'courtly love'). This was the beginning of the golden age of Occitan literature when the songs of the troubadours were performed throughout southern France and northern Spain, and when their art form was exported to England, Germany and the land of the *langue d'oil.*

They also wrote in other genres. One of the best-known works of Occitan literature is an epic poem, '*Canso de la Crosada*' or '*The Song of the Crusade*', started by Guilhem de Tudela around 1210 and completed by an anonymous author ten or so years later. It is written from the viewpoint of the Cathars and provides a counter-balance to the narrative composed in Latin by the crusading monk, Pierre des Vaux-de-Cernay.

Post-Guillaume IX, the typical troubadour song, or *canso*, is a monologue in which an amorous knight swears devotion to an aristocratic married lady. Around 2,500 such compositions survive. Although some troubadours performed their own works, it was more common for the *cansos* to be sung by wandering minstrels called *joglars* in Occitan, or *jongleurs* in French. Some troubadours had their preferred *joglars* whom they sent on tour in what might be regarded as an early example of the tribute act. On stage, the *joglar* introduced each song with a short speech about the life of the troubadour-composer (his *vida*) and the story behind the composition (the *razo*). In this way, a troubadour's music could reach a wider audience and continue to be performed after the composer had retired or expired.

The reason so many troubadour songs survive is that, in the mid-thirteenth century, scribes began compiling them into songbooks called *chansonniers*. They also included the *joglar* supplements which were further embellished to the point where some of the *vidas* and *razos* are undoubtedly as imaginative as the official biography of a modern rock star or the sleeve notes to his or her latest album. Unreliable though they may be, they remain our prime source of information about the lives of the troubadours.

So did any of them come from the Lauragais? I trawl through various articles and websites and then, to my delight, I discover a fourteenth-century prizewinner.

The oldest literary institution in the western world is called the Acadèmia dels Jòcs Florals, or the Academy of the Floral Games. It was founded in 1323 by seven troubadour-citizens of Toulouse, and it organised its first Occitan poetry competition the following year. The proud winner of the inaugural gilded violet was Arnaud Vidal de Castelnaudary who, as his name suggests, came from Castelnaudary, a town in the heart of the Lauragais. Unfortunately my excitement soon evaporates when I discover that only one of Arnaud's compositions has survived: an adventure story he had written a few years before his prize-winning poem. I track down a nineteenth-century copy, but even the editor describes it as mediocre. That won't do! I continue my search, and find the names of five more troubadours from the Lauragais, but they offer only a single surviving work between them. I need to find a more prolific and talented songsmith, even if I have to stray slightly further afield.

Raimon de Miraval soon catches my attention when I realise I have unknowingly cycled past his front door dozens of times, and he would have been a regular traveller through the Lauragais on his way to the court of Count Raymond VI in Toulouse. He would also have known Jourdain de Roquefort and the Count of Foix and all the other Cathar nobles, and he had good reason to hate Simon de Montfort as vehemently as they did.

Even better for my purposes, Raimon de Miraval was a troubadour who truly lived his art. He was a knight so poor he only owned a quarter-share of an insignificant castle hidden in a lost valley of the Montagne Noire. No wonder he fell hopelessly in love with the wives of the two brothers who owned the bigger château next door. And in his old age he was tempted to come out of retirement in a bid to save the world, the Cathar world, from destruction by the crusaders.

I study my maps of the Montagne Noire and plan a visit to Raimon's modest home. I shall go there as soon as Dr Alibert has visited mine.

9

AN OCCITAN TUTORIAL

I am waiting on my terrace for Laurent to arrive. In the distance, hungry combine harvesters chew their way through golden crops and throw up clouds of dust. I try to ignore the sounds of mechanised farming and, like an anxious student revising on the morning of an important exam, I scan a few lines from *'The Song of the Crusade'*. They describe the death of Simon de Montfort at the siege of Toulouse in 1218 where a rock fired from a catapult by the women of the town *'struck the count [Simon] so squarely on his steel helmet that it smashed his eyes, brain, teeth, forehead, jaw; and the count fell dead on the ground, bleeding and black'*.[5]

The sound of footsteps on gravel drags me back to the present. It is only ten o'clock but the sun is crushingly hot so we sit beneath the awning. I pour coffee and offer Laurent a plate of chocolate biscuits which are already beginning to melt. I shuffle my papers and turn on my voice recorder. Laurent is half the age of anyone

5 Translated from : Meyer, Paul. *La Chanson de la Croisade Contre les Albigeois commencé par Guillaume de Tudèle et continué par un poète anonyme. Tome Second.* Paris : Librairie Renouard, 1879 (page 419).

else I know who speaks the language of the troubadours, and my first question is obvious.

'Why did you want to learn Occitan?'

I know he has been asked this question countless times, by his parents, his friends, and even by me, but there is nothing tired about the smile that accompanies his reply, and on this occasion I shall pay more attention and record his answer for safe measure.

'In the beginning it was childhood curiosity. I used to come here every summer to stay with my grandparents. They spoke French with us, but with each other they spoke something else. They didn't give it a name, but to my ears it was a distinct language, not a patois, because in French *patois* is a pejorative term meaning a corrupted or sick version of a true language. I started to pick up a few words, but my grandfather didn't want to teach me. He used to ask, "Why do you want to learn this language?" But I persevered and in the end he was pleased. When I was in my early twenties I began to study it seriously.'

'Why was he reluctant to teach you?'

'He remembered how he had suffered like most of the local children when he first went to school. Before the age of seven he didn't speak any French.'

Eloi Alibert was born in 1914. I have read that on the eve of the Great War more than ten million people spoke Occitan. That was around a quarter of the French population, but I always assumed they could speak the national language as well.

'Surely he understood French?'

'No, because it was never spoken at home. So at the age of seven, children like my grandfather suddenly found themselves in a strange new environment where they couldn't say a word. It was strictly forbidden to use Occitan in the classroom or in the playground. They were told it wasn't a proper language, it was only patois, and they had to learn French.'

Being struck dumb, even temporarily, at the age of seven must have been a shock for Eloi. I imagine how the smug minority of children who already knew French would have mocked him cruelly, and sniggered every time the schoolmaster rapped his knuckles for daring to let slip a word of Occitan.

'What exactly did your grandfather speak at home?'

'He spoke the Occitan dialect of this area: the Lauragais is in the Languedoc so he spoke Languedocian.'

'So does that mean Provençal is the Occitan dialect of Provence?'

'That depends on whom you ask.' Laurent grins and fiddles with the gold Occitan cross around his neck. 'A friend of mine teaches at Aix-Marseille University. When I speak Occitan with him he uses exactly the same language as I do, but when he writes his Provençal poetry he uses different spellings and claims it's a different language. I admit Provençal and Languedocian are not identical, but to my ear they are closer than Languedocian and Gascon, and everyone accepts both of those are Occitan dialects. Whether we choose to be united or not seems to be mainly a question of spelling and ideology.'

I take a sip of coffee and reflect that the century-long conflict between the Provençalists and the Occitanists is complicated, politically charged, and frankly mystifying to most outsiders. Its roots go back to 1854 when the most famous and successful Occitan, or Provençal, writer since the troubadours became one of the founders of a movement called 'Lou Felibrige' in Provençal, or 'Lo Felibritge' in Occitan. Frédéric Mistral dedicated his life to promoting and protecting the language and culture of Provence. In 1904 he received the ultimate accolade when he won the Nobel Prize for Literature for his Provençal compositions. By then, the Félibrige movement had established itself throughout the south of France. It favoured Provence in all matters and tried to impose Mistral's spelling system on all the other dialects of Occitan. In the first half of the twentieth century, scholars, linguists and writers in these other Occitan-speaking areas rejected Mistral's dictature and moved instead towards a classical spelling system based on the medieval language of the troubadours. These learned disputes were irrelevant to most of the ten million Occitan speakers of the day because they didn't know how to read or write in either system, but the two movements argued anyway and have continued to do so ever since.

'Today we Occitanists are largely reconciled with the Félibriges, but more recently a large group has split away in Provence and persists in believing Provençal is a separate language.' Dr Alibert is smiling, but the tone of his voice reveals his frustration. 'Unfortunately they remain very popular.'

'Are relations with the Catalans any better?'

'Oh, the Catalans are in another world. They have succeeded beyond our wildest dreams. We look to them for inspiration.'

'But can you understand them?'

'Yes, if they speak slowly, and to be honest I find Gascon more difficult. Catalan has the same origins as Occitan, and when spoken Catalan first appeared in the twelfth and thirteenth centuries, they still wrote in Occitan. One of the most prolific troubadours of the period came from Girona.'

I look him up later and discover that 114 of Cerveri de Girona's compositions survive, but none of his music. I also discover that Catalonia is the only place in the world where an Occitan dialect enjoys the status of an official language. In the Aran Valley of the central Pyrenees they speak something similar to Gascon called Aranese.

I ask Laurent another question. 'Would your grandfather have been able to read the works of the troubadours?'

'No, because the written use of Occitan died out in the sixteenth century and after that it was thought of as an oral language. I can read them because I have studied the medieval language, but most modern Occitan speakers find the vocabulary and syntax of the troubadours as challenging as you would find Chaucer or *"Sir Gawain and the Green Knight"*.'

'Was that the point at which Occitan fragmented into different dialects – Provençal, Languedocian and all the rest – when there was no longer a unifying written language?'

'No. We have non-literary written records which suggest the current range of spoken dialects existed even in medieval times, but it seems everyone could understand the troubadours. They wrote a standardised form of Occitan and their songs were understood throughout the Occitan-speaking world.'

The demise of written Occitan dates very precisely from 10 August 1539. In the Edict of Villers-Cotterêts, named after the village where it was signed, François I decreed that all administrative and legal business in his kingdom should henceforth be conducted in French. This edict was primarily directed against Latin, but it had a dramatic side-effect on Occitan. After 1550 there is virtually no trace of Occitan in the judicial and administrative archives of Toulouse or Bordeaux. Despite this, Occitan remained the dominant spoken language in the south of France. Like Laurent's grandfather, generation after generation learned the local dialect at home. Then the French Revolution brought a more deliberate attack.

Abbé Henri Grégoire, Bishop of Blois, was an influential and, in many ways, an enlightened revolutionary leader who called for the abolition of slavery, the ending of privileges for the nobility and the introduction of universal suffrage. But he also called for the death of all regional languages and dialects in a paper presented to the government in 1794: '*Report on the need and means to annihilate patois and to make the use of the French language universal.*' Abbé Grégoire was convinced that imposing a common language was the best way to spread knowledge among the masses, counteract superstition and create one nation. In his report he indicated the scale of the task: at that time roughly half the population was unable to conduct a conversation in French; instead they spoke one of thirty dialects, many of which were mutually unintelligible. France, he observed, was a Tower of Babel.

During the next century, primary education became universal, obligatory and free, and local schoolmasters, who had often grown up speaking Occitan themselves, were obliged to ensure their pupils never spoke the shameful patois at school. Only the activism of movements such as the Félibriges and the Occitanists, and the curiosity and enthusiasm of people like Laurent, have saved Occitan from the fate wished upon it by Abbé Grégoire.

Dr Alibert's thoughts on the present state and future prospects of Occitan logically belong at the end of these chapters about the language of the troubadours. Before then, I shall go in search of Raimon de Miraval and some music.

10

At Home with Raimon de Miraval

On my previous visits to Miraval-Cabardès I have cycled through the village with no more thought for its château than a rather bored, 'Oh look! More ruins!' In my own defence I shall add that, on my usual circuit, by the time I reach Raimon's home, I am hot and tired and have already passed the more impressive ruins of the four châteaux guarding the hills around Lastours, the Château de Roquefère (if I make a slight detour for an ice-cream), the grassy terraces of the Château de Mas-Cabardès, and the surprisingly extensive ruins of a thirteenth-century church abandoned in the middle of nowhere. When I spot my seventh medieval castle in about as many kilometres, the insignificant remains of the Château de Miraval make little impression on me.

Today is different. First, I am travelling by car. Second, I am playing my collection of Raimon's songs at disco volume and I intend to listen to my favourite tune when I reach the top of his castle mound. Third, I am following a different route which takes me across the plain from Puylaurens to Revel and up through the westernmost forests of the Montagne Noire.

I pause in Saissac and admire another splendid panorama of Pyrenean peaks. The old town and its ruined château lie a stone's throw below me, and in the time of the Cathars, this was the home of Bernard de Saissac, a patron of Raimon de Miraval and several other troubadours.

I resume my journey and follow the route Raimon would have taken between Saissac and his own château, a sinuous and undulating ribbon that winds its way through mountain pastures and dense oak forests. Soon after Cuxac-Cabardès the road begins a treacherous descent into the valley of the Orbiel. Early morning shadows and fallen leaves from a recent storm camouflage the fine line between tarmac and catastrophe. I have to breathe in when I squeeze my way through the narrow streets of La Tourette, but I reach the river without mishap and soon arrive in Miraval-Cabardès. I park my car by a pretty roadside *lavoir* adorned with hanging baskets. These stone buildings are common in the Lauragais, a reminder of how the village women did their laundry before the invention of the washing machine. A concrete footbridge leads me over the river and into a narrow street. On the wall of the house next door to the *mairie* some joker has mounted a metal plaque: *'Ici le 17 avril 1891 il ne se passa strictement rien'*, *'Here on 17 April 1891 absolutely nothing happened'*. What a relief! I don't want another important historical event gatecrashing my troubadour party.

I cross a second bridge and enter a tiny *place*. Ahead of me is a mound. Steps are cut into the rock, and their worn, rounded edges tell me they were fashioned a long, long time ago. Attached to the rockface beside the steps is another plaque which informs me in Occitan that the troubadour Raimon de Miraval was born here sometime in the twelfth century. Even the most basic details of his life are intriguingly vague. He was born in 1135, or maybe 1160, or even 1165. He died in 1216, 1220, or perhaps 1229, aged somewhere between fifty-one and ninety-four, probably at the monastery of Santa Clara in Lerida, Spain. Fortunately there is no dispute about *where* he was born, and I have managed to track down recordings of some of his songs. He wrote most of them between 1191 and 1213. Twenty-two of these compositions survive complete with lyrics and melodies, and they are still performed today.

I look beyond the plaque. Far above me, a white effigy of Christ gleams on a wooden cross against the pale blue morning sky. I begin to climb the castle mound, and after the first turn the steps vanish and I struggle up a slope of slippery grass until I reach the cross. A flat area roughly the size of a tennis court is strewn with wildflowers. When their barbs scratch my legs and dig into my feet and ankles, I decide someone in a less poetic frame of mind would probably call them weeds.

In front of me stands an 'L' shaped section of battlement, and I speculate that this may have been Raimon's quarter-share of the castle. Arrow slits pierce the crenellations, and there is another row of them at the height of my knees. I deduce that the ground has risen over the centuries and that the grass and wildflowers around my feet cover the rubble of Raimon's ruined château.

It is easy to see why someone built a castle on this piece of rock. It is a *presqu'île*, nearly an island, a natural defensive position. Below me, the river describes a loop like the Greek letter 'Ω' and the walls of the château seem to grow out of steep cliffs that rise from the river's edge. For me there is one major drawback with this location: there is no view. The château and the village lie in a natural bowl surrounded by steep slopes and forests of evergreen oak. Due to the twists in the river, you cannot see more than a few hundred metres up or down the valley. Miraval-Cabardès is a lost and lonely spot. In Raimon's day, the meagre lands of his estate supported forty men and their families. The 2013 census counted a total population of thirty-seven.

From my vantage point, I have a clear view of the road where it bends around the rocky base of the village church far below me.

Since I have arrived, half a dozen bicycles have passed by, and they far outnumber the motorised traffic. Not one of the riders has looked up at me standing on this forlorn castle mound.

I peer through one of the arrow slits and all I can see are trees. It is easy to believe that absolutely nothing happened here on 17 April 1891, or on any other day in history. You need imagination to bring the Château de Miraval back to life, and perhaps some music.

If you are a celebrity-watcher, by now you may be thinking, this doesn't sound like the Château de Miraval where Angelina Jolie and Brad Pitt secretly married in 2014. And indeed it isn't. The other one lies 390 kilometres to the east on an estate of 400 hectares complete with vineyards and a recording studio. Before Angelina and Brad bought the place, artists who recorded there included Pink Floyd, Sting and AC/DC, and this explains why the estate has the cheek to label one of its wines 'Pink Floyd rosé'. But I can't help wondering if all these musicians made the same mistake, if they were seeking inspiration from Raimon de Miraval, but when they drove down from Paris they took a wrong turn just before Avignon.

In contrast, I have come to the older Château de Miraval, the one with a musical heritage stretching back eight centuries. I sit on my grassy throne like a prince and I have no hesitation about which song I shall command my troubadour to play. I already know from my visits to medieval fairs that much of the music from Raimon's era sounds irritatingly repetitive to modern ears. I have also been struck by the fact that most performances of Raimon's songs sound as if they were recorded in a church, which is inappropriate because they were in no way religious. I have unearthed only one recording with an articulation and a dynamic and a variation of tempo that match my idea of a troubadour song. Perhaps a purist would tell me the original work has been corrupted to please modern tastes, and that a lute or vielle was easier to carry on horseback than a harp, but I don't care. I am sure each *joglar* had his own way of playing a song to please his audience.

I rest my back against the castle wall and listen to '*Apenas sai don m'apreing*' performed by the Italian harpist Matteo Zenatti. I know the piece well enough to be able to hum along with the melody, but I suspect I shall never master the Occitan lyrics, or even the title which translates as *'I scarcely know where I learn...'*

The sound of the harp dies away and all I can hear is the wind. Down in the *mairie* someone is working with the light on, and I watch another weary cyclist labour up the hill by the church. Otherwise I am alone with my thoughts of Raimon and his songs. I glance around me and remember the ghost of Montgey. I rub my arms and they are covered in goose-bumps. It is the wind, I tell myself, but I shiver with the eerie thought that I am sitting on the ruins of Raimon de Miraval's home listening to music he wrote 800 years ago.

I pull his picture out of my pocket. It comes from a thirteenth-century illustrated manuscript, a *chansonnier,* and it shows a cheerful-looking, clean-shaven young man riding a pink horse. He wears no hat and his chestnut hair is cut above his ears. His riding habit is blue, and he holds the reins in one hand and with the other he appears to be marking time to his latest melody. I picture him putting the finishing touches to my favourite song while he and his pink mount gallop along the road that brought me here, and it occurs to me that many of the characters in the story of Montgey will almost certainly have listened to this same composition: Jourdain de Roquefort, Count Raymond VI, and the Count of Foix and his son Roger-Bernard.

Raimon de Miraval was a frequent visitor to the court in Toulouse, and in many of his compositions he uses the pseudonym Audiart to represent Count Raymond. In return, he was honoured by the count who gave him gifts of horses, arms and other finery. He was also admired by his contemporaries, but according to the *vidas* and *razos*, his romantic life was often a disaster. He divorced his wife Gaudairença, allegedly because she composed dances and it was too much to have two poets under one roof. So for much of his musical career, Raimon travelled around the Lauragais a free man and a celebrated troubadour, and he composed his songs of courtly love for ladies who pleased him.

Despite the platonic affection so revered in many troubadour songs, in real life neither the ladies nor the gentlemen of the nobility were able to resist the temptation to explore the more physical aspects of their love. As René Nelli suggests in his book, '*Raimon de Miraval – Du jeu subtil à l'amour fou*', '*Raimon de Miraval – from a subtle game to uncontrollable passion*', it may have been tempting for a lady of the time to practise platonic love with the men she did not find attractive, and carnal love with those who were more to her taste. This certainly seems to have been the case with two of the women Raimon courted through his songs.

First came Etiennette de Pennautier. She was reputed to have a voracious appetite for men, and she is better known as Lady Loba, '*loba*' being the Occitan for 'she-wolf'. She was the wife of Jourdain de Cabaret who, with his brother Pierre-Roger, owned the eponymous château down the road above what is today called Lastours. Lady Loba was famed for her beauty, and Raimon was not the only troubadour to sing her praises. In his song '*D'Amor es totz mos cossiriers*', '*Love is all I think about*', Raimon beseeches her to return his love, which has been long and loyal for five whole years, and not to keep him hanging on in such uncertainty. Deaf to his entreaty, she chose instead to become the long-term mistress of the Count of Foix, to whom she bore a child. Presumably this was a clear enough rebuttal, even for romantic Raimon.

After that setback, sometime around 1206 Raimon de Miraval turned his attention to Azalaïs de Boissézon, wife of the lord of

Lombers. Azalaïs was a lady in search of fame, or at least notoriety, and she was delighted when such a famous troubadour agreed to write songs about her. With Raimon's help her beauty would be celebrated far and wide, not easy to achieve at a time when there were no tabloids, no celebrity magazines and no selfies.

Unfortunately for Raimon, he excelled himself in his songwriting and soon found himself a victim of his own game. He fell in love with her himself, but Azalaïs was aiming higher than a poor knight with a minority stake in a tiny château. She wanted to attract the attention of the King of Aragon who was also the Count of Barcelona and therefore ruled most of northern Spain. When she asked Raimon to extol her charms in a new song, our troubadour duly obliged and probably wished he hadn't. '*Ar'ab la forsa del freis*', '*Now that the cold [of winter] is in all its force*' did not seek to hide its objectives; it was a very direct form of marketing. '*If the king [of Aragon] comes a courting to Lombers, joy will always be with him...because the courtesy and gaiety of the beautiful Madame Azalaïs, her fresh complexion and her blonde hair bring happiness to the whole world.*'

When King Pedro II first heard it, he rushed hot-footed and hot-blooded all the way to Lombers, situated between Castres and Albi. According to the song's *razo*, '*And she [Azalaïs] granted him permission to do anything he wished, and that night the king took everything he desired.*'

Poor Raimon soon consoled himself with the other noble spouse down the road at the Château de Cabaret. His songs about Lady Brunessen were more discreet, maybe because he was older and wiser, or perhaps because her husband, Pierre-Roger de Cabaret, was a powerful friend and protector. Ultimately the strength of this neighbour proved to be a double-edged sword because, if Pierre-Roger had not proved such a thorn in the side of Simon de Montfort, the crusaders may not have destroyed the Château de Miraval.

11

An Occitan Swansong

I pack away my affairs and take a last look around the ruins of Raimon's home. It seems ironic that today the symbol of the crusaders – the crucifix – should dominate the site from a plinth built with stones torn from his château.

I stroll back to my car and continue my journey through Raimon de Miraval's world. I head downstream alongside the Orbiel towards the Château de Cabaret where Lady Loba and Lady Brunessen once lived. The road twists and turns in the shade alongside the river, and after a kilometre I pause at the ruined church of Saint-Pierre-de-Vals, lost in the forest at the midpoint between Miraval-Cabardès and La Tourette. It was built to serve the two villages, probably a few years after Raimon lost his château, and it was abandoned towards the end of the seventeenth century after a long argument about which village should pay for its upkeep. Only the cemetery is still in use, and when I wander among the tombstones the most recent grave I can find is dated 2012. There is something disconcerting about the sight of silk and plastic flowers and shiny marble tombs alongside the ivy-covered ruins of a roofless church.

Two kilometres further and I pass through Mas-Cabardès, a much larger community than Miraval. The village existed in Raimon's time, but the ruined château on the rocky heights above the town was built a century after his death. It may stand on the site of an older castle, but if it did, the owner's wife wasn't pretty enough for Raimon to mention her in any of his songs.

After Mas-Cabardès, the valley opens out and the countryside responds to an increasingly Mediterranean climate. These are the southern slopes of the Montagne Noire, and the dense oak forests give way to the scrubby vegetation and rocky hillsides of the *garrigue*. Shade is much harder to find and the landscape reflects a harsher light. I pass a vineyard and then I am in Lastours. Red flags bearing the Occitan cross flutter from lampposts beside colourful hanging baskets. High above me a line of ruined châteaux gleam from a dazzling blue sky. The rocky spur above Lastours dwarfs the castle mounds of Miraval and Mas-Cabardès. Squeezed between the valley of the Orbiel to the east and the ravine of the Grésilhou to the west, it rises abruptly to a height of 300 metres. On its lower slopes lie the excavated remains of a medieval village, and on the highest points of the ridge four separate châteaux stand in a line: Cabaret, Tour Régine, Surdespine and Quertinheux.

Today, the tourist leaflets describe Lastours as the only site in France with four châteaux. I pay a modest entry fee and start climbing, and my visit proves to be the perfect way to spend a couple of energetic hours, particularly with tales from the past spinning around inside my head. The hillside is riddled with caves, and before I can reach the first château I am forced to scamper through a thirty-five metre long cavern which no doubt helped deter unwelcome visitors in earlier times.

Beyond the cavern, cypress trees stand guard on the rocky hillside below the line of stone towers. I would like to imagine

Raimon de Miraval admiring this same view while he perfected the lines of his latest composition for Lady Loba or Lady Brunessen, but unfortunately all four châteaux were built shortly after he fled the country. Raimon would have entered the site from the north on the old Roman road to Carcassonne, and from where I am standing I can still see its trace on the other side of the Grésilhou.

I skirt around low cliffs on a dusty path and march off through the *garrigue* until I reach a fork. To my right the path climbs up to the remains of the thirteenth-century Château de Cabaret, built twenty or thirty years after Raimon last visited his neighbours. To my left, the path zigzags down the hillside towards the river. The older Château de Cabaret, where Pierre-Roger, Jourdain, and their wives lived, was built on a small promontory half way between the river and the newer château. Below it, their village was built on eight or nine terraces leading down to the water.

I explore the ruins and lose myself in a maze of paths among the pine trees. The air tastes hot, even in the shade, and the scent of the conifers is overpowering. I would welcome the sound of running water and the freshness a river brings to the air, but at this time of year the Grésilhou is no more than a dried-up bed of pebbles. I sit down on a wall and take a long drink of water. I notice a discreet sign which tells me I am in what was once the forge. Excavations during the last thirty years have also identified a stable, a workshop, a quarry, a water cistern and numerous houses where a vibrant community once flourished.

Today, all I can hear is the song of the cicadas in the trees above my head. Their voices are so loud and insistent, I decide to drown them out with the opening lines of one of Raimon's more pastoral compositions, *'Be m'agrada-l bels tems d'estiu'*. I slip on my headphones and imagine Raimon is sitting beside me. The breeze carries his serenade up the hillside and through the open window of a stone tower to the unreceptive ears of Lady Loba.

'Fine summer weather pleases me so well
And the song of the birds pleases me too
The leaves and the branches, they please me
And the green meadows make me pleased.'

Hmm! Raimon has been described as a good songwriter but a poor poet, and his overuse of the verb '*agradar*' brings another song title to mind: '*Please Please Me*'. Perhaps he has more in common with The Beatles than Bob Dylan. His song soon reaches a more typical troubadour theme. *'But you [madame], it doesn't please you to give me what I need; what pleases you is to see me dying from desire'.*

These lines remind me of another troubadour who courted the insatiable Lady Loba, but who was even more unlucky in love than Raimon. With admirable logic, Peire Vidal concluded that the best way to come close to the She-Wolf was to dress up – as a wolf! Unfortunately for Peire, his disguise was so convincing that the local shepherds mistook him for a real one and nearly killed him.

Cabaret is an idyllic spot, a place to enjoy songs of courtly love, a place to dream. For me, the whole journey between Saissac, Miraval and Lastours has been a voyage through an enchanted landscape of forbidden forests, brooding castles and timeless villages. But in 1209, this halcyon world was shattered by the cataclysmic arrival of Simon de Montfort and his crusaders.

Pierre-Roger de Cabaret put up a stronger resistance than most of his contemporaries. Around this spot where I am sitting, he provided shelter for Cathars and dispossessed knights who fled from the crusaders after the fall of Carcassonne on 15 August 1209. A few weeks later, Simon de Montfort marched up the valley of the Orbiel with his troops and launched an attack on Cabaret, but he had underestimated the strength of its natural defences and the determination of its defenders. He soon retreated.

Some historians suggest this was the moment when Raimon de Miraval's château was destroyed, but my journey this morning along the twisty, cliff-lined road between Miraval and Lastours convinces me it would have been extremely foolhardy for Simon de Montfort to march further up the valley while Cabaret remained in the hands of the Cathars. Simon would have known that at some point he would be obliged to turn around and head back to his base in Carcassonne, and there could be little doubt that he would be ambushed somewhere along the way.

What happened shortly afterwards supports my case. After his failed attack on Cabaret, Simon put his wife's cousin, Bouchard de Marly, in charge of the Château de Saissac and tasked him with keeping an eye on the rebellious neighbours. One day, Bouchard and fifty of his men were ambushed while they were patrolling the hills around Cabaret. Several were killed, and Bouchard himself was captured and carried off to Pierre-Roger's château where he spent the next eighteen months a prisoner.

The following August, Simon began a four month siege of the Château de Termes to the south-east of Carcassonne. He started with a modest army, but before long, new crusaders embarking on their forty days began to arrive in such large numbers that they created a new problem: how to feed them all. The surrounding countryside was a land of forests and mines, and it offered little nourishment for a mighty army, so Simon was obliged to organise convoys to bring food from Carcassonne. These provided a perfect target for Pierre-Roger de Cabaret and his knights. They repeatedly ambushed and robbed the supply trains, and either killed their enemies or mutilated them as a warning to the others.

Towards the end of November 1210, the château's remaining defenders – including Jourdain de Roquefort's father, Guillaume – fled in the night, probably due to an outbreak of dysentery. This left Simon de Montfort firmly in control of the lands around Carcassonne and much of the Lauragais, apart from one painful thorn in his side: the impregnable Château de Cabaret where his friend and relative was still being held captive. Worse still, by this time Simon's wife and Bouchard de Marly's mother had travelled south to join him. I can imagine the two women giving him a hard time that winter. 'Come on Simon! You're leader of the crusade, aren't you? Surely you can do *something* to rescue poor Bouchard from his dungeon!'

The truth of the matter was that the leader of the crusade found himself almost powerless each winter. The forty-day pilgrim-soldiers were no fools: like modern tourists, they began to arrive each spring with the good weather, and by the end of November they had all gone home. Simon de Montfort was obliged to hide himself away during the cold, dark months of winter, along with a couple of dozen knights and three or four thousand men. It was barely enough to defend the châteaux and towns they had already captured, and certainly didn't allow him to contemplate attacking anywhere new.

Sometime around 13 March 1211, the first crusaders of the new season arrived. Simon could now resume the war. His first priority was to deal with the Château de Cabaret and try to rescue his friend. He was about to set out from Carcassonne and mount a siege, when Bouchard de Marly unexpectedly turned up at one of the city gates. Even more surprising, he was freshly-shaven, dressed in new clothes and riding a fine horse.

Pierre-Roger de Cabaret had evidently taken good care of his prisoner, and I'm sure he would have asked his musical neighbour to call in now and again to provide some light entertainment. Raimon would no doubt have been delighted to spend more time with Lady Brunessen, and I am convinced that when Bouchard de Marly rode up to the gates of Carcassonne he was humming one of our troubadour's greatest hits, '*Lonc temps ai agutz cossiriers*', because the opening lines roughly translate as: *'I've been worried and troubled for ages…but now all that has changed'*.

Why had Pierre-Roger played the good host and released his enemy unharmed? Because many of the fugitive knights had abandoned him during the winter, and he knew his château was too isolated to resist indefinitely. He had sent Bouchard de Marly to negotiate an honourable surrender. The enemies soon reached an agreement: Pierre-Roger de Cabaret rode east to take possession of a new estate near Béziers, and Simon de Montfort took over the Château de Cabaret and set off to lay siege to Lavaur. On his way he destroyed Raimon de Miraval's home, and in despair our troubadour swore never to sing again until he had won it back. A few weeks later the Cathars massacred the crusader-pilgrims at Montgey.

We do not know if Raimon de Miraval was at home when the crusaders came calling, but soon afterwards he was in Toulouse with Count Raymond, and it was in Toulouse that he wrote his final song two years later, shortly before the biggest battle of the Albigensian Crusade.

On 27 January 1213, a strange ceremony took place in Toulouse. Count Raymond, his son and the consuls of Toulouse broke their feudal ties to the French crown. Instead, they swore an oath of loyalty to the man who had been so inflamed by Raimon's song about Lady Azalaïs: Pedro II, King of Aragon and Count of Barcelona. In the same ceremony, the counts of Béarn, Comminges and Foix, who were already vassals of Pedro, renewed their oaths of allegiance. This ceremony created a mighty trans-Pyrenean kingdom. It was also another step in Count Raymond's plan to persuade King Pedro to join him in the fight against the northern invaders. He had already married one of Pedro's sisters, Eleanor of Aragon, and his son had married Eleanor's younger sister, Sancha, a few weeks before the massacre at Montgey.

When Pedro headed south a few days after the ceremony of allegiance, the governor of Catalonia remained in Toulouse and the city began to prepare for war. Lords and knights and men-at-arms from the surrounding lands began to gather in the city, and they soon became impatient for the king's return. Of course he would come back and help them, wouldn't he?

Perhaps remembering how one of his previous compositions had brought King Pedro rushing north to conquer Lady Azalaïs, Raimon de Miraval decided, or was persuaded, to write a song with a more political motive. '*Bel m'es qu'ieu cant e coindei*', '*It pleases me to sing and court*', was ostensibly addressed to Eleanor of Aragon, but after half a dozen verses of the usual troubadour compliments to the lady, Raimon's lyrics get down to business.

Our troubadour exhorts King Pedro to recapture the city of Carcassonne, and to make the French invaders fear him as much as the Moors whom he had defeated at the Battle of Las Navas de Tolosa a year earlier. In conclusion, Raimon says he didn't believe he would write another song until he had regained Miraval, but he has written this one because King Pedro has promised to win it back for him.

Pedro was unable to resist the triple pull of family ties, personal ambition and Raimon's lyrics. At the end of August, he recrossed the Pyrenees with a thousand knights from Aragon and Catalonia and joined up with the armies of his vassals, old and new, outside the town of Muret to the south of Toulouse.

The Battle of Muret was a disaster for the Cathars despite outnumbering their enemies by about four to one. Before the fighting started, King Pedro took the elementary precaution of swapping armour with one of his knights, but when his men saw the fake king fall, the real one uncovered himself to reassure them and shouted, 'I'm the king and I'll show them how I won the Battle of Las Navas de Tolosa!' At that moment, Pedro was struck by a lance and the true king was as dead as the false one. His armies panicked and fled, and thousands were cut down by the crusaders or drowned when they tried to escape across the Garonne. The number of deceased was somewhere between 7,000 and 17,000, but whichever figure you believe, Muret was the most crushing defeat or victory of the crusade.

Did Raimon de Miraval follow King Pedro and Count Raymond into battle? No one knows and it is difficult even to guess because, depending on which date of birth you favour, Raimon was somewhere between the ages of forty-eight and seventy-eight. What is more certain is that after the battle our troubadour went into exile on the other side of the Pyrenees. He never saw Miraval again, and if he wrote any more songs, they have not survived. Even the death of Simon de Montfort in 1218 failed to entice him home or inspire a new composition.

12
SURVIVAL

How many people speak Occitan today? I have come across estimates ranging from a hundred thousand to several million, all from seemingly reputable sources. Perhaps this disparity is explained by the difficulty of defining exactly how much Occitan a person must speak before they can be classed as an Occitan-speaker. In my experience, people like Dr Alibert are rare, and he is far outnumbered by those who would like to think they can speak the language of the troubadours, but are in fact limited to a few stock phrases with which they try to impress the *étrangers*, meaning anyone who was born outside Occitania.

Whatever the true figure, the overwhelming majority of speakers undoubtedly belongs to the more mature section of the population. If the future of Occitan is to be any less gloomy than the future of the Cathars after the Battle of Muret, it needs to attract new, more youthful practitioners.

At the end of our coffee break I quizzed Laurent about his daughter. Although she is still too young to start school, she already speaks the mother tongues of both her parents: French and Ossetian.[6] But will Laurent's daughter learn Occitan as well?

'She already understands a little bit, and she can sing an Occitan song. Beyond that she'll have to decide for herself when she's older.'

'Where would she be able to learn Occitan, apart from with you?'

'It's an option in schools and colleges in Aquitaine and Provence as well as in Occitania. In fact, nowadays it's rare for children to learn Occitan from their parents. We are also beginning to see a strange phenomenon: until recently, the only people who spoke Occitan lived in the villages, and no one in town spoke it at all. But now, it's the townsfolk who show the most interest; they want to learn Occitan and discover their heritage. For those who want to take it further, universities in Montpellier and Toulouse offer degree-level courses.'

'What on earth can you do with a degree in Occitan?'

I bite my tongue. I should have phrased my question in a more neutral manner. Fortunately, Laurent has become accustomed to this sort of attitude after twenty years of studying and teaching a minority language.

'So far, all my graduates have found work, which is quite an achievement in France. Some use the language directly, either in teaching or in Occitan newspapers and television, and there are three publishers dedicated to producing novels and poetry in Occitan. Others find it invaluable for historical research because it allows them to read the original Occitan texts. Even staff in retirement homes find it useful because people with conditions such as Alzheimer's often revert to the first language they learned. And of course there's a growing demand for Occitan speakers in tourism and local government.'

6 To satisfy the curious, Ossetian is a language spoken by half-a-million people living in the Caucasus Mountains between Georgia and Russia.

I remember those dual-language road signs like Bertre, *Bèrtre*, and my thoughts naturally turn towards the creation of our new region. 'What about the future? Will the rebirth of Occitania help the language survive?'

Laurent pauses to think; only a few weeks have passed since the referendum to rename our region. 'I believe we can use it positively. Globalisation makes it difficult for all minority languages, and the death of Occitan has been announced many times. But we are determined to keep it alive, although sometimes I think if we were realists we would give up the fight.'

A few weeks later I bump into Laurent at our village fête. We stand inside a long marquee which shades us from the sun's rays but traps its heat. This gives us a raging thirst, and we are obliged to drink chilled rosé wine from white plastic cups in a misguided attempt to stay hydrated. After a couple of cupfuls, Laurent asks if I am making progress with my Occitan studies.

'I believe so. I've listened to the recordings of our conversation several times, and I'm still studying the troubadours.'

'Can you read them in Occitan yet?'

Laurent has clearly overestimated my level of interest in his subject. It was never my intention to read the troubadours in Occitan, but I don't want to disappoint him.

'I'm picking up a few words that please me, like *agradar*.'

For a moment he looks mystified, but then he takes another slurp from his plastic cup, swallows the cool liquid and grins. 'See if you recognise this.'

He begins to recite lines of what I presume is a troubadour *canso* and I wonder why he isn't singing. After a verse or two he stops and looks at me expectantly.

'Um…no, I'm not sure I recognise that one.'

Laurent grins again and switches to English.

' "*Now is the winter of our discontent*
Made glorious summer by this sun of York;
And all the clouds that lour'd upon our house
In the deep bosom of the ocean buried." '

I stare at him in amazement. Sometimes it is easy to be a prophet, and I can predict with absolute certainty that the number of people who are able to quote Shakespeare's '*Richard III*' in Occitan will be forever minuscule. On the other hand, with this type of enthusiasm the cultural treasures of the troubadours will never be lost, and people like Laurent give me hope that an Occitania where no one speaks Occitan will remain as unthinkable as a Catalonia where no one speaks Catalan, or a Wales where no one speaks Welsh.

Part III

Of Bastides and Adulterers

13

Market Day

One evening, I put away my books about Occitan, pour a glass of wine and go outside to clear my head. The air is motionless and it smells of honeysuckle and sun-baked straw. I hear the snort of a horse, and through a gap in the poplars beyond our stables I spot the Château de Montgey standing proudly on its ridge as it has done for a thousand years. This reminds me that, so far, all my tales of medieval history have revolved around lords and ladies and their châteaux, with the occasional cleric playing a bit part, and a horde of peasants filling in as anonymous extras. In some ways this is inevitable because, as my host observed when I was in the great hall at Montgey, a château is a physical point of reference that makes people think of the past. The same could also be said of ecclesiastical buildings – the abbeys, monasteries and churches.

Today, many people are tempted to buy a piece of this history, and they invariably choose a château over a church. In the Lauragais they are spoiled for choice. In my department of the Tarn, which stretches from the edge of Revel in the south to beyond Albi in the north, there are around 350 châteaux. That's a generous one per thousand inhabitants, and at the moment of writing, fifty-three of them are up for sale on one website alone with prices starting at a modest €198,000. Quite clearly the heirs of Madame Delamy were not alone in their desire to sell their inheritance, although nowadays it is more common for the purchaser to be a foreigner than a native like Pierre Bouyssou. In my immediate area I know of modern-day *châtelains* or *châtelaines* who are Australian, Austrian, Belgian, English, German, Greek, Irish, Scottish and Swiss.

This type of project presents numerous pitfalls, not least of which is the fact that in many cases the purchase price should be regarded as a small down payment on the horrendous sums of money that will be required to transform an ancient dwelling into an agreeable home for a demanding foreigner in the twenty-first century. Another important question is, how do you know you are buying a château?

Imagine the scene: you are comfortably installed in your new home somewhere in the Lauragais – or as comfortably as is possible until you have fixed the electrics, heating, plumbing, roof timbers, roof slates, septic tank and windows – and you decide to invite your neighbours over for an aperitif. You lean on the crumbling stone balustrade of your terrace and chat to your guests and admire the lofty trees in your shady park and hope no more of them blow down in the next storm. You feel very much like the lord or lady of the château until you overhear a couple of peasants muttering behind your back after a few glasses of pastis. 'Of course, it's not really a château, is it? It hasn't got any towers.'

So what is a château? Is it a castle, a manor, a stately home, or merely a rather oversized house? I have put this question to many of my friends on the premise that, in a department boasting so many so-called châteaux, someone should know. The most common answer I receive is that a château must have at least two defensive towers.

I have found support for this definition in dictionaries and encyclopaedias from the eighteenth and nineteenth centuries, but

I can think of several friends who live in large houses constructed in those times that have been called châteaux since their inception but are woefully deficient in the tower department, or if there is a tower or two, one of them is supporting a large cistern at a suitable height to provide running water. Curiously, the French word for 'water tower' is '*château d'eau*', something which can only add to the confusion.

Once in desperation I consulted Larousse, a highly regarded French dictionary, and I discovered three modern definitions which I shall translate into English as follows: (i) the home of a lord or royalty; (ii) a large and beautiful country mansion; (iii) formerly a fortified feudal dwelling defended by a ditch, walls and towers.

The second of these definitions should in theory silence the two-tower brigade, but I can assure you it won't, unless perhaps you let them finish the entire bottle of pastis.

My quest for historical points of reference will inevitably take me inside plenty more châteaux, with or without towers, but in the meantime I decide to award myself a château-free day. Tomorrow I shall accompany my wife, Donna, to one of France's finest markets and explore the lives of the common people in medieval times.

Saturday is market day in Revel, and we join a stream of people flowing from the car parks towards the centre of town. We cross the boulevard by the fountain of the Three Graces, where horses and cattle once took their refreshment on market day, and we enter the Rue Victor Hugo. Above our heads, ancient buildings protrude over the pavement and reveal their ancient joists scarred by the passage of centuries and pockmarked by woodworm. At street level, we pass my favourite shop window. A single sheet of plate glass fills the entire ground floor façade, and this unbroken expanse of prime display space is devoted exclusively to clothes airers. Nothing in this window has changed in fifteen years. In my mind, the display has acquired a timeless quality that almost matches the medieval street leading us towards the market square.

I slow down to inspect a tempting display of cakes outside a patisserie and I forget about the clothes airers. The road opens out before us, and our view is filled by a sea of colourful awnings and a swirling crowd of people who clutch wicker baskets or drag heavy shopping trolleys behind them like reluctant dogs.

The square is surrounded at street level by arcades and shady walkways which seem generously wide for pedestrians, but were in fact designed to cope with two-way horse-drawn traffic. The centre of the square is dominated by the fourteenth-century covered market, forty metres along each side. A forest of ancient oak timbers holds up the roof which provides shelter for buyers and sellers alike. Their voices echo off the surrounding façades and fill the enclosed space with a potpourri of accents and languages.

We skirt around the square in the shade of the Galerie du Couchant. Above our heads, massive oak joists are painted green or yellow or pastel blue. I catch the scent of flowers, the odour of strong cheese, the aroma of coffee mixed with spices, and I am sure I could find my way to the *boulangerie* with my eyes closed. We approach the south-west corner of the square where clouds of fragrant steam rise from a line of paella dishes so large they could feed a whole army of hungry crusaders.

We reach the point where we separate because my wife takes great pleasure in making several circuits of this market. Apparently it is essential to check the price and quality of apples and carrots on all the stalls that face onto the square from the arcades, and those that look out from the edge of the market hall, and obviously all the others that huddle together beneath its colossal roof. Much of the produce she buys is destined to be chomped indiscriminately by her horses, so I can't see the point of more than half a lap and I make for our usual café.

I find a table in the shade outside Le Centre and order a *café allongé*. My eyes roam over the swarm of people who buzz hither and thither like bees in search of nectar. Their ancestors have been coming to this market for over 600 years. If I could travel back in time and sit on this same corner in the fourteenth century, the scene would not be so very different. The market hall, the buildings and the arcades around the square would all be familiar, even if much of the original wood has been replaced by stone. Everyone would be chattering away in Occitan, a language which I am convinced the two elderly gentlemen at the table behind me are using this morning.

My coffee arrives on a saucer with a couple of sugar sachets and a small dark chocolate, and they jolt me out of the past. None of these items were known in Revel in those days: the first credible evidence of coffee drinking dates from fifteenth-century Yemen, sugar was prohibitively expensive in Europe where honey was the main sweetener, and as for tasting chocolate, you would have had to cross the Atlantic. I would have had no more luck if I had ordered a cup of tea any time before the seventeenth century. On market day in medieval Revel you were obliged to enjoy a pint of wine, so I catch the waiter's eye and order a glass of red in the interests of historical authenticity.

A man walks past me with a sack of potatoes slung over his shoulder, and my train of thought follows in his tracks. There were no potatoes in fourteenth-century Revel so there were no French fries. No tomatoes meant no ketchup. Aubergines, courgettes and peppers were unknown, so ratatouille was off the menu. Also missing were avocadoes, Brussels sprouts, butter beans, cauliflowers, kidney beans, pumpkins, runner beans, sweetcorn and sweet potatoes. And that is not an exhaustive list.

Mentally I remove all of these vegetables from the brightly coloured display of the market stall opposite me, and it begins to look rather bare. The fruit department is more promising. In the absence of bananas, kiwis, mangoes and anything vaguely tropical, I would have been able to enjoy oranges and lemons, cherries, figs, grapes, medlars, plums, pomegranates, quinces and strawberries, but only in season. Nothing was grown under glass or plastic or flown in from the other side of the world. No wonder the peasants ate a lot of bread, cabbage and chick peas, and the rich ate so much meat.

I sip my coffee and discover its flavour has acquired a new piquancy. A clucking sound attracts my attention and I glance into the shadows of the covered market and spot what today is a rare sight: a pair of live chickens in a wire cage. I cannot help wondering how modern sensibilities would cope with the practices of old when, in the absence of refrigeration, the best way to ensure your meat was fresh was to witness the slaughter of your dinner.

In Revel, beasts were butchered in the shelter of the market hall until the seventeenth century and you can still see hooks in the roof timbers where the meat was hung. On market day, the gutters around the edge of the square ran red with blood. There were two butchers' benches: one opposite where I am sitting and the other on the north-east corner. They belonged to the town and the rights to use them were auctioned every three years. Annually at Easter all the butchers were obliged to swear that they would only sell good meat and that during summer months they would not keep it for more than two days.

A double ding-dong marks half-past eleven. A square building – the bell tower – protrudes from the red-tiled roof of the market hall. It is crowned by a cylindrical domed belfry, and I can see the heads of tourists peeping over the parapet below the clock. This building was once the administrative centre of Revel. The consuls used to meet in the council chamber on the ground floor, above them was the prison, and above that, the platform around the belfry provided a lookout for the town's guards. Officially it stopped being a jail long ago, but I cannot look at it without thinking of a bitterly cold November day when the president of the Revel history society imprisoned me at the top for failing to pay sufficient attention to his account of the founding of the bastide of Revel.

14

THE BIRTH OF A BASTIDE

The day after the death of Simon de Montfort in 1218, his son Amaury was appointed military leader of the Albigensian Crusade, but it was the new captain of the Cathars who proved to be the more skilful in the art of war. Over the next six years Raymond VII won back all the territory his father had lost to Simon de Montfort.

In 1222, the young Raymond founded the town of Cordes as a means of rehousing and protecting his people after the ravages of the crusade. Now known as Cordes-sur-Ciel, it was the first example of a new type of community that would soon spread all across south-west France: the bastide.

Earlier medieval towns and villages such as Puylaurens or Montgey grew up in a haphazard fashion around a central strong point – a castle or a keep – and the lord of the castle enjoyed almost total control over the peasants who huddled around his walls. In contrast, the layout of a bastide was planned from the outset and the rights of its citizens were enshrined in a charter.

During the 150 years that followed the founding of Cordes, more than 300 other bastides were built in south-west France, often from nothing. In the second half of this period, nearly all of them were instigated by the kings of France or England (at that time Aquitaine belonged to the English). Revel was among the last, and it provides a classic example of a *bastide royale*.

In the early fourteenth century much of the plain at the foot of the Montagne Noire was covered by the forest of Vauré, a lawless place full of bandits and wild beasts where Robin Hood would have felt perfectly at home. The local villagers had asked a succession of kings to evict the outlaws, but it wasn't until Philippe VI de Valois was on the throne that anyone listened, and even he took ten years to do anything about it.

According to local legend, on 8 June 1342 the king's seneschal of Toulouse, Agot de Baux, took a walk in this shady forest, presumably keeping a careful lookout for wolves, wild boar and brigands. When he found a place that pleased him, he thrust a wooden stake into the ground and declared that this would be the centre of the next *bastide royale*. Assuming the usual protocol was followed, this spot now lies immediately below the spiral staircase in the tourist office on the ground floor of the bell tower. From this central point, the king's man traced out the plan of Revel that we see today with its regular grid pattern of streets so typical of the bastides.

Why, an amateur town planner may ask, did the king's seneschal choose this particular part of the forest located on a wide plain with no natural defences? Perhaps because there was a convenient water supply nearby, but not so close that the town would be at risk of flooding, and because there were deposits of clay and plenty of trees to provide building materials for houses, town gates and ramparts.

Revel grew rapidly, and some sources suggest that within three or four years the population had grown to 3,000, so another reasonable question is, why were the locals so keen to leave the countryside for a new town? There were several attractions, starting with security. These were violent and uncertain times. It was the beginning of the Hundred Years' War, and a larger community would be better able to defend itself against an English invasion, or attacks by the unsavoury characters who were still hanging around in the forest.

Second was the prospect of escaping the vagaries of feudalism and instead becoming a property owner. Each family taking up residence in Revel was given a building plot on which they could erect their new home, and another piece of land for a garden, orchard or vineyard. Inheritance laws allowed them to bequeath this property to their heirs.

The third attraction was the prospect of civic services. The consuls diverted part of the Sor from Sorèze to provide an abundant water supply, and this attracted tanners, dyers and clothmakers. As well as benches for the butchers, the charter obliged the consuls to build communal water mills and bread ovens, and they were also tasked with maintaining the streets and keeping them clear of manure and rubbish. On top of all this, there was a jolly nice market every Thursday, and the square of Revel has been compared to the forum of a Roman city, a place to exchange gossip or goods, or to share a jug of wine with friends. Revel's new citizens could shop and conduct their business secure in the knowledge that the consuls monitored weights and measures and the freshness of the meat, and that the baker's profit and the notaire's fee were all regulated by the charter. There was even a forerunner of welfare benefits: if the consuls caught a butcher selling dubious meat or a baker fleecing his customers, the guilty man's goods were confiscated and distributed among the poor.

In return, the *bastides royales* enabled the king to extend his power into an area formerly controlled by feudal lords, religious orders or bandits. Revel's charter defined levels of taxes, duties and fines for residents, merchants and businesses, and it specified what monies would be due to the king, because the creation of bastides like Revel was also a way for the crown to reinvigorate the local economy and raise more taxes to help fight the English.

15

Prisoners in the Tower

Revel is often windswept and each wind has a name. The meanest of them all is the *vent d'autan*, and folklore claims it can drive a man mad or make a woman give birth prematurely. It certainly blows down trees and snaps telegraph poles, and in 1916 it killed Madame Anna Stein when it blew the train off the tracks just as it was leaving Revel. The *vent d'autan* is a gusty wind and it rushes in from the Mediterranean and sweeps around the end of the Montagne Noire. In summer it brings warm air that dries and fries the vegetation, and in winter it sends cold draughts through every crack and keyhole in your home.

When I first met the president of the Revel history society, the *vent d'autan* was blowing with enough force to penetrate every layer of my winter clothing. Jean-Paul Calvet was showing our shivering group around town, and the cold became more and more unbearable at each point of interest where we huddled together to listen to the president's erudite explanations. The chill started at my extremities – feet, hands, nose and ears – and insidiously crept up my legs towards the parts I generally prefer to keep warm and cosy. For nearly an hour, I leaned against the gusts and tried to catch his words on the wind. Then, to my relief, he led us into the market square and into the warmth of the bell tower, through the tourist office on the ground floor and up the stairs to where the former prison has been converted into a modest museum. Jean-Paul proudly showed us the most important exhibit.

My French was not so fluent in those days, and it took me a while to work out its pedigree, but eventually I understood that the long roll of paper behind the sheet of Perspex on the wall was a photocopy of a parchment dating back to 1462. In case you don't know your parchment from your paper, the former is made from animal skin, and after nearly 600 years the original of the one on the wall has become rather fragile so it is kept safely locked away in the municipal archives. But that parchment is itself a copy of an older French translation of the original Royal Charter of Revel which was written in Latin on another parchment which has long since disappeared.

Somewhat pleased with myself for following this contorted explanation, I half-listened to Jean-Paul explaining the structure of the charter. It contained eighty-nine articles, and most of them are rather dull unless you happen to specialise in the art of medieval civic governance. Just when my attention was wavering under the effect of the sudden transition from the windswept exterior to the warm interior, I heard the word 'adultery'. I opened my eyes and saw a grin on Jean-Paul's face. Article 50, he said, always amuses visitors.

'If someone is caught in the act of adultery,' Article 50 begins, *'he will have to choose as his punishment either to run across the town as is the custom in other towns of His Majesty the King, or to pay for each guilty party sixty* sous toulousains *within two days.'*

The charters of other *bastides royales* clarify that if the adulterers opted for the run across town, they were tied together and forced to perform their sprint of shame in a state of total nudity. Worse still, the punishment was usually inflicted on market day. This ensured maximum humiliation for the guilty, and maximum entertainment for the righteous who used to take great pleasure in throwing rotten vegetables and other missiles at the sinners as they scuttled past.

Later, I tried to assess the severity of the financial option: what was sixty *sous* worth in medieval France? If you were a craftsman, it was between a fortnight's and a month's salary, or you could rent a nice cottage for a hundred *sous* a year. Further examination of Revel's charter throws up other comparisons. If, instead of being caught in your neighbour's bed enjoying his wife, you were caught in his orchard enjoying his fruit after dark, you were fined twenty *sous* plus damages. If you pulled a knife on your neighbour without provocation and mutilated one of his limbs, the fine was sixty *sous*, the same as for adultery.

To conclude our visit, Jean-Paul took us up to the platform at the top of the bell tower, and I shivered and admired the panoramic view of the countryside beyond the rooftops surrounding the square. Before long I found myself deep in conversation with another man. Naturally we discussed adultery. He seemed to know a lot more about medieval charters than I did, and he observed that the adulterers of Revel would have been well-advised to move to Le Fossat south of Toulouse where the fine was only five *sous*. There was no fixed price for sin.

A few minutes later we turned around and everyone had disappeared. We scampered across the platform to the door leading back into the warmth of the tower, but it was locked. We were trapped. In the days when the tower was built of wood, the prison was not always so secure. The wooden walls were sometimes unsound, and so was the jailer, and escape was common. Unfortunately for us, the stone construction of the nineteenth century was much more solid, and so was the door upon which we were skinning our frozen knuckles in an attempt to attract attention. I tried shouting through the keyhole and I placed my ear against the door, but all I could hear was the wind. It was cold at street level, and it was much colder in the icy gusts that swept around the top of the bell tower.

My fellow-prisoner and I peered over the parapet. I had come alone on this visit, but he had been accompanied by his wife, and I assumed she would soon notice the absence of her husband and raise the alarm.

'There she is!' My companion pointed towards the south-west corner of the square, and I caught a glimpse of someone wearing a red jacket with the hood up. She disappeared out of the square and out of sight without a backwards glance.

'Do you have a phone with you?' I asked.

'No, we leave it in the car for emergencies. What about you?'

'No, I leave it at home to remind me I no longer work.' (For incredulous younger readers, I should perhaps explain that this was back in the days when mobile phones did little more than make phone calls and send text messages.)

There was another blast of wind and dusk began to fall early. 'How soon do you think your wife will notice you are missing?'

He shrugged. 'When she runs out of money?'

I pulled the zip of my coat as high as it would go and wished it had a triple lining and a hood. Meanwhile, my companion was gesticulating at the sky. Silly man, did he think our saviour would descend from the heavens? I glanced in the same direction and saw three angels. The wind made my eyes water and I blinked and wiped away the tears and looked more closely. Three wretched souls were working on a perishing roof above the south arcade of the market square. '*Allo*!' shouted my companion. '*Coucou*!'

Eventually he caught their attention and succeeded in communicating our plight through sign language. I saw one of the roofers make a call on the mobile phone which he sensibly carried in his pocket, and a few moments later a smiling and breathless young lady from the tourist office opened the door to freedom. There was no sign of our president-guide. We shivered our way downstairs through the old prison, and I tried to imagine what my cellmate would say to his wife and what excuse she would come up with for failing to notice she had lost her spouse. Fortunately she lives in twenty-first century Revel where, although we may be more tolerant of adultery, we are far less tolerant of domestic violence. In the days when the town's charter was written, a husband could legally treat members of his household as badly as he wished and inflict the harshest of punishments for the most trifling of misdemeanours. Article 62 stated: '*If someone while correcting his wife or a member of his family has beaten or injured them, he will have nothing to pay as long as the punishment has not killed them.*'

16

The Lost Ramparts

The clock in the belfry strikes midday and brings me back to the present. My own wife will be near at hand waiting for the late morning bulk-buy bargains. There is no danger of her wandering off without me; her purchases will be heavy and I shall have to carry them back to the car. I take another sip of wine and allow my thoughts to turn to Article 50 of Revel's charter as they often do when I sit alone in the square.

In my imagination, the shouts of the market traders become the taunts of the crowd, and I grimace at the idea of being forced to flounder naked across the cobblestones beneath the scornful eyes of my fellow citizens. Perhaps the wise adulterer set aside sixty *sous* just in case, and the considerate adulterer allocated another sixty to spare the blushes of his lover.

'*Bonjour*, Colin.' A couple of German friends sit down opposite me and interrupt my thoughts. They order tea and coffee, and I try to focus on the present. Stefan likes to tell me about economics and politics, and I toy with the idea of testing him on the price of immorality in the fourteenth century. But I am sure that as soon as I mention Article 50 he will think of the other one and lecture me on the perils of Brexit, so instead I express a hint of sympathy for the French head of state who has just hit an all-time low in the approval ratings.

'You know what they say about French presidents, don't you?' says Stefan.

'No,' I say, and wait for the joke.

'If you walk into a busy bar anywhere in France and announce, "*Bonjour, Monsieur le President,*" a dozen people will look up and acknowledge your greeting. There'll be the president of the local rabbit breeders association, the president of the boules club…'

For a moment, I forget to laugh. Is he making fun of my friend Jean-Pierre, the president of the Puylaurens tennis club? He has a point though. Because the word '*président*' can also mean 'chairman', there are more than a million of them in France, one for every sporting club, cultural association or voluntary body in the country. I smile and Stefan laughs and I think of another president who is much more popular than the big French cheese. I forgave Jean-Paul Calvet long ago for my enforced sojourn in the bell tower, and I have even joined the Revel history society. You never know when it may pay to be on good terms with a president or two, and it now occurs to me that Jean-Paul is the ideal person to complete the story of the founding of his home town. He can explain how he discovered the only remaining section of Revel's ramparts hidden away inside someone's garage. Even better, he can give me a guided tour. It will be like visiting the Americas with Columbus, or Troy with Heinrich Schliemann.

The first part of the Albigensian Crusade reached its conclusion in January 1224 when Amaury de Montfort and the last few crusaders surrendered at Carcassonne to Count Raymond VII of Toulouse and Count Roger-Bernard of Foix (the young man who killed the priest in the church at Montgey had succeeded his father a few months earlier).

The two young counts did not enjoy their victory for long. In 1226 a new king of France, Louis VIII, relaunched the Albigensian Crusade. Three years later, Count Raymond's lands were devastated once again and his people were exhausted by twenty years of war. He capitulated, and the Treaty of Meaux obliged him to dismantle the ramparts of Toulouse, Puylaurens and twenty-eight other fortified towns. Count Raymond was also forbidden from building walls around any of his new bastides, but by the time Revel was founded in 1342, the Hundred Years' War was underway and most towns were granted the right to fortify themselves.

We do not know exactly when the townsfolk of Revel started work on their civic defences, but it was probably sometime in the 1350s or 1360s. For the next 400 years the town was protected by over a kilometre of good thick ramparts that rose to a height of six metres. Four gates were positioned at the cardinal points of the compass, and because there was no ring road outside the ramparts, traffic was obliged to pass through the gates and across the centre of town underneath the arcades where it could be inspected and taxed.

The ramparts proved their worth on many occasions up until the end of the Wars of Religion in the early seventeenth century. By the time of Napoleon, their defensive role was redundant. They had become a physical restriction on the growth of the town, and the associated moats and ditches were a disgusting mess of stagnant water and rubbish, colonised by rats. Over the next few decades, Revel gradually demolished its defences and replaced them with the wide boulevards that encircle the town today. Before long, no one was quite sure where the ramparts had once stood.

In 2009, a gentleman called Charles Maguès was sorting through his family archives in Toulouse. His was not a trivial task. Two generations of his ancestors had been the architects responsible for maintaining the Canal du Midi. Over a period of sixty years they had amassed a mountain of paperwork relating to the canal, and hidden away among these documents Monsieur Maguès discovered three plans of Revel dating from around 1760. In May 2009 he donated them to the town of Revel, and the mayor immediately realised who would be able to make best use of them: the president of the Revel history society.

I arrive early in the Place du Patty for my rendezvous with Jean-Paul Calvet. While I wait, I try to imagine what I would do if someone presented me with an ancient map of my home town. No doubt I would search for my own house, and idly note the presence or absence of the homes of my neighbours. After that, I would probably frame it and hang it in the downstairs cloakroom where the occasional visitor would remark, 'What a nice old map!' I certainly wouldn't pore over it for days on end, or superimpose it on a more recent plan, or carry it around town to measure and verify its accuracy. And therefore I would never exclaim, 'Hold on! Maybe the town walls haven't disappeared after all!'

I decide to take a stroll around the block between the Place du Patty and the Boulevard Denfert Rochereau. I pass an osteopath, a beautician, a driving school, an antiques shop, a dentist, a kebab takeaway and an accountant. I arrive back at my starting point by the entrance to a physiotherapist. There is not the slightest indication that hidden away behind these façades are forty-five metres of medieval ramparts.

To the left of the physiotherapist's front door is an edifice that looks like an old warehouse or factory. A modern roll-down garage door firmly seals an opening large enough for a horse-and-carriage. It has been defaced with blue and mustard-coloured graffiti, and above it the painted letters spelling out the name of a long-deceased business are faded and illegible.

To the right, a pedestrian door hangs open and invites me to enter the building.

My eyes adjust to the gloomy interior. I am standing in a rectangular space a little larger than a basketball court, and the rear section is open to the sky. The structure is an eclectic mixture of building materials from across the ages, or to put it another way, the place is a mess. Wood, cast iron and concrete. Cut stone blocks with carefully rounded corners, stone rubble, medieval red brick and modern hollow brick. The mortar and rendering of lime are pale and crumbling, and the modern equivalents of cement are grey and ugly. The floor is covered by a soft carpet of dried guano, and inexplicably a couple of pigeons flap around inside a tiny cage on a table in the middle of this forgotten space. Who on earth feeds them, and why? At the far end of the roof, loose planks of wood hang like daggers at precarious angles from a failing fascia. I realise that if one of them falls on my head I will be impaled, and I jump to one side. This building not only looks ripe for demolition: it seems as if self-destruction has already begun. And where are the ramparts? I need an enthusiast to bring this dismal shambles to life, and luckily one is standing in front of me.

'*Bonjour*, Jean-Paul!'

Monsieur Calvet is a perfect example of the type of historian who has so enriched our knowledge of the Lauragais, a true amateur in the original sense of the word. At the end of a professional career in which he spent twenty-five years working in Revel hospital, he was at last able to devote himself wholeheartedly to what had long been his passion: the archaeology and history of our region.

We shake hands and he introduces me to another man who has come to see the ramparts. I exchange greetings with the president of the speleological-archaeological research society of Sorèze, and I thank my good fortune. I can profit from the knowledge of two presidents for the price of one.

Jean-Paul wastes no more time and he points at the wall to my right. It is sheltered by a long stretch of roof held up by four wooden pillars. 'This,' he says, 'is the last remaining section of the ramparts of Revel.'

His voice sounds unnaturally loud in the cavernous silence of the abandoned warehouse. I turn to look, and dried guano crunches to dust beneath my shoes and the pigeons fidget noisily in their cage. I squirm in disgust. 'What was this place?'

Jean-Paul is a tall man, and he stoops to address me. 'Over the years it has been many things: a warehouse for coal and firewood, a garage, and most recently a car park. We are lucky it was never developed into something more substantial. Otherwise we would not be able to see any of this.'

He points again and I listen to his commentary, and the wall which at first sight could be part of my own eighteenth-century farmhouse takes on a new aspect. It rises to a height of around five metres, and with Jean-Paul's guidance I spot the slots in the stonework where a wooden walkway allowed the guards to patrol the perimeter of Revel. A square stone structure with numbered parking spaces for two cars becomes the barracks where the guards took shelter from the rain or the *vent d'autan*. I notice three arrow slits which overlooked the area outside the gate of Saint-Antoine. One of them is angled to provide a perfect vantage point for the defenders to fire upon anyone who tried to hold their breath and sneak in where the stream of the Mayral flowed out beneath the ramparts.

I take a look at the detailed plan Jean-Paul has given me, and I realise that what was once the outside of the ramparts now forms the inside back wall of the driving school and antiques shop I walked past earlier.

'I still don't understand why you thought of looking in here.'

He smiles apologetically. 'I already knew from other texts that there might be a section of ramparts hidden away somewhere near the Place du Patty, but no one knew exactly where. I always assumed they had by now been absorbed into the surrounding buildings, but the plans of Maguès inspired me to take a closer look because they mapped the town's old defences in extraordinary detail. They showed me the exact position of the gates, the walls, the guard towers, the barracks, and even the stairs leading up to the walkways. I came down here with the plans in my hands and soon realised there might be something inside this building. It was all closed up, but I tracked down the owner and obtained the key and took a look inside.'

Jean-Paul opens his arms in an expansive gesture. 'When I first saw all this, I was flabbergasted. I couldn't believe the ramparts were simply standing here, totally forgotten. Of course I have seen better – it's not Carcassonne, is it? – but for me these are the most beautiful ramparts in the world. These are the ramparts of Revel! I started to tell people about my find, and before long the whole town was saying, "Jean-Paul Calvet has discovered the ramparts of Revel!" In reality I had discovered nothing at all!'

'You rediscovered them,' I suggest.

'I had certainly discovered a problem. The owner wanted to sell the building. He didn't care about the ramparts and I was afraid that, if a developer bought the site, the past would disappear forever behind plasterboard and concrete. We've already lost the other side.'

'So what did you do?'

'I started writing. The press covered the story and I published a long article in the history society's periodical. For me, it was unthinkable we could simply abandon the last remaining section of our ramparts. Apart from the market square, there's not much left from the town's medieval past. So we lobbied the *mairie* to exercise its *droit de préemption*.' He gives me a sideways glance; he always doubts my ability to understand French. 'Do you know what that is?'

'No, not exactly.'

'In France, once a buyer and a seller sign a pre-sale contract for any piece of land or building, the *mairie* has the right to buy it for the same price. That's what happened here, and now the ramparts belong to the town of Revel. All we have to do is make them safe and presentable, and then everyone can enjoy them.'

At the time of writing, unless you are fortunate enough to have presidential connections or friends at the *mairie*, you can only glimpse a tiny section of rampart. It is visible beyond a head-height wall that blocks off an alleyway beside the antiques shop on the Boulevard Denfert Rochereau. A plastic drainpipe runs down the middle. For now, you have to imagine the rest.

We lock the warehouse door and stroll back towards the market square deep in conversation. It is a slow walk because Jean-Paul keeps pausing to point out other historical features that would escape the casual passer-by. Eventually, we reach the square and I profit from his presence to solve a mystery. Some time ago I heard that the stone base supporting one of the wooden posts of the market hall has been fashioned from an old tombstone, but there are eighty-five posts, each with a stone base, and I still haven't found the one with the inscription.

'I'll show you,' says Jean-Paul, 'but haven't you read our book *"The Bell Tower of Revel"*? It's all in there.'

'I've read extracts,' I mumble, 'but I'm rather inundated with history books at present.'

He smiles. 'I always wanted to write about the bell tower; my mother was born up there.'

I glance up at the clock in surprise. Born in the bell tower? I picture Jean-Paul's heavily pregnant grandmother labouring her way up the steep stairs to enjoy a view over the rooftops, and I wonder if it was the strain of the climb or the *vent d'autan* that sent her into premature labour.

'Your poor grandmother!'

'Not really. That's where she lived.'

I glance at Jean-Paul again, and the memory of my own chilly experience at the top of the tower reminds me of its former role as a prison. Am I mistranslating the sense of his words?

'Do you mean she was in jail? They wouldn't lock up a pregnant woman would they, not even in those days?'

'No, it was nothing like that. The bell tower ceased being a prison in the second half of the nineteenth century, long before my grandparents lived there. My grandfather was the town crier and his job was to march around town beating a drum and shouting out public announcements. You know the sort of thing: "Tomorrow morning a cloth merchant from Castres will display his wares under the market hall." My mother was one of eight children and the whole family lived in the bell tower. My mother first met my father at the bottom of the steps, and later my uncles turned the place into a workshop. In those days Revel was famous for its furniture, and to get the finished pieces down to the ground my uncles had to lower them on a rope through a trapdoor in the floor.'

I cannot restrain a smile when it occurs to me that Jean-Paul's family has been at the centre of life in Revel for generations, literally and figuratively speaking. Town crier was one of the first civic posts in the bastide, and Article 30 of the charter contains a rough job description.

We find the tombstone. It supports the fourth outermost pillar from the north-west corner, and the inscription faces eastwards into the dark interior. No wonder I missed it on market day. I squint to decipher the letters chiselled by a stonemason in another century, and somewhere in the shadows of the market hall I am sure I catch sight of a ghostly figure. Unlike the phantom of

Montgey, this one is not silent. He beats a drum and cries out his message. 'Oyez, oyez, oyez! Long-lost ramparts of Revel found in a garage! By my grandson!'

17

As Easy as Buying a Baguette

By now you may be thinking that uncovering the past in the Lauragais is as easy as buying a baguette, but not everyone is as lucky as Pierre Bouyssou or Jean-Paul Calvet. In the interests of balanced reporting I shall recount a less-successful quest, even if it does take me to another château.

Every year in the month of September, fifty countries participate in the European Heritage Days, or *les journéees du patrimoine* as they are called in France. For the amateur historian, the parsimonious, or the plain nosy, this is a time of great excitement. On this one weekend of the year, a host of private châteaux and other establishments throw open their doors to the public, usually for free.

A few years ago we took advantage of this annual generosity to pay a visit to the Château de Massaguel, fifteen kilometres east-north-east of Revel. It stands at the foot of the Montagne Noire and guards the entrance to a steep-sided valley. The day was wet, and Jean Fabre de Massaguel and his wife stood outside their ancient walls in the shelter of a camouflaged marquee and waited for anyone foolish enough to brave what the locals would call the English weather.

Jean is descended from a family of wealthy cloth merchants who, in 1768, bought the château, its four towers and its estate. As a child, he was convinced that somewhere within its ancient walls he would find buried treasure, but rare indeed are the parents who encourage their offspring to demolish parts of the family home in pursuit of a childish fantasy. Personally, I can understand Jean's belief, even as a rational adult. My own house may only date back to the eighteenth century, but when I was renovating parts of it, I experienced a frisson of excitement each time I found a void inside its thick walls. In the absence of banks, even the peasants had to hide their gold somewhere, and in the case of the Château de Massaguel, it could be much more thrilling. Some people believe the Cathars possessed the Holy Grail and smuggled it out of Montségur in 1244 to a place of safety. But where? The walls inside which Jean grew up probably date back to the fifteenth century, but they are believed to have been built on the site of a more ancient fortress, and who knows what treasure may have been buried there.

Jean's childhood dream persisted into adulthood, and when he inherited the ancestral home he seized both his opportunity and his pickaxe. He invited his friends to come over for a treasure hunt. My own memory of such events is that they usually involved wasting a lot of time in pub gardens trying to decipher cryptic clues, interspersed with crazy motorised jaunts around the countryside. In contrast, the Château de Massaguel's quest was a much more physical pastime, better suited to the navvies who dug the Canal du Midi than Jean's unfortunate friends.

Our treasure-hunting *chatelain* had identified a room just inside the château's main entrance where it seemed the floor level had been raised by the height of at least a dozen gold bars. The room was as big as a swimming pool, and the treasure hunters eventually dug down more than a metre and carried away back-breaking tonnes of soil and stone. They uncovered a flight of ancient steps, but no treasure. Undeterred, Jean issued a second call to arms, or perhaps that should be 'picks'. This time, the ranks of his treasure-hunting army were significantly depleted, but there were still enough willing hands to excavate another part of the château. Once again they unearthed nothing of value or interest.

Persistence is a virtue in these matters, and hunting for treasure in a château is like looking for a black cat in a coal cellar: you can never prove it isn't there. So Jean announced a third treasure hunt, but this time it proved to be a solitary affair, and just as fruitless as the others.

Part IV

A Hundred Years of Misery

18

The Black Prince

At the beginning of the fourteenth century, Europe's weather took a dramatic turn for the worse. Summers were unusually cold and wet, and it was often impossible to plough or sow or harvest or make hay. In the Lauragais, one historian estimates that between 1300 and 1346 there were twenty-five years when winter reserves were exhausted before the new crops were ready to harvest.[7] The worst period was the Great Famine of 1315, when somewhere between ten and twenty-five percent of Europe's population died of starvation.

It was during these times of hunger that the first citizens of Revel set to work and began to build their new town around the seneschal's stake in the centre of the market square. They chopped down trees in the forest of Vauré and erected their timber-framed houses. From the safety of the new bastide they would be able to face the future with more optimism. The consuls had appointed guards to defend the town, and others to protect the crops in their orchards, vineyards and fields from marauders and wild beasts. One day soon they would find time to profit from Article 22 of the

7 Gauvard, Claude. *La France au Moyen âge du Ve au XVe siècle*. Paris: Presse universitaire de France, 2010.

charter by raising ramparts and digging moats which they would stock with fish.

I can picture members of the new bourgeoisie going about their business and meeting friends or neighbours at the market or in the street. Life would improve now, wouldn't it? And indeed, the inclement weather that had so often ruined their agriculture since the start of the century began to improve. The rain clouds became less prevalent and the temperatures began to climb, and people dared to hope the worst was behind them. But there are Four Horsemen of the Apocalypse, and famine was not the only one who was circling the Lauragais. Death was always close at hand, and the Hundred Years' War had rumbled away in the north for ten years and would soon come much nearer, but first came pestilence.

In Europe as a whole, the Black Death is believed to have killed a third of the population. The causes of the plague and its calamitous effects on society have been debated and documented elsewhere, so I shall restrict myself to observing that in Revel and much of the Lauragais, the epidemic reached its peak in the summer of 1348 and gradually died out the following year along with half the population. The plague took no notice of age, profession or position. In the space of a few short months, on average, half the mothers, half the children, half the bakers, half the butchers, half the carpenters, half the stonemasons, half the gravediggers, half the town guards were all dead.

The survivors barely had time to bury all the corpses and adapt to life with one-in-two people missing before another calamity hit the Lauragais. In the Book of Revelations war is represented by a red horse, but in 1355 it manifested itself in the shape of the Black Prince. The length of his visit could be counted in days, but the unforeseen effects of his subsequent actions would afflict the Lauragais for sixty years.

Edward Woodstock was Prince of Wales and eldest son of Edward III of England, but he became better-known as the Black

Prince, some say because of the colour of his armour, others because of his brutal reputation. In the summer of 1355 his father sent him off to France with strict instructions to cause mayhem. The king planned to cross over to Calais later in the year and invade northern France. He wanted his son to create a diversion that would draw the French armies south, and that would decimate the king of France's tax revenues.

In French, the type of expedition the Black Prince was planning was known as a *chevauchée*, a romantic-sounding word which can mean a pleasant horse ride, but in the medieval military context it meant a fast-moving raid that created as much destruction and chaos as possible and did not waste its time besieging well-defended towns. If the locals resisted, they were massacred, and if they didn't, they were ransomed. Either way, their portable possessions were looted and everything else set ablaze.

The Black Prince sailed into Bordeaux on 20 September 1355 and immediately began to make his preparations. Two weeks later he set off with an army of around 10,000 men. Historical accounts of this expedition often refer to the English and French armies, which is convenient but misleading. It is more accurate to think of whose side someone was on rather than his nationality.

The people of Armagnac, Toulouse and the Lauragais owed their allegiance to the French crown, a link that had been strengthened by the creation of bastides such as Revel with their royal charters.

The Black Prince was accompanied by around fifteen hundred English knights and a couple of thousand archers, but most of his troops came from Gascony, an area which had been under English rule for two centuries and today forms part of Nouvelle Aquitaine.

Then there were the lands in the foothills of the central Pyrenees which belonged to Gaston Phoebus, Count of Foix, whose great-great-great grandfather had murdered the priest in the church at Montgey. Gaston was a wily character who protected his lands from the worst ravages of the Hundred Years' War by playing off one king against the other. Neither side trusted him, but neither side wanted him as an enemy.

In the second week of October the Black Prince left English-controlled territory and entered Armagnac. He met no resistance and sacked several towns. The forces loyal to the French crown were under the command of the Count of Armagnac and they took refuge inside Toulouse. They also destroyed the bridges across the Garonne, but after a long dry summer the river was exceptionally low and the Black Prince found a ford to the south of the city. He decided Toulouse was too well-defended, so he camped for the night in a pretty vineyard in the village of La Croix-Falgarde and prepared to ransack the fertile countryside of the Lauragais.

19

Burning the Lauragais

Today, if you take the D813 and then the D6113 from the edge of Toulouse towards Castelnaudary, you will be following the Roman road – the Via Aquitania – and the destructive trail of the Black Prince.

One fascinating aspect of this expedition is that the Black Prince described it himself in letters he dispatched to England as soon as he was safely back in Bordeaux. His steward, Sir John Wingfield, sent other letters which stressed the economic impact of the great raid. Both men wrote in French. A third contemporary account of the expedition was written in Latin by a chronicler called Geoffrey the Baker. In this chapter I shall quote excerpts from all three sources, based on the translations in Richard Barber's book *'Life and Campaigns of the Black Prince'*.

It took the invaders five days to traverse the Lauragais, and they systematically destroyed and looted most of the towns along their route. According to the Black Prince: '*And we marched through the country round Toulouse where many good towns and fortresses were burnt and destroyed, because the region is very rich and fertile; and not a day passed without a town, castle or fortress being taken by one or other of our battalions or by all of them'.*[8]

First to go up in smoke were Castanet, Montgiscard and Ayguesvives. The next stop was Baziège where, if you are lucky enough to visit the town when the church is open, you can view the stone that once marked the fifteenth Roman mile from Toulouse (in case 'milestone' conjures up the image of a small lump of rock at the roadside, this one is a hefty granite column the height of a tall centurion, although not many centurions had a fifty-inch waist).

After Baziège, the towns of Villenouvelle and Villefranche-Lauragais were set ablaze, and the army marched on as far as Avignonet-Lauragais. The Black Prince described Avignonet as a large and strong town which his army easily took by assault (most of its defences had been destroyed a century earlier after the massacre of Bernard de Roquefort and his fellow-inquisitors). The town also boasted a fleet of twenty windmills because, since Roman times, the main crop in this part of the Lauragais had been wheat. Predictably the invaders set fire to all of them.

It was at this point that someone told the Black Prince about the Château de Montgey. Exactly what he was told and by whom we do not know, but it prompted him to send one of his captains and a company of soldiers on a forty kilometre round trip to investigate. Maybe he too imagined Cathar treasure was buried in the Lauragais.

Pierre Bouyssou tells me about the second battle of Montgey one day when we are sitting in his study in the heart of the château.

---

8 Barber, Richard. *The Life and Campaigns of the Black Prince: from contemporary letters, diaries and chronicles, including Chandos Herald's 'Life of the Black Prince'.* Boydell Press, 1979, 1986, 9780851154350, (page 53). Reprinted by permission of Boydell & Brewer Ltd.

Bizarrely, the room makes me claustrophobic despite its lofty ceiling and view of the Pyrenees. Bookshelves tower above my head and the top row would be out of reach even if I stood on my own shoulders. I am being crushed against Pierre's leather top desk by the weight of all the history contained in his library. In a moment of clarity I measure the scale of my audacity. How can I hope to distil the spirit of the Lauragais into a single volume?

I glare out of the window towards the route taken by the Black Prince seven centuries earlier. I imagine how the defenders of the château would have spent two agonising days watching the southern sky fill with smoke, and two fearful nights staring at the glow of the fires raging in the ransacked towns and villages. As long as the enemy kept moving east, the Château de Montgey would be safe, but if the invaders turned north, how could they defend themselves? Aymeric VI de Roquefort had taken his men to Toulouse to join the Count of Armagnac, and his wife remained in the château with only a skeleton staff to protect her.

Their fears soon became all too real. The Black Prince's men rode into view and surrounded the château. They mounted their siege ladders against the towering stone walls and began to climb. Luckily for Montgey and its defenders, Lady Roquefort had a sudden moment of inspiration.

'They didn't have sugar in those days,' Pierre reminds me. 'If you wanted something sweet, you took a spoonful of honey, and it was common to keep beehives inside the castle walls somewhere near the kitchen.'

I remember my musings about medieval food and drink when I was sitting in the market square in Revel, and I nod wisely, but I have no idea why this is relevant to the Black Prince's attack. And why is Pierre smiling like that?

'Lady Roquefort knew her bees were patriotic and she had every confidence they would be able to tell the difference between a soldier loyal to the English king and one loyal to the French crown. She and her servants hauled the beehives up onto the battlements and emptied them over the heads of their enemies.'

I return Pierre's smile, and my mind fills with an image of battle-hardened men sliding down their siege ladders and running away and flapping their arms to ward off swarms of furious insects. And what if the bees had got inside their honey-coated armour? More than their pride would have been stung.

'I heard the story from people in the village when I was a child,' says Pierre. 'It always struck me as too original not to be true, but I could never find any documentary evidence. Then, ten years ago I was showing some visitors around the château. When I came to the story of the bees, an English aerospace engineer said he had read all about it in the archives in Oxford. When the unfortunate captain reported back to the Black Prince he was demoted in disgrace. How dare he allow himself to be beaten by a woman and a swarm of bees!'

After those sticky moments at Montgey, the Black Prince renounced any more side trips and continued to march east with his army. The citizens of Revel were able to breathe a sigh of relief, but it was obvious that eventually the invaders would turn around and head back to Bordeaux, and who knew what route they would take for their return journey.

Some sources speculate that this was the moment when the people of Revel decided to start work on that town wall project they had been putting off for so long. To me, this either seems unlikely or was an extraordinary feat because a mere fourteen years after its birth Revel had fallen into a sorry state. In an additional charter dating from a few months after the Black Prince's *chevauchée*, the French king was so moved by the town's plight that he gave all its present and future citizens permission to hunt or fish in the surrounding forests for wolves, wild boar, deer, foxes, hare, rabbits, other wild animals, and any type of bird. The text of this charter describes a town and countryside devastated and depopulated by plague, starvation and war; a town where the survivors were reduced to misery; a town where many of the agricultural lands had been abandoned to an encroaching forest in which wild and dangerous beasts roamed at will because the citizens were too frightened to hunt them without permission from the king.

If the people of Revel built their ramparts under these conditions, even if their initial efforts were limited to earthworks topped by sunbaked bricks of clay, it was a Herculean labour that truly demonstrates their immense terror of the Black Prince.

When the English and Gascon invaders reached Castelnaudary, the entire army stayed in town for two nights. The day after their arrival was All Saint's Day, but all the saints were unable to save the religious establishments. Sir John Wingfield reports that during their weekend stay, his master's men set fire to the church of Saint Michael, the convents of the Minorites and Carmelites, the hospital of Saint Antony, and an Augustinian convent in the nearby town of Mas-Saintes-Puelles.

After Castelnaudary the modern road splits in two. One route tracks the north bank of the Canal du Midi, and the other follows the Via Aquitania along the south bank all the way to Carcassonne. But work on the canal would not start until 1667, so the Black Prince's battalions were able to meander through the countryside and destroy towns along both routes: Saint-Martin-Lalande, Pexiora, Villepinte and Bram. In the space of five days they had devastated the Lauragais. Its people were left demoralised and terrified, their homes razed, their reserves plundered and their valuables stolen.

On 3 November, the Black Prince arrived at Carcassonne and the whole population took refuge inside the citadel. Geoffrey the Baker described Carcassonne as a beautiful and extremely wealthy city that was larger than London. Its leaders tried to buy their way out of trouble: they promised to pay the Black Prince 250,000 gold *écus* if he spared the lower town. In those days, the annual cost of maintaining a man-at-arms was around 180 *écus*, so this would have covered the Black Prince's entire wage bill for the duration of the *chevauchée*, or alternatively it would have bought him 50,000 horses. He declined the offer, and his army devoted an entire day to burning the town so that it was completely destroyed.

The invaders reached Narbonne on 8 November where for the first time since leaving Bordeaux they encountered serious resistance. The inhabitants had abandoned the town and taken refuge in the château with the Count of Narbonne and a garrison of five hundred. The defenders refused to surrender, and after two days of fighting, the Black Prince received two pieces of news. First, his father had landed in Calais so his decoy mission was accomplished. Second, the Count of Armagnac had left the safety of Toulouse and was waiting for him somewhere in the Lauragais. It was time to take his army back to Bordeaux and seek to join battle with the Count of Armagnac on the way.

By now the invaders were tired and weighed down by plunder, but there was no question of taking the easy road home. Thousands of men and horses would need to find food, and they had destroyed everything on their outbound journey. Initially they followed a more northerly route, and the Black Prince's army marched through the arid countryside of the Minervois accompanied by a thousand carts laden with booty. Geoffrey the Baker noted that food was not the only problem: *'On Wednesday, Saint Martin's day [11 November], the march was long and difficult, particularly bad for horses because it was rocky and there was no water or other supplies; the horses had to drink wine instead of water, and the food was cooked in wine, because no other liquid except wine or oil was to be had*'.[9]

When they reached the remains of Carcassonne the invaders switched to a more southerly route and sacked more towns on the southern edge of the Lauragais – Limoux, Fanjeaux and Villesavary – but the Count of Armagnac was nowhere to be seen. They learned from captured enemy scouts that he was retreating back to the safety of Toulouse. On Tuesday 17 November, the Black Prince crossed the River Hers and was met at the Abbey of Boulbonne by the Count of Foix.

Edward Woodstock and Gaston Phoebus were both ambitious young men in their mid-twenties and they shared a common enemy: the Count of Armagnac. They soon struck a deal: Gaston's men would guide the Black Prince's army through the county of Foix and across the rivers without hindrance as long as they promised to take a break from destruction and pillage while they were on Gaston's lands. The deal done, the two men went off hunting for the afternoon.

The next day, the Black Prince re-entered lands loyal to the French king, but to his disappointment the Count of Armagnac was still hiding in Toulouse. At the age of sixteen the Black Prince had distinguished himself at the battle of Crécy, and now he was longing for a pitched battle rather than all these tiresome weeks of arson and looting. For him, the *chevauchée* was a triumph without glory, and he complained about his enemies in a letter to the Bishop of Winchester: '*That same night we encamped outside the town [of Gimont], and waited there the whole of the next day, hoping that a battle might take place. And the same [next] day we and the whole army were in battle order before sunrise, when news came that before daybreak most of the enemy had left; only the commanders remained in the town, which was large and strong and could have been held*

9 Barber, Richard (page 66).

against large numbers of men. So we returned to our quarters and had a council as to what to do. It was clear that the enemy did not want a battle, so it was agreed that we should return towards our own lands'.[10]

On 28 November the Black Prince was back in English-controlled territory. In forty-seven days his army had reduced more than 500 towns and villages to charred and smoking ruins. The expedition had been a hopelessly one-sided affair. Sir John reported that during the whole *chevauchée* his master's army lost a single knight. He also noted that the economic impact was devastating, and based on tax records he had inspected in various towns along the way, he estimated: '*…the countryside and towns which have been destroyed in this raid produced more revenue for the king of France in aid of his wars than half his kingdom*'.[11]

Back in Bordeaux the Black Prince received a hero's welcome. He sent his Gascons home on leave and told them to come back for another sortie in the spring.

---

10 Barber, Richard (page 54).
11 Barber, Richard (page 52).

20

A Secret Retreat

I leave the village of Durfort and begin to climb into the Montagne Noire. I am only a few kilometres from Revel and my road follows the shady right bank of the Sor. It rained last night and the river is loud and fast and the air is clear and blue. Willow, ash and elder grow alongside the river, and their freshly-washed young leaves glisten green in the sunlight. Here and there I spot the dark green needles of a conifer hiding among the deciduous foliage. Oak trees dominate the hillside, and there are chestnuts by the narrow lane where the old folk will congregate in autumn to gather the harvest in wicker baskets.

Houses are squeezed into the narrow strip of land between the road and the river. They are spaced at intervals which promise solitude and threaten loneliness. Some homes have tried to reclaim a garden from the forest while others make do with dense undergrowth and perpetual shade. In summer, the trees cast dark shadows, and in winter, the sun rarely penetrates the bottom of this steep-sided valley. It feels like a road into the past, or a road to nowhere. Half a century ago, a local writer described it as the road to the end of the world, *le bout du monde.*[12]

---

12 Mistler, Jean. *Le Bout du Monde.* Paris: B Grasset, 1964.

After the last house I cross a bridge by a dilapidated hydroelectric station. A couple of zigzags later and the road clings to the mountainside high above the river. The strip of tarmac is barely wide enough for a single car and the drop is vertiginous, but it is rarely troubled by traffic.

Three kilometres out of Durfort, I branch off onto a grassy track and follow an old water pipeline that has been painted green by lichen and moss. Even beneath the trees it is hot, and all I can hear is distant birdsong and a sound that may be the wind in the trees or the Sor dancing along its rocky bed far below me. I am lost in the timeless tranquillity of ancient woodland. Up on my right in the Forest of the Aiguille stands an enormous beech tree more than three centuries old. Beyond the ridge on the north side of the valley by the ruined chapel of Saint-Jammes you will find an even older specimen: the doyen of the forest is in its fifth century and measures six metres around the trunk. But these venerable monsters are the exception because the valley has not always been like this. The forest has waxed and waned as the human population has waned and waxed.

I round a bend and glance behind me. On the other side of the valley stands a rocky knoll with cliffs of pale granite submerged beneath verdant foliage. Peeping out of the trees at the highest point, an observant or forewarned eye can make out the top of a stone tower.

I have a sepia photograph of this same view. A couple dressed in their Sunday Best are driving a carriage pulled by a pair of horses. A century ago, Sunday was the only peaceful day of the week. The rest of the time the valley resonated to the din of hydraulic hammers. Powered by the Sor, they pounded pieces of copper at two beats a second to manufacture cauldrons, saucepans and other utensils. Durfort was Copper City, and 500 cauldron-makers banged away for twelve hours a day. At the end of the nineteenth century, a doctor noted that deafness was common among the workers, and that their forearms and hair took on a greenish tinge and their gums became reddish-brown. It was hot work too. The furnaces were heated to 1,200 degrees Celsius to melt the copper, and each piece was reheated several times while it was being hammered into shape. The heat was generated by charcoal produced in the surrounding forests, and for much of the year the smoke of the charcoal burners drifted through the trees. Today you can still see the rusting remains of their iron kilns dotted around in the woods on both sides of the valley.

In the days when my sepia photograph was taken, there were no trees to hide the rocky knoll's granite charms, and the full height of the stone tower stood naked against the sky. This is my destination, a place that was once a sanctuary for those seeking to escape persecution, or a hideout for those seeking to escape justice. To reach it, I must cross the river, and before long I leave the track beside the pipeline and plunge down a steep footpath. The undergrowth is thick with new brambles and stinging nettles and super-sized dandelion leaves. The sun illuminates a ford to my left. I see hoofprints in the dark peaty soil, but I am not an errant knight and I keep my feet dry by using the footbridge. I pass the ruins of a building where a millstone leans against an ivy-covered wall, and I follow a stony path that winds its way up the north side of the valley. I reach a thick-trunked conifer and see that someone has helpfully marked on the bark in yellow paint '*Variante tour*'. This is the way to the ruins of Roquefort, but you won't find it in the guidebooks.

My path undulates along a steep hillside and the river falls away below me until it is a distant whisper. Through the gaps in the oak tree canopy I glimpse a circling crow, and its call breaks the eerie silence of the forest. I know I shall have only my imagination for company when I reach the fortified village. No one comes here. I march for another five minutes, then moss-covered banks squeeze the path into a narrow cutting through slabs of rock. At the far end I enter a clearing. A hand-painted sign nailed to a tree confirms that I have found the Castrum de Roquefort and that Monsieur Pierre Clement declines all responsibility if I suffer an accident while visiting his ruins. I glance up from the sign at a steep cliff. It is covered in vegetation and the leaves sparkle in the sunlight. I squint against the glare and can just make out the blurred outline of the tower.

I also have an old photograph of this view, and at the time it was taken, barely a twig obscured the tower. The appetite of the charcoal kilns kept the forest tamed because it took around half-a-tonne of wood to produce the charcoal to melt the copper for a single cauldron.

In the photo, a man stands proudly on the edge of the cliff and stares into the distance. He is the perfect cliché of a French peasant: he wears a beret and below his bushy eyebrows he sports a bushy moustache; in his hand he holds a cane at an angle which suggests he is about to prod a reluctant cow. Below him, a women in a hat sits on top of a wall at the entrance to the fortified village. Her head is turned, but I cannot tell if she is looking at the camera or admiring the man on the cliff above her.

I climb a short section of steep rocky path and pass through an archway in the wall beneath the lady's petticoats. I glance up, half-expecting to see her, but instead I notice the crumbling stonework above the gateway has been shored up with a wooden frame to stop stray rocks falling on my head. The path continues to climb and I reach the first moss-covered foundations of medieval village houses. I follow the faint trace of a street and then turn back on myself and continue climbing over treacherous overgrown rubble onto a flat grassy area which would once have been the enclosed courtyard or bailey. In a castrum, the majority of the population lived inside the walls, and the stone tower or keep served as the last line of defence. Roquefort's tower is in front of me, built on the highest point of the outcrop, and its walls are pierced by a solitary window. In contrast with the rest of the site, the cut stones of the tower are so clean they look as if they have been sandblasted. In reality, they have been fried and dried by the sun and the *vent d'autan* for a thousand years.

As its name may suggest, I am standing in Jourdain de Roquefort's family home. His father and uncles lived here – including the ones who were *parfaits* – and it was probably his birthplace.

In some ways it was an unusual spot to build a fortress. At a time when agriculture dominated the economy, it was far from ideal for farming. The surrounding land was mountainous and its soil was poor, and the valley floor was prone to flooding. Most of the medieval châteaux in the Lauragais enjoy commanding positions from where the local lord could survey and control the countryside around him, but from where I am standing the steep sides of the valley restrict my view of the Lauragais to a narrow triangle. On the other side of the plain lies the ridge of Montgey. I can imagine one of Jourdain's forefathers looking out from where I am standing and thinking that if he were to build another château over there in the sunshine, he would be able to see all the way to the Pyrenees.

In Jourdain's day, the two communities would have been able to signal to each other and warn of approaching crusaders, inquisitors or other enemies. I try to spot the Château de Montgey, but thick green foliage impedes my view. I start to climb the wall of the tower in search of a higher vantage point. With binoculars, I can see the top of the tower from my bedroom window, so I should be able to see my house and Montgey if I climb high enough. The handholds and footholds are flawless, and barely a grain of sand or grit comes off on my fingertips. The stone and mortar are indestructible, but when my toes are three metres off the ground, I remember I am not. I remember Monsieur Clement's warning about accidents and responsibility, and I remember how isolated this spot is. It has been abandoned and barely touched for 600 years, one of the least-investigated Cathar castles. I have heard from Jean-Paul Calvet that a team of archaeologists plans to excavate the site in a few months' time, and I don't want mine to be the first skeleton they discover.

I descend carefully to the ground and tell myself it is disrespectful to climb the walls of ancient monuments. My face burns hot in the sunshine and I lean against the stones of the keep and swig warm water from my bottle. The crow still caws and circles overhead, but otherwise the valley is at peace and the Castrum de Roquefort seems more like a hiding place than a command post. And so it proved to be on many occasions. In 1209, after the massacre at Béziers and the fall of Carcassonne, 300 *parfaits* took refuge here on what must have been a very crowded hilltop. After that, fleeing heretics regularly found temporary shelter at Roquefort during the era of the Albigensian Crusade and the Inquisition.

Starting in the 1370s Roquefort played a darker role. For over forty years it was the hideout of a band of brigands, fearsome men who terrorised the surrounding countryside as far as the gates of Toulouse. At least part of the blame for their unwelcome presence can be laid at the door of the Black Prince.

21

A PLAGUE OF BANDITS

After a few weeks of celebrations and letter writing at the end of 1355, the Black Prince began to prepare for another expedition. He ordered new weapons and armour from the workshops of Bordeaux and requested more archers and longbows from England. When he set off in the spring of 1356, he headed north. His plan was to join up with two other invading English armies, but after a long campaign of looting he found himself cornered near Poitiers by the army of King Jean le Bon, or John the Good if you prefer.

In the Lauragais the previous autumn, the Black Prince's army had been stronger and more experienced than the enemy, and he had been itching for a battle. At Poitiers his men were outnumbered two-to-one, and when the Cardinal of Perigord offered to negotiate, he accepted. The cardinal spent all of Sunday riding back and forth between the two armies carrying proposals and counter-proposals, but to no avail. The following day, 19 September 1356, the two armies joined battle.

Poitiers was even more of a disaster for the French crown than Crécy ten years earlier. Jean le Bon was not quite as good as his name might suggest, and he was captured on the battlefield, along with his son. Even worse, the French king proved to be worth far more than his weight in gold. The Black Prince took him back to Bordeaux, shipped him off to London, and demanded a ransom of three million gold crowns, or over thirteen tonnes of the precious metal.

Jean le Bon spent four years in London while the two countries tried to reach an agreement. Eventually they signed the Treaty of Brétigny. In return for keeping possession of half of France, Edward III generously renounced his claim to the French crown and accepted that Jean le Bon could pay his ransom over a period of five years. The first instalment of 600,000 crowns was paid on 25 October 1360, and Jean le Bon took a boat back to Calais and started to think about how he could raise the rest of the money.

For over twenty years the kingdom of France had been ravaged by war and ransacked by English armies. Now its king had negotiated peace, but at an economically crippling price. Still worse, peace did not bring tranquillity.

Les Grandes Compagnies, or the Free Companies, plagued France throughout the Middle Ages. They were bands of mercenaries of mixed nationalities and no fixed loyalties who would fight for anyone who paid them, and when they were dismissed during intervals of peace, they devoted themselves to private plunder. One of the side effects of the Treaty of Brétigny was to throw thousands more soldiers out of work, and they swelled the ranks of *les Grandes Compagnies* still further. Because of the nature of their activities, these brigands were generally men of no fixed abode. They wandered around the kingdom spreading terror and despair among the already impoverished population.

Sometime in the 1370s, one of these *Grandes Compagnies* found a place that was so remote, so safe, but which offered such rich pickings, they decided to set up a permanent home there. For the next forty years they lived in the Castrum de Roquefort. They also occupied a similar settlement on a rocky spur just above modern-day Durfort, and they kept an eye on the plain from a third castrum on the hilltop of the Berniquaut. It would have been a brave, or perhaps foolhardy, attacker who rode up the valley to try to expel them. On my walk to Roquefort I passed numerous places ideal for an ambush long before I reached the castrum.

From the safety of their rocky refuge the brigands could pass over the Montagne Noire and attack the countryside towards Castelnaudary and Carcassonne, or they could follow the Sor down onto the plain and ravage the Lauragais. They maintained good relations with a neighbouring band of outlaws in the mountain above Dourgne, and together they made expeditions as far afield as Castres, Albi and the gates of Toulouse. Any merchant who travelled the country had to pay a levy or risk forfeiting his wares and his life, and nearly all the towns and villages of the Lauragais had to buy off the plunderers – in some cases several times – or risk destruction. This financial burden followed on from the more legal but no less onerous contributions demanded by the king's men to help pay off the royal ransom.

In the immediate neighbourhood, the brigands sacked Sorèze, Saint-Chameau (now Saint-Amancet), Dourgne and Massaguel. Only the town of Revel was able to resist, thanks to the valour of its inhabitants and those fine new ramparts, but the six watermills outside the safety of its walls were ransacked and fell into such a state of ruin that the king auctioned them off in 1402 for the price of a few horses.

I leave the granite walls of the castle keep and stroll down through the bailey. Peeping out of the undergrowth around me are the foundations of a dozen tiny houses. They were simple dwellings with drystone walls and roofs covered with flat stones instead of tiles. This is where *la Grande Compagnie de Roquefort* lived.

Writing two hundred years ago in his '*Notice historique sur Sorèze et ses environs*', Jean-Antoine Clos was in no doubt about their nationality: '*the memories conserved among the people tell us they were English*'.[13] He then tells us their captains were called Ribes, Galard and Rodrigo, but these are not names I usually associate with my compatriots, so it is perhaps more accurate to say that they were a mixed bunch who may at times have been in the pay of the English. Whatever their nationality, they formed a well-organised community that engaged in a far wider range of activities than mere thieving. Over recent decades local enthusiasts have discovered iron ore, slag, metal shoes for horses and mules, bobbins and needles. These suggest the presence of blacksmiths, saddlemakers, tanners and tailors. Other bandits became secondhand dealers who resold the plunder, principally livestock, grain, furniture and jewels.

The kings of France made numerous attempts to disperse *les Grandes Compagnies* in general and the brigands of Roquefort in particular. Some of them were recruited into the French armies that invaded Spain and Italy, but many of the brigands preferred to continue with their easy life of crime.

In the Lauragais, the common people grew more and more desperate, and in 1393 they raised enough money to bribe the brigands of Dourgne to go away. They then tried the same trick at Roquefort, but this time the bandits took the cash, went on holiday, and came back a few months later to resume business as usual.

In 1415 the king ordered his lieutenants to clear them out by force. They succeeded, but the following year the brigands rolled back into Roquefort like a pocketful of bad pennies. The king's men evicted them a second time, and realised the only way to

13 Translated from : Clos, Jean-Antoine. *Notice historique sur Sorèze et ses environs*. Rev. ed. 1845. Reprint. Nîmes: Editions Lacour, 2003 (page 67).

stop the brigands coming back was to destroy both the Castrum de Roquefort and the Castrum de Durfort. This particular *Grande Compagnie* finally dispersed, and the historic home of the Roquefort family was abandoned forever.

I hurry through the crumbling archway in the defensive walls and pause in the clearing by Monsieur Clement's warning sign. I take a last look at the ruins left behind by the king's men. What became of the brigands who lived here? Forty years was long enough to put down roots, and some of the bandits married local girls so presumably they had children who were raised into a life of crime. After their final eviction, some of the outlaws are believed to have settled in Durfort where they took to beating seven bells out of pieces of copper instead of their neighbours. As for the rest, they may have joined groups elsewhere because *les Grandes Compagnies* continued to plague the kingdom of France for another thirty years.

I take a different route back to Durfort, and after a steep descent I come out of the forest near the mill at the entrance to the village. I can see traces of the brigands' advance post on a rocky ridge running up the mountainside to my right, but I won't visit it today. The remains of the Castrum de Durfort are even sparser than those of Roquefort, but they were subjected to lengthy archaeological investigation in the 1980s and 1990s. Since then, bushes and scrubby trees and wild flowers have reclaimed the site. The ruined walls of its tiny keep come up to your waist, and it is fiendishly difficult to get into the site and even harder to get out.

A few paces further and I pause in a *place* beside a shallow rectangular pool where the coppersmiths once washed their new cauldrons in clear mountain water. From here the route splits into three. You can choose between the Rue des Martineurs (the hammersmiths), the Rue des Recureurs (the men who cleaned the finished cauldrons with acid) and the Rue du Castlar. I choose Hammersmith Road, which is really more of a narrow lane squeezed between half-timbered houses. A stream courses down a channel in the centre of the street, and at its lower end the lane opens out onto a larger *place*. After a mountain walk on a day like this, it is impossible to pass the tables outside Le Cyrano without stopping for a drink. Chasing bandits is thirsty work, even if you are only chasing their ghosts.

I turn my chair and look up the valley from the comfort of the twenty-first century with a glass of cold beer in my hand. From here I can see no sign of the Castrum de Roquefort, but my head resounds with the echoes of hydraulic hammers and more than a hundred years of misery. Throughout this terrible period, the lords and the knights and the men-at-arms of the Lauragais were almost constantly at war with the English, the Gascons, the Spanish, the French king, or one another, and the entire population suffered from famine, the Black Death, the Black Prince, raising a king's ransom and paying off *les Grandes Compagnies*.

The Hundred Years' War effectively ground to an end in 1453 when the English lost the Battle of Castillon near Bordeaux. Soon afterwards, life changed out of all recognition for the Lauragais. It was about to enjoy a century of peace and prosperity, a golden age when dark times would be banished by blue.

Part V

In Search of *Pastel*

22

Taking Root in the Lauragais

I drop a white flannel into the evil-looking brew and swirl it around with the end of a stick. The virgin cotton erupts in ugly spots, like the skin of someone who has caught a nasty disease. Warily I continue to stir the contents of my plastic bowl. The liquid looks as if it has been squeezed from the bladder of a thirsty horse and I give it a cautious sniff.

'You don't still use human urine, do you?' I have heard the story of the *pisseurs* many times, those enviable men whose profession required them to drink large quantities of beer and urinate copiously into the vats of dye.

There is a touch of irony, or perhaps apology, in the smile that accompanies Jean-Louis Fragasso's response. He assures me that modern science has found a less pleasurable way to produce a liquid with a high concentration of ammonia. Breathing more easily, I give my sickly flannel a good prod to remove any air pockets. The dye may be yellow, but the spots have spread and the whole flannel now appears to be green.

Through the open doors of the workshop, a fountain plays in

the village moat and the church bells of Roumens chime the hour. The lady opposite me smiles and her disposable plastic apron flutters around her waist. She's pretty, but Jean-Louis looks much more fetching in his blue cotton apron. He tells us now is the time. I fish out one end of the flannel with my stick and seize it with latex-covered fingers. I allow it to hang vertically over the container and it begins to drip-dry. The cloth is an unpleasant yellowy-green, but after a few seconds oxygenation begins to take effect and a miracle is performed before my eyes. Over the next couple of minutes, my once white, once seasick flannel turns a delicate shade of blue. When the colour is uniform, I hang it on the washing line outside and look around me.

I have cycled or driven through the centre of Roumens countless times without paying any attention to the building beside the moat which houses the workshop and offices of Carré Bleu. Instead, my eyes are usually drawn to the other side of the road where a menagerie of painted plaster figures – human and animal – portray idyllic scenes of country life from long ago, and my mind tries to guess what the artist had been drinking the day he decided to sculpt an elephant, a giraffe and a lion, or the buxom mermaid with heart-shaped areolae around her nipples.

Today, with fresh eyes I see that many of the human figures are wearing clothes of *bleu de pastel*, or pastel blue. Nearer to hand, I notice the blue lettering on the blue sign above the workshop's blue doors, and the blue shutters of the office windows, and the blue of the cart in the garden where my blue flannel drips and dries in the sunshine. Other garments – dyed by professionals rather than dippers like me – are drying under cover at the end of the building. All of them are blue, but the intensity of colour varies according to a complex range of factors including the weather, the fabric, the water and the bacteria in the vat of the day. My flannel is the darkest tint in sight, but it will lighten as it dries and then it will fade no further.

Surrounded as I am by *pastel*-dyed fabrics, plaster peasants with their beasts of burden, and the sound of the old village pump dribbling water into an old stone trough, I feel as if I have taken another step back into the past. To complete the effect, there is even a *pastel* plant growing at my feet. This is the perfect place to start my journey through the golden age of blue.

In English, *isatis tinctoria* was commonly known as woad, and in the north of France it was *guède*. In the Lauragais it was *pastel*, and I have lived here far too long to think of it as anything else. *Pastel* sounds much more romantic to my ears, even when I remember that the word derives from '*pasta*', meaning 'paste' in Latin, because the first stage of the medieval process involved grinding the leaves of the plant into a pulp.

The specimen in front of me has been allowed to flower. Multiple stems as high as my waist rise from a clump of dark green leaves at the base. From a distance, the clusters of tiny bright yellow flowers could be mistaken for mustard or rapeseed, and indeed, all three plants are members of the brassica family. I inhale a faint scent of honey, but the flowers are of no interest to the dyers – except to produce seed for planting next year's crop. The colour resides in the oblong-elliptical foliage. On closer inspection, I see that the tips of the more mature leaves look ill. They are turning blue-black like fingers that have suffered from frostbite, but it was the product of these sickly-looking leaves that made my flannel turn blue and brought a century of immense prosperity to the Lauragais. It was thanks to *isatis tinctoria* that, between 1460 and 1560, the *pastel* merchants of Toulouse built their magnificent mansions; new châteaux and dovecotes sprang up across the countryside; and village churches were rebuilt or extended.

I leave the workshop with my flannel stowed safely inside a plastic bag. It won't be colourfast until it dries, and I don't want to decorate the upholstery of my car with patches of blue.

'Put it in the washing machine on its own the first time,' Jean-Louis calls after me. 'After that, you can wash it like anything else.'

I drop off the flannel, grab a hat and my camera, and stroll up the road beside the moat. I want to see if I can find the *pastel* fields. I want to know how the countryside looked in the fifteenth century. When I asked Jean-Louis where they were, he said cagily, somewhere near the village. I didn't push the point. I can understand his reluctance to see hordes of visitors trampling his crop beneath their inquisitive feet, and several hectares can't be that hard to find, particularly as I now realise I am not looking for fields of yellow flowers. I am looking for fields of dark green lettuce.

In medieval times, *pastel* was grown all over Europe, including the north of France, England, Germany, Holland, Italy, even Russia, but in terms of productivity the Lauragais beat them all. In Thuringia, which was an important area of *pastel* production in central Germany, there was one harvest a year. In the Lauragais there were up to six, and the quality was among the best. The reason? The soil of the Lauragais is known as *terrefort*, a chalky clay that holds its humidity and is highly fertile. The *pastel* plant was particularly fond of *terrefort* and it adored the climate of the Lauragais. The brighter the blue of the skies under which the plants grew, the brighter the blue of the dyes they produced.

Half a dozen harvests between mid-June and early November made it a profitable crop, but an exhausting one for the peasants. The hard work started well before the grains of *pastel* were sown in February or March. *Terrefort* is heavy to plough, and the *pastel* plants demanded finely tilled soil. As soon as the seedlings broke the surface, the Battle of the Weeds began. This relentless struggle lasted seven months until the final harvest in November. Another problem with chalky clay is that after it has rained, a thin surface layer compacts and sets like cement. I know this from my own vegetable garden. No further rain can penetrate and the peasants had to break up the soil with a hoe.

Six harvests and ten months of ploughing, weeding and hoeing consumed huge quantities of labour, particularly those who were cheap to hire such as women, children and paupers in search of daywork. I can imagine many a scorching summer's day when the peasants must have rubbed their aching backs and wondered why they didn't grow wheat instead. But then, no doubt, they reminded themselves that *pastel* earned them four times as much as wheat, and they numbed their pain with visions of the shiny copper cauldrons they would buy in Durfort before Christmas, and those new pewter plates that would be the envy of their work-shy neighbours.

Back in the present, I leave the last house of Roumens behind me and begin to labour up a dusty track through fields of sunflowers, sorghum and maize, and a dark green plant that may be soya but certainly isn't *pastel*. I reach the top of an escarpment where a platoon of wind turbines faces the *vent d'autan*. From here, I can see most of the fields around Roumens and on the plain of Revel. So where are the fields of dark green lettuce? I should be able to see something from up here, even if the crop is split into small parcels like it was in the olden days.

Eventually, I locate a dark green field less than a kilometre away and I descend by a different path. It leads me in the direction of Montégut-Lauragais, but long before I reach the field I can see the dark green plants are much too tall to be *pastel* and I halt at a parting of the ways. There is no shade, I am sweating profusely, and I stare at the crop of young maize in irritation. In an earlier career, I could unfailingly navigate my way across moor and mountain in the dark, in the mist, or with a balaclava worn back-to-front. How can I fail to locate a field of *pastel* in broad daylight? I must be searching in the wrong place.

With a sense of resignation, I choose the fork that will take me back to Roumens. If I can't find the source of the region's medieval wealth, I shall go to Toulouse and see what the rich merchants built on the sore backs of the peasants.

After a dozen paces, I cheer up. I spot hoofprints in the dust and they remind me that Roumens has another page in its history. I am walking over another battlefield, and the actors in this drama included the ramparts of Revel and the Black Prince's hunting partner, Gaston Phoebus, Count of Foix.

In 1380, Gaston Phoebus was not a happy man. Jean le Bon's son, Charles V, had promised to make him governor of the Languedoc but had then inconveniently died before the parchment-work could be completed. The new king, Charles VI, was only twelve years old, and his elder uncle, the Duke of Anjou, became regent, and his younger uncle, the Duke of Berry, decided to appoint himself governor of the Languedoc.

Gaston Phoebus was a popular lord and, along with most of the local nobility, he refused to recognise the self-appointed royal governor. The following spring, the Duke of Berry marched south with an army to deal with what he viewed as a rebellion. Gaston Phoebus gathered his troops in Toulouse and prepared for battle.

There is some disagreement among historians about the place where the two armies met. According to Gustave Doumerc in his 1976 book '*Histoire de Revel en Lauragais*', it took place in these same fields between Roumens and Montégut-Lauragais where I was hoping to find some *pastel* plants. To support his case, Doumerc cites the large number of horseshoes discovered somewhere beneath my feet at the beginning of the nineteenth century.

The battle was fought on 15 or 16 June 1381. Gaston Phoebus had a much larger army, and when one of the Duke of Berry's officers saw how heavily his side was outnumbered, he advised his commander to avoid a fight. The duke replied, 'It won't please God if a son of the king shows so much cowardice. *Au contraire!* I swear I shall not move from this spot until we have done battle!'

I pause in the shade of a walnut tree and idly turn over the soil with the toe of my shoe. Maybe this was the spot! History is never far below the surface in the Lauragais, and I am almost disappointed when I fail to unearth any military souvenirs.

The proud duke's army was soon overcome. Three hundred soldiers lay dead or dying in the fields around my walnut tree, and their comrades fled five kilometres across the plain towards Revel where they hoped to find refuge. Men fleeing for their lives will not necessarily take the most obvious route, but even so, local geography suggests the fugitives approached Revel on the old Toulouse road which today is called the Rue de la Liberté. This would have led them to the gate of Saint-Antoine which stood next to the section of ramparts rediscovered by Jean-Paul Calvet. Unfortunately for the Duke of Berry's men, this gate and all the others were firmly shut. The citizens of Revel quickly realised that for once they were not dealing with *la Grande Compagnie de Roquefort*, but they still looked down on the duke's men from their lofty walls and said, 'Go away!', or less polite Occitan words to similar effect. Infuriated but powerless in the face of such opposition, the Duke of Berry paid off some of his troops, and retreated with the rest to Carcassonne where he hoped to find a warmer welcome.

Soon afterwards, peace was restored and Gaston Phoebus renounced his claim to govern the Languedoc and instead devoted himself to more leisurely activities. He had always been a great hunter and he started writing his '*Livre de Chasse*' in 1387. Today, you can turn the pages of an imaginatively projected electronic copy in the Round Tower of his château in Foix, or there are forty-four physical copies of this wonderfully illuminated guide to medieval hunting in various libraries and museums around the world including Brussels, Geneva, London, Los Angeles, New York, Paris, Stuttgart and Turin.

Gaston Phoebus was also lord of the old French province of Béarn. It lies to the west of his château in Foix, further along the Pyrenees towards the Atlantic Ocean, and today its principal city is Pau. From the middle of the fourteenth century the Béarnese took advantage of their neutrality during the Hundred Years' War to export *pastel* to England. They bought it in the countryside around Albi, and in villages such as Auterive, Le Fauga and Muret to the south of Toulouse, and they took it over the Pyrenees or shipped it out through the port of Bayonne. At the beginning of the fifteenth century, another export route developed eastwards to Catalonia and this was principally controlled by merchants based in Barcelona or Narbonne.

The merchants of Toulouse had little involvement with this early trade. Like the Lauragais, the city had suffered from a hundred years of misery. The population had declined, many of the buildings were abandoned, the lone bridge across the Garonne was falling into ruin and the ramparts had been patched up with unbaked clay. In 1463, a great fire burned for fifteen days, and with the help of the *vent d'autan* it destroyed two-thirds of the city.

Around the time of this ruinous blaze the merchants of Toulouse woke up to the business opportunity growing on their doorstep. They took on the Béarnese, and within a few years they had wrested control of the export trade through Bayonne, which was still mainly bound for England. Between 1475 and 1480, merchants from northern Spain arrived in the city and began to buy up *pastel* for Castile's textile industry. Most of them came from the city of Burgos, located midway between Bilbao and Madrid, and before long some of them settled in Toulouse. One of the best known was Jean de Bernuy, and by 1503 he had grown so rich he began to build the most impressive house the city had ever seen.

23

STRATOSPHERICALLY RICH

I arrive in Toulouse on the metro and jump out at Jean Jaurès. This is not the nearest station to my destination, but I want to visit a statue on the way. I exchange subterranean gloom for dazzling sunlight and stroll past the multiplex cinemas to the green islet of the Place Wilson. In its centre, a marble figure of a man sits on a mound of marble rocks and holds a marble book in his left hand. His hat lies on a boulder by his right foot and his muse reclines naked below his left. The monument sits in the middle of an ornamental pond, and soothing fountains of water rise and fall in the morning air.

The man's name is carved on the back of the monument but there is nothing to tell you what he did. Thanks to Dr Alibert and his reading list, I know that Pèire Goudouli, or Pierre Godolin, was Toulouse's most prominent Occitan poet of the seventeenth century, and that his marble hand is holding his most famous work, '*Ramelet Moundi*'. Ironically, his first known composition was a poem written in French and it won him a prize at the Floral Games of 1609. The following year he switched to Occitan, but he never won another prize from the Acadèmia dels Jòcs Florals.

I take a few photos, and then I sit on a bench and contemplate Pèire Goudouli. I watch passers-by taking pictures of the monument with their mobile phones. None of them look like tourists, or students of history, or Occitan specialists, and I can't help wondering if they know anything about this poet, or perhaps they are merely taking pictures of a pretty fountain and a marble statue set against the backdrop of a brick building which, in the morning sunlight, illustrates perfectly why Toulouse is known as *la ville rose*, the pink city.

Unlike Revel with its orderly grid of streets, the heart of old Toulouse is an anarchy of disorientating angles. I zigzag my way through narrow back streets and eventually wriggle my way out onto the Rue Léon Gambetta. In front of me stands the Hôtel de Bernuy.

I should perhaps explain at this point that I am not seeking a room for the night, or for an early siesta. In medieval times, the French word *hostel* meant a guesthouse. Then it lost its 's' and acquired a circumflex accent, and *hôtel* came to signify a grand townhouse like the one built by Jean de Bernuy. It was only in the nineteenth century that the word reclaimed its original meaning as a place where you could rent a room with a bed.

A helpful stone plaque next to Jean de Bernuy's front door tells me the façade dates from 1504. This is among the first of eighty mansions built in the city by the rich *pastel* merchants. Its ornate sculpted doorway and iron-studded double wooden doors seem more suited to a church than a private mansion. This may not be entirely accidental because they were added a hundred years later, by which time the building had become a Jesuit college. The Hôtel de Bernuy has remained an educational establishment of one sort or another ever since – religious, royal or imperial – and today it is a *lycée*, or high school.

While I am reading the plaque, a man presses a button and opens one of the ancient doors and steps inside. I casually drift to my left and glimpse the courtyard inside. The man glares at me and waits for the door to shut. I resign myself to staying on the outside, and I follow the façade to the right. On the corner, a row of iron railings imprisons oversized trees in a tiny cell of a garden. I follow the walls down the Rue Lakanal. Above a brick wall as high as the ramparts of Revel, I can see the hexagonal tower built by Jean de Bernuy to show off his importance to his fellow citizens. Attached to the hexagon is an even taller round tower with a steeply-pointed conical roof, and the ensemble looks rather like an Ariane space rocket on its launchpad. This strikes me as appropriate for two reasons: Toulouse is at the heart of the French aerospace industry, and Jean de Bernuy was stratospherically rich. Some sources suggest his personal contribution accounted for twenty per cent of the total taxes raised in Toulouse, and after the Battle of Pavia in 1525 when another French king was captured on the battlefield, Jean de Bernuy was so wealthy he personally guaranteed the entire ransom payment. A few years later, the newly-liberated François I visited the sumptuous Hôtel de Bernuy as a mark of his appreciation. This, incidentally, is the same king who issued the Edict of Villers-Cotterêts in 1539 and brought an end to the official use of Occitan and Latin in his kingdom.

It is only natural to wonder how someone could grow so rich from those dark green plants I was trying to find in the fields around Roumens. The key to becoming a successful *pastel* merchant was good finance: the business worked on a three-year cycle and had a voracious appetite for capital. The peasants demanded cash for their *pastel* leaves, which then went through a lengthy process to transform them into a non-perishable, transportable product, and the buyers, particularly those overseas, bought on credit. Only well-financed merchants could afford to tie up their money for so long, and this stifled competition and allowed the rich to grow steadily richer.

In the case of Jean de Bernuy, he came from a family of wealthy merchants and over time he expanded his activities to include all stages of the business cycle. He grew his own *pastel* plants, processed the leaves in his own mills and exported the finished product to the textile industries of Spain, England and Holland. One Spanish academic studied the family's 1546 accounts and calculated that Jean de Bernuy earned a profit of thirty-six per cent from the *pastel* he sold in Spain. This compared with a typical profit of around thirteen per cent for wool or cloth.[14]

So how exactly were those off-colour *pastel* leaves transformed into gold and silver and luxurious mansions with rocket ship towers? During each of the multiple harvests in the Lauragais, the pickers took their baskets of leaves to the nearest water course where the *terrefort* was washed off. The peasants then spread out the clean leaves to dry, and within hours they took them to the *pastel* mill where they were ground into a paste. Unlike wheat, *pastel* could not wait for a windy day; the leaves had to be processed immediately or the colour was lost. The windmills which the Black Prince had set alight in such large numbers a century earlier were too weather-dependant, and the hydrography of the Lauragais was unsuited to water mills, so most of the *pastel* mills used bovines or equines to turn the stone wheel. Today, for a fee you can see an example of this type of mill in the Musée du Pastel at the Château de Magrin near Puylaurens, or if you don't mind a climb, you can inspect one without charge near the windmill in Lautrec.

After crushing, as much liquid as possible was drained from the paste and it was formed by hand into balls called *cocagnes*. These were placed in racks in a well-ventilated area sheltered from the rain and left to dry for several weeks. I have a *cocagne* on my desk as I write. It looks like one of those fat balls people hang out in their gardens for the birds, only darker. If I pick it up, it weighs

14 Casado Alonso, Hilario. *Finance et commerce international au milieu du XVIeme siècle : la compagnie des Bernuy.* Annales du Midi, Année 1991, Volume 103, numéro 195. (pages 337 – 338).

about the same as a small bag of crisps; if I tap it, it sounds like a hollowed-out gourd; if I sniff it, there is the faintest aroma of dried foliage.

Once the *cocagnes* were dry, they were stored until the end of the season. Until then, everyone was too busy weeding and hoeing and picking the next harvest to have time to work on the least pleasant stage of production.

It took four months of smelly work to transform the *cocagnes* into a product which could be shipped and sold to the textile industry. Early in the New Year the *cocagnes* were taken back to the same mills where the same beasts turned the same millstones. The ground-up *cocagnes* were then mixed with impure water, and the mushy mass began to ferment, usually on the brick-paved floor of the *pastel*-maker's workshop where it was easier to stir or turn with a shovel. For several weeks the unpleasant mixture festered away and gave off noxious and revolting fumes. It took skill to control this process. The fermentation had to be lively enough to oxidise the glucose in the leaves and make them release their pigment, but if it went too far, there was a risk of destroying the colour. Adding human urine was the simplest way to speed things up, and cold weather or adding pure water slowed it down. The *pastel*-maker's art lay in striking the right balance to obtain a product of the highest quality.

The rich *pastel* merchants like Jean de Bernuy made sure this malodorous activity stayed in the countryside of the Lauragais and came nowhere near their fine mansions in Toulouse. Once the fermentation was finished, the paste was left to dry and then it was broken up to form something like fine gravel. The granules were very dark – almost black – and the first sacks of *agranat* were ready for shipping in May.

Sometime around 1517 Jean de Bernuy bought the estate of Villeneuve-la-Comptal, just outside Castelnaudary, and the title of baron which went with it. As well as producing *pastel* on these lands, he bought *cocagnes* and *agranat* in many parts of the Lauragais to the north-west of his estates, principally in the villages of Cambiac, Caraman, Le Vaux and Maurens. To give an idea of the scale of his production, early one year he bought eighteen kilometres of cloth to make the sacks for that season's *pastel*, and in 1525 he exported over 800 tonnes. In those days, one hectare of good Lauragais land typically produced around thirty kilograms of *agranat*, so he was extracting the pigment from 250 square kilometres of *isatis tinctoria*. That's twice the size of Toulouse, or four times the area of Manhattan. Even I would be able to find a *pastel* field that big.

Jean de Bernuy died in his princely home in 1556, but he did not pass away peacefully in his bed. True to his Spanish roots, he threw a party for his nephew which included a bullfight. The animal escaped and Jean de Bernuy took the bull by the horns – unfortunately for him, in a literal sense – and he died of his injuries. Ten years later, commercial and religious misfortunes obliged his family to sell the Hôtel de Bernuy to three rich men of the city who gave it to the consuls on the condition it should become a Jesuit college.

I retrace my steps to the accidental matador's front door, and then I head south to see how another rich *pastel* merchant, Pierre Assézat, outdid his neighbour by building one of the masterpieces of European Renaissance architecture. This time I shall be able to go inside.

I make a slight deviation to see the river because it is from here, from the Quai de la Daurade, that the *pastel* merchants dispatched their goods in flat-bottomed barges to Bordeaux where they were transferred to ocean-going ships. Jean de Bernuy was one of the first to make use of this route, and this comparatively easy transport was another of the factors that helped Toulouse and the Lauragais attain such prominence in the European *pastel* trade.

I turn inland at the Pont Neuf and within a few paces I reach the Hôtel d'Assézat. Open gates welcome me, so I enter the courtyard and sit down in the shade of the loggia and order a coffee. Through one of the three airy arches of this comfortable café terrace, I inspect the exquisite home of Pierre Assézat.

The loggia encloses one side of a cobbled courtyard which is not quite square. To my right, a blank wall soars skywards and supports a covered walkway which connects the first floor above my head with the first floor of the main building. The other two sides of the courtyard are enclosed by three stories of grandiose Renaissance stonework and brickwork. Each window is framed by columns of the classical order; Doric on the ground floor, Ionic on the first and Corinthian at the top. Above the intersection between these two façades rises an octagonal red brick tower with two terraces and a small temple. Pierre Assézat made his tower the same height as Jean de Bernuy's, give or take a few centimetres.

Pierre Assézat must have thought himself a lucky man when he began building this extravagant home in 1555. His two older brothers were *pastel* merchants, and when they died in swift succession in 1545 and 1546, he found himself head of a wealthy family at the age of twenty-five (the exact year of his birth is uncertain, but it was probably around 1520). Two years later he married into one of the leading families of Toulouse, and in 1551 he became one of the city's consuls. Like many of the rich *pastel* merchants, Pierre Assézat used his wealth to expand into financial services such as money lending and insurance. Before long he was so successful and so well-connected that he was underwriting the income of the Queen Mother in all of south-west France. By this time, Jean de Bernuy had found out the painful way that possessing a great fortune is no guarantee of good fortune, and Pierre Assézat was about to make the same discovery.

24

A Spectacular Fall

At its heart, the *pastel* trade was an agricultural business, and the weather always played a big role in determining the volume and quality of the crop in much the same way as it does with vines and wine. A wet season produced a large volume of poor quality *pastel*, whereas hot, dry weather produced smaller quantities of leaves that were packed with pigment.

In 1559 there was a drought in the Lauragais. The smaller-than-usual crop was picked and turned into *cocagnes* between June and early November. Everyone was convinced that the finished product, the *agranat*, would be of the highest quality, and as a result, speculators pushed up the price of *cocagnes* to some of the highest levels ever seen.

During the first few months of 1560 the *cocagnes* were ground up, and by May the *agranat* was ready for sale. Between August and October it was shipped down the Garonne to Bordeaux, and in November and December ocean-going vessels took it to England or Holland. In those markets, the buyers were most active in May and June, so it was not until the summer of 1561 that they began to buy the *pastel* grown in 1559, the *pastel* which everyone had expected to be of the highest quality.

Before long, buyers were complaining that the pigment was not as good as they had been promised. Some of the *pastel* merchants blamed the peasants in the mills: the fools had added too much fresh water to slow down the fermentation, and then the cool spring of 1560 had slowed it down still further. But it seems unlikely everyone in the Lauragais would have made the same mistake, and no one really knows why the quality was poor.

By this time the buyers had read the weather reports for 1560 and 1561. The spring of both years had been unusually rainy, so they anticipated two more years of low quality *pastel*, but this time in greater abundance. The market slowed to a crawl and prices in London and Antwerp slumped. Confidence in the blue skies and blue dyes of the Lauragais began to fade in a way the colour never does, and the buyers waited for prices to fall still further. Some of the *pastel* merchants duly obliged in a desperate attempt to recoup some of their capital, but to little effect. The buyers knew they now had a choice – a new competitor called indigo.

Small quantities of indigo had reached Europe from Asia since the time of the Ancient Greeks. In the early sixteenth century the Portuguese began growing it in their colonies in India. By the early 1560s, supplies to Europe became more reliable and more voluminous, and in 1561 the product appeared in significant quantities on the London market.

The ostentatious wealth of the de Bernuys and the Assézats had undoubtedly created envy, and some merchants saw indigo as an opportunity, a chance to break the monopoly of these rich and powerful dynasties. It would take several more decades for indigo to truly topple *isatis tinctoria*, but its arrival was another blow to confidence in the *pastel* market.

If you pay to visit the *pastel* mill at Magrin, you will also see an indigo bush in the château's garden. It grows a couple of metres high and has leaves like a false acacia. Although *indigofera tinctoria* could not produce the glorious blues of *pastel*, it enjoyed overwhelming commercial advantages. Its cultivation was much simpler and therefore cheaper; its pigment was far easier for the dyers to work with; its transport was much more economic because it was a stronger, more concentrated product than *pastel.* This last advantage was particularly important for the Spanish market where transport to the interior of the country was on the back of a mule.

Pierre Assézat was still grappling with these *pastel* problems when, in 1562, he was hit by a third catastrophe: the Wars of Religion. Two or three years earlier he had converted to Protestantism, and on 11 May 1562, he and his fellow-believers in Toulouse seized control of public buildings and strategic points across the city. A week of fighting on the streets left 3,000 dead, and Pierre Assézat was forced to flee along with all the other Protestant consuls and their supporters.

Overseas confidence in *pastel* from south-west France had now taken a triple hit: unreliable quality; the emergence of a fierce competitor; and the start of a bloody civil war.

The following year, the Protestant consuls were reinstated but Pierre Assézat never felt safe in the city again. He had too many enemies, including Catholic members of his own family. Like many of the Protestants he also encountered endless legal and administrative difficulties, including punitive taxes and confiscation or pillaging of his goods and possessions. At the end of September 1572, he gave up the struggle and renounced his faith. Like many of his fellow-believers, he was probably encouraged to take this step by the Saint Bartholomew's Day massacre in Paris a month earlier.

In return for re-embracing Catholicism, Pierre Assézat's confiscated possessions were returned to him, but during the last ten years of his life he rarely came back to the Hôtel d'Assézat and instead spent most of his time in Bordeaux from where he continued to trade in *pastel.* He was able to do this because indigo did not replace *pastel* overnight. Its supply route by sea around the Cape of Good Hope was long and unpredictable, and the price fluctuated wildly. For many years dyers used both products, often mixing them together, and they played off the competing suppliers against one another. Nevertheless, *pastel* gradually lost its pre-eminence and disappeared from the countryside of the Lauragais.

I finish my coffee and take a last look at the glorious home which Pierre Assézat was forced to abandon after his failed coup. He had planned to surround his courtyard with four equally opulent façades. Whether it was the exorbitant cost or uncertainty about the future that stopped him at the halfway point we do not know.

Today, anyone can visit the interior of the Hôtel d'Assézat because it is not only home to the restaurant and café where I have comfortably reflected on its creator's life. It also provides a home for six learned societies, including the Academy of the Floral Games, and museum space for my next destination: the splendid art collection of a rich Argentinian, Georges Bemberg.

25

TWO QUEENS CALLED ELIZABETH

I spend a couple of hours with Tintoretto, Monet, Gauguin and Toulouse-Lautrec. Señor Bemberg also acquired some sketches by Picasso, but unfortunately nothing from his Blue Period. This reminds me that long before Picasso's time, *pastel* began to play a role in the world of art. When the dyers were at work, a dark blue substance called *la fleurée de pastel* formed on the surface of the dye and around the edges of the vats. It was skimmed off and used as a pigment to make blue paint. It was also mixed with a binder and dried to form what later came to be known as pastel sticks, whatever their colour.

I step outside the gates of the Hôtel d'Assézat, but there is no escape from *pastel*. Attached to the corner of the building is a shop, Terre de Pastel, selling *pastel*-dyed clothing and household linen, and *pastel* cosmetics. I peep inside, and I am convinced the flannel sitting on my desk at home looks almost as good as the professional products. With a sense of misplaced pride – all I did was dip a cloth in a bowl of dye, and it truly is far more complicated than that – I stride up the Rue de la Bourse. Within seconds I find myself outside another shop, La Fleurée de Pastel. I hesitate in front of the window. I rarely enter pretty shops on my own, certainly not two within a hundred paces of each other, but then I remind myself I have come to Toulouse on a mission and I step inside.

I head to the back of the store and peer into a courtyard. The doors are ajar, but there is a chain across the opening and a sign forbids me from going any further inside what was once the home of another rich *pastel* merchant. To my left is a hanging rail, and I am rather taken by a *pastel*-dyed polo shirt. I turn to ask the shop assistant if I can try it on, but she is deep in conversation with another customer, so I continue browsing. A framed certificate on a pillar catches my eye. The ink is blue, like most things in this shop, and below the heading, 'Académie des Arts et des Sciences du Pastel', the certificate informs me that Her Majesty Elizabeth II Queen of England was received as an honorary member on Wednesday 7 April 2004. I smile and wonder if it was explained to Her Majesty how the first Queen Elizabeth tried to stop *pastel* spreading across her green and pleasant land.

The problems of the *pastel* trade in Toulouse and the Lauragais in the 1560s prompted large scale planting of *pastel*, or woad, in the south of England and then in the Midlands. Unfortunately, this coincided with a period of food shortages across the country. Part of the blame was laid at the door of *pastel*: too much fertile land that should have been producing food was being turned over to the more profitable *isatis tinctoria*. In 1585, the government carried out a woad census and found that in Hampshire, one of the most successful woad-growing counties, 1,748 acres of land were devoted to the crop. That was about seven square kilometres, a drop in the ocean compared with the vast territory once exploited by Jean de Bernuy, but Queen Elizabeth was still sufficiently concerned to issue a '*Proclamation against the sowing of woade*' in which she forbade anyone from sowing *isatis tinctoria* within four miles of a market or clothing town. In addition, she imposed an eight mile exclusion zone around all her own houses because of the smell of the extraction process. This leads me to suspect she was more concerned about the royal nose than her people's stomachs, and indeed, she soon decided money smells so sweet it can mask even the most putrid stench. When the queen and her advisors realised they could fill the royal coffers by licensing woad-growing and taxing its production, the laws were rescinded.

Meanwhile, the decline of *pastel* in the Lauragais continued and the French king, Henri IV, saw things differently. He wanted to protect his indigenous *pastel* industry from the new Asian competitor. In 1609 he pronounced the use of indigo to be a crime punishable by death.

Despite these royal interventions on both sides of the Channel, *pastel* continued to lose ground until all natural dyes whatever their colour were commercially doomed by the invention of synthetic pigments in the late nineteenth century.

I take a photo of my queen's certificate, and I wonder if she too dyed her own flannel, and if so, where she keeps it. I check my photo; the light is poor so I try again using flash. The shop assistant breaks off from talking to the only other customer and wags a finger at me.

'It's forbidden to take photos.'

I peer around the pillar towards the till. 'What? Even of Her Majesty's certificate? Even if I am one of her subjects?'

'Yes. It's forbidden.'

'Why?'

'There might be copyright issues. We can't let people take photos inside the shop.'

I bite my tongue and take another look at the certificate. It seems remarkably kind, or forgetful, of Queen Elizabeth to have left it behind. No, it couldn't have been forgetfulness. She has people with her who take care of practicalities such as carrying her money and gifts. Maybe she already has too many certificates on her walls, or perhaps it is only a copy, but surely no one would mind me taking a photo of a copy? Whatever the reason, it's a wonderful memento, and if it were my shop I would be delighted to have it photographed and posted on social media as often as possible.

I study it more closely. Two people have signed the Royal Certificate: one, inevitably, is the president of the academy, and the other is the permanent secretary. I note down both their names, but for once it is not the president who catches my eye. The name of the secretary rings a bell: Henri Lambert. He'll know why Queen Elizabeth's lackeys failed to carry away her certificate in a cardboard tube.

Back at home, some rapid research reveals my memory was not playing me tricks. In the mid-1990s, Henri Lambert and his wife Denise decided to leave Belgium and settle in France. They bought a fifteenth-century tannery by the river in a place called Lectoure to the north-west of Toulouse. What began as idle curiosity about the blue paint on their ancient shutters led them to invent a much faster process for extracting the pigment from *pastel*.

I need to talk to them, and not only about the royal certificate, but I quickly discover Henri died of a heart attack in 2010. He was only fifty-five. When I read this, my first thoughts are naturally for his family: a sudden loss at a comparatively young age is always tragic. But Denise has continued to work with *isatis tinctoria* and, if her television and press coverage are anything to go by, she can tell me more about the renaissance and future of *pastel* than anyone else alive.

I dial her number and make an appointment to visit the old tannery next week. Our conversation will be different from all the others I have conducted so far for this book. This one will be in English because Denise is from Chicago.

Before I visit Lectoure, I continue my research and discover that the shop in Toulouse where Queen Elizabeth's certificate hangs on the wall was founded by the Lamberts. After Henri's death, Denise sold it to the owners of Carré Bleu in Roumens, and this reminds me I still haven't seen a *pastel* field.

I send an email to Jean-Louis Fragasso and ask him if I can watch the next harvest and take some photos of his crop. He replies that unfortunately they have just finished the final harvest of the season and his field is now being prepared for sowing. Maybe next year…

But we are in early September and I don't want to wait until next year. Perhaps I can find one elsewhere. After more research I stumble across an article published in a local paper, '*Voix du Midi*', in May 2016. The commune of Montgeard has planted a field of *pastel!* The village lies in the southern half of the Lauragais and is notable for its eponymous château, also known as the Hôtel Durand after the man who started building it in 1555. Naturally Guillaume Durand's money came from *pastel.* According to the press article, tourists used to ask if they could see a field of *isatis tinctoria.*

'You see?' I jab a finger at my computer screen. 'I am not the only one!'

After a small-scale experiment in 2015, the *mairie* of Montgeard took the initiative of planting 3,000 square metres of this ancient crop – that's about a third of a football pitch – to satisfy the curiosity of its visitors.

This will be easy, I think. The mayor has publicised her *pastel* field in the press. She wants people to see it. But when I read on, my excitement evaporates. The whole field has been allowed to flower and there's talk of making *miel de pastel*, or woad honey. The tourists are being shown fields of flowers! What about authenticity? Neither the Hôtel de Bernuy, nor the Hôtel d'Assézat, nor the Hôtel Durand was built with the proceeds of flowers and honey.

I shut down my computer in disgust. Perhaps Denise can help.

26

Renaissance

'Twenty years ago we read an article about the quality of life in south-west France and decided to move here. So we drove down one rainy day, saw the house and fell in love with it, not knowing what we were going to do with the place. We had ideas, but nothing specific.'

I am sitting with Denise in the kitchen of her old tannery. The back door is open and the sound of the river is barely audible at the end of the garden. Her home is a rambling old place built on three levels. From the outside, the roof tiles form a patchwork of pinks and reds. Blocks of pale stone surround the window openings, and honey-tinted lime rendering covers the walls. You cannot miss the blue paint. It is on all the woodwork: window frames, shutters, doors, and the slatted shutters on the second floor where the tanners used to hang their skins to dry.

'My husband and I had spent twenty years in Redu in Belgium running a gallery specialising in second-hand art books and musical scores. So we were accustomed to colours, and when we saw the shutters we were curious about the blue paint and why it was used here.'

Denise hands me a cup of coffee and I decline the sugar. I am almost disappointed she is not dressed in blue.

'We started with all the usual tourist visits – the mansions of the *pastel* merchants in Toulouse, the Musée du Pastel at the Château de Magrin. We soon realised no one had made *bleu de pastel* paint since about 1871 when chemical dyes were invented. But in countries throughout Europe everyone continued to paint their shutters blue because they thought the colour repelled insects. In fact, it's a transparent substance in the *pastel* plant that provides a natural protection against insects and some types of fungus. Later, we worked with the wood department of the University of Vienna, and they were able to dissociate these properties from the colour, but old habits often continue without questioning the reason why.

'At first we were astonished no one could show us paint made from *pastel*. Ochre and madder and various minerals are still used in dyes and paints, but Europe's only natural blue had disappeared. It had been forgotten. So it became our passion to rediscover how to make it and to find a more industrial method of extracting the pigment. We came across a few people who were dyeing with *pastel*, but they all worked in isolation and grew a few plants in their gardens and wouldn't talk to us. It was like a closed door, and we quickly realised we would have to do it on our own, but I don't think anyone believed a crazy American and Belgian couple would be able to figure it out.'

Undeterred, the Lamberts tracked down some *pastel* seeds. They bought 450 grams from a museum, the Conservatoire National des Plantes à Parfum, Médicinales et Aromatiques, at Milly-la-Forêt to the west of Paris.

Denise frowns. 'The seeds probably dated back to the time of Napoleon and they were very expensive.'

'Why did you buy them there? I read that a few years before you started, a cooperative near Castelnaudary had started growing *pastel* for its seeds, and that the oil was used in cosmetics.'

'Oh, we went to them, and they closed all the doors on us too. Someone suggested, why not go to the local café and find an employee who has just been fired. So that's what my husband did and he got a bit of information, but it was like Fort Knox. We couldn't understand why it was all such a big secret.'

Now it is my turn to frown, and I recall my own difficulties trying to find a field of *pastel*, or even taking a photo of a certificate in a shop.

Denise is still talking and I make an effort to catch up. 'We convinced a local farmer to plant our seeds, but when it came to trying to extract the pigment we discovered another problem. Despite its long history, nothing much was ever written down about *pastel*, partly because it's not like a simple recipe. There are too many factors you can only learn to understand through experience, and knowledge was passed down orally. We decided we would have to work it out by trial and error. We weren't scientists, but we knew about colours.'

'How did you even know where to begin?' I ask.

'We found some old books from Napoleon's time which talked about the extraction process, and one of them had the design drawings for a *pastel* mill and a dyeing facility. They gave us a starting point, and then my husband went to see Professor Vilarem at the School of Chemistry in Toulouse. He thought we were completely crazy.'

At the end of the 1980s, Gérard Vilarem and his scientists had developed a process to extract the oil from *pastel* seeds, and this was then used by Bourjois/Chanel in some of their cosmetics. Now, Denise and Henri asked him to help them find a faster method of extracting the plant's pigment.

'The scientists worked in their laboratory and Henri did his little chemistry thing down here in our basement. In fact, he discovered how to precipitate the pigment before they did. They asked to see how he was doing it, and then they realised their mistake: they were using purified water. *Pastel* needs bacteria, and the bacteria need impurities to make them work.'

Between them, the Lamberts and the School of Chemistry perfected a new process that is over a hundred times quicker than the medieval method. The pigment can be extracted from the *pastel* leaves in less than a day.

'Did you patent your invention?' I ask.

'No. We didn't think it was worth the cost, and we wanted to share our knowledge. We wanted as many people as possible to use the process. We wanted the *pastel* industry to grow. None of that was going to happen if we kept our work secret.'

There is a commotion above my head. It sounds as if a pack of huskies is dragging a sledge across bare floorboards. Denise excuses herself and goes upstairs to calm her canine companions who, I am surprised to discover later, number only two.

During her temporary absence, I drain my coffee cup and seize the opportunity to inspect her kitchen without any obligation to hide my curiosity. I see blue lampshades, blue tassels tied to the drawer handles, blue floorboards set into the stone slabs near my feet, blue window frames, blue leather chairs, blue and white kitchen tiles, blue paint between the joists, blue kitchen towels. This is the home of someone who has been bewitched by *bleu de pastel*.

Denise sits back down at her kitchen table. 'Where were we? Oh yes, we wanted the *pastel* industry to grow. Our original aim was to produce decorative paints, but we soon realised that in order to expand the market we would need to find as many applications as possible, even where *pastel* had never been used before. If we could do that, the farmers would grow more *pastel* and prices would come down and the whole thing would take off.

'We only started dyeing fabrics because a fashion designer asked us to try it. Now it's my main activity and I have customers in France, England, Italy, Japan and other countries. For this year's Cannes Film Festival, I hand-dyed all the table cloths with the help of my daughter. Designers like the fact that they are buying a French colour grown in France, extracted in France and dyed in France. And they are prepared to pay for hand-dyed quality.'

'Is it particularly difficult to dye with *pastel*?'

'With other natural colours you just stick the product in water and there's your dye. But with *pastel*, the powdered pigment won't dissolve in anything. It's dense and very hard like lapis lazuli. It's difficult to work with, and you have to work around the problems. It always amazes me that Stone Age man worked out how to do it. It's such a complex colour, and dyeing with *pastel* depends on the water, the bacteria, the weather, so many outside factors. It also depends on the porosity of the material. Back in the fifteenth century they only worked with wool and silk, but nowadays we dye other natural fabrics such as cotton, linen and bamboo fibre. They are all different and that's why I only do blues.'

Denise then introduces me to a new French word: *ennoblissement*. This is what you do when you dye with *pastel*, you make the fabric more noble.

'Don't forget that from the time of Louis IX, or Saint Louis, this was the colour of the kings of France. They and their nobles wore rich fabrics to dissociate themselves from the people. They wanted prestige and they thought, blue is the colour of the sky and the ocean, blue is the colour of the gods. But when we started our project, although everyone seemed to know blue was the French colour, no one knew where it came from. And no one knew that Colbert had the charge of regulating thirteen royal shades of blue. Who in the world would order a minister to do that?'

I know the answer to that one: Louis XIV, a king who truly cared about his colours. In 1669 his finance minister, Jean-Baptiste Colbert, introduced regulations covering all the colours used by the textile industry, and when it came to blue he excelled himself: *bleu blanc, bleu naissant, bleu alazado, bleu mourant, bleu mignon, bleu céleste, bleu turquin, bleu de reine, bleu de roi, bleu fleur de guède, bleu pers, bleu aldego, bleu d'enfer*. The last one is the darkest – the blue of hell – and it would be a devil of a job to translate the whole list.

This talk of royalty naturally reminds me of Queen Elizabeth II's *pastel* certificate.

'How did you come to meet Her Majesty the Queen?'

'Because we were well-known. She came on a visit to Toulouse and she asked to meet us. I'm always amazed when that happens, but anyway…'

'You mean Her Majesty requested an audience?'

Denise laughs. 'She wanted us to explain about *pastel*, which annoyed a lot of people who thought they were more qualified than us. She came to the Place du Capitole in the centre of Toulouse and visited our tent with *pastel*, another tent with fruits of the area, one with wines, and that was it. It was funny because all morning we had to listen to the English school practising "*God Bless the Queen*". But when she arrived, she already knew practically everything about what we were doing, so we made her an honorary member of the academy and offered her several gifts – a scarf and a medal and so forth. I didn't realise how small she was by the way, that was hilarious too.'

For a moment I wonder if it will be treason to report Denise's last comment, and I hope the schoolchildren sang '*God* Save *the Queen*'.

'How did she know about you?'

'Through the press, the British press. Sometimes I am astonished how well-known we are, but I believe it's because we work with, first, a passion, second, history, and third, a craft that was more important in France than in any other European country.'

'Why didn't Queen Elizabeth take her certificate away with her?'

'Oh, she took it. The one in the shop is a copy. I left it there when I sold the shop.'

I knew it! I was scolded for taking a photo of a copy!

There is another interruption, this time from the telephone. Denise may be from Chicago, but she was raised in France and has spent most of her life in Europe. To my ears she speaks perfect French, and I listen to her chattering away about an old gypsy caravan she is selling. I noticed it as soon as I arrived at her home. It stands in the garden painted as blue as all the other woodwork.

Denise hangs up, and I decide that this is the moment to find out if she has a field of *pastel* that I can see and touch and smell.

'Where do you get your pigment? Is it extracted from your own *pastel*?'

'In the beginning, we worked with a farming cooperative near Saverdun south of Toulouse and extracted small quantities of pigment here at home. Back then, so few people wanted it, a few hundred kilos was enough for everyone. But demand grew quickly and the farmers took too long to respond. Now we have new farmers who are interested in growing *pastel* but we don't have enough good quality seed. So at present I am buying pigment in Italy, but I can only obtain it in small quantities. You can find some in France but it's triple the price. Everyone is in the same position.'

Later, I discover you can buy a kilo of powdered pigment for slightly under a thousand euros, although it won't be of much use unless you have Denise's knowledge of dyeing.

'Isn't it odd to be buying pigment from Italy? I thought this was about the renaissance of *pastel* around Toulouse.'

'Historically, the Toulouse merchants bought in Italy and the Azores as well as the Lauragais. Gascony produced a lot too, and so did the north of France where they called it *guède*. I even have photos of woad mills and people making *cocagnes* in England as recently as the early twentieth century. But the blues of the north were never as good as those of the south because of the climate. The other big advantage for Toulouse and the Lauragais was having the Garonne for transport. If I think about the way a *pastel* trader would reason, if you had a farmer from somewhere like Lectoure who took his *cocagnes* to the *pastel* market in Toulouse, it would have taken him about a month in his horse cart, and on the way he might have been robbed or killed because *pastel* was worth its weight in gold. So it was logical for the rich merchants to buy up land and estates close to Toulouse where they could grow their own *pastel* and manage the source of their wealth.'

We continue to chat and I have no doubt Denise could talk about *pastel* all day long. She is clearly obsessed by blue and she tells me about her latest projects.

'I'm working with a new farmer down the road in Fleurance. Next year we will plant twenty-three hectares and build a new extraction facility. And next month I'm opening a new workshop in the village of Montjoi where the public will be able to watch me at work dyeing with *pastel*. I'm determined to make this industry grow. I'm tired of *pastel* being a craft.'

On the drive home, I reflect on the similarities between the efforts of the Lamberts to breathe new life into *pastel* and the work of Dr Alibert to promote the use of Occitan. Both the dye and the language have been close to extinction, and both have experienced renewed interest in the last couple of decades. They are two of the most important features of the history of the Lauragais, but despite the best efforts of their enthusiastic supporters, both remain something of a curiosity, or in the case of *pastel*, a cottage industry.

Isatis tinctoria has one major advantage over Occitan: it has multiple strings to its bow, and it is this diversity that makes me suspect it has the greater chance of flourishing in the future. As well as interior and exterior paints, art products, cosmetics and dyes, there are medical opportunities.

Pastel has been used in Chinese medicine for two thousand years, and today it is widely grown in the north of the country. In China, they dry the roots and call it Ban Lan Gen, and they dry the leaves and call it Da Qing Ye. According to the Chinese, these *pastel*-based medicines can cure anything from the common cold and AIDS to encephalitis and prostate cancer.

Denise told me she is working with Austrian, German, Swiss and Japanese researchers to investigate medical uses, such as treating burns and skin complaints with *pastel* oil. Other laboratory trials have shown that a substance in *pastel* called indirubin can, among other things, stop the growth of tumours, and that *pastel* has an antibiotic effect and can help wounds to heal. This last finding has led some historians to suggest that when Queen Boudica and her Iceni warriors daubed their bodies in woad paint, it was not to frighten the Romans but to reduce the risk of infection if they were stabbed by a centurion's spear.

Everyone I have met during my *pastel* adventure talks excitedly about these possibilities, but the harsh reality is this: there are thousands of scientific papers out there reporting on promising laboratory tests that have used all manner of natural substances. Commercialising a new pharmaceutical product takes a level of investment that would cause even Jean de Bernuy to blink, and it is impossible to predict if one day *isatis tinctoria* will form the basis of a new medical treatment.

27

A FIELD OF *PASTEL*

When I finish listening to the recordings of my morning spent with Denise, I am left with one huge disappointment. I still haven't seen a field of *pastel*. Yes, Denise will be able to show me twenty-three hectares next year, and others have made similar claims, but what about this year? Why is *isatis tinctoria* proving to be as elusive as the Scarlet Pimpernel? I wouldn't write about growing rice without seeing a paddy field; neither would I write about Raimon de Miraval without visiting the ruins of his château or listening to his music. I can't write about the renaissance of *pastel* without seeing a field of the stuff. In fact, that's my minimum requirement. Witnessing a harvest would be better, and seeing the extraction of the pigment would be ideal.

The largest concentration of *pastel* plants I have seen numbered two whole specimens, and they were in my own garden. Many years ago, someone gave a brace of them to my wife as a present. I knew much less about *isatis tinctoria* in those days, and when their leaves began to look off-colour I accidentally ran over them with the lawnmower. I am beginning to wish I had been more careful.

I decide to call a few friends. Someone must know where I can find a field of *pastel* this year rather than next, but instead, my week goes from bad to worse. I speak to one old killjoy who suggests the story of the beer-quaffing *pisseurs* is probably a myth. As the gentlemen in question is an expert in the practice of *pastel* dyeing, I feel obliged to take his suggestion seriously and to carry out some more research.

I have heard the *pisseurs* mentioned during every tourist visit I have made, and the story is repeated in numerous documents and websites relating to *pastel*, but no one cites a source. Before the emergence of modern chemistry, urine had been valued and carefully collected since Roman times. It was widely used in the textile industry; by tanners and dyers; by washerwomen to clean the laundry; by farmers as a fertiliser; and by makers of gunpowder to make things go 'bang', or '*pan*' if they were French. But the idea that there was a *métier de pisseur*, a trade or profession where the practitioner was *paid* to do nothing more onerous than stand around drinking beer and answering the call of nature in the appointed place – well, it sounds too good to be true, doesn't it? And the word *métier* is usually reserved for an activity that requires at least a modicum of knowledge or skill.

To resolve the matter, I write an email in my best French and send it to Francis Brumont. He is a widely-published professor of modern history, and his academic papers have been among my main sources of information about the *pastel* trade and the rich merchants of Toulouse. I feel a trifle foolish putting such a base question to such an eminent expert, but I go ahead anyway: did the profession of *pisseur* exist?

I receive a charming reply in which Professor Brumont says, '*It is true that some people in our tourist industry and those who seek to exploit the rich vein of pastel's past treat historical truth rather lightly (very lightly, even). It is true that one mentions that under certain conditions, notably relating to temperature and according to the state of the mixture's fermentation, it was advised to add urine. But to turn that idea into a true profession! And besides, at that time beer wasn't a drink known in the south of France where one was happy with wine.'*

I turn off my computer, lob my *cocagne* into the bin and sulk off towards the kitchen. It is a hot Friday afternoon, but I ignore the fridge of cold beer and open a bottle of red wine instead.

I hear about David Santandreu and his *pastel* field from a contact in Revel. When I speak to him on the telephone, David says he still has one more harvest to cut. We fix a provisional date for a visit and I agree to call him a couple of days beforehand to confirm our arrangement.

The date approaches and I make countless calls, but I only speak to his answerphone. I leave messages, but I receive no reply. Here we go again, I think. Another *pastel* field that vanishes as soon as I express a desire to see it, let alone touch it, smell it, taste it. With a sense of foreboding, I make one last call on the morning of my proposed visit. When David answers in person, I almost drop the phone.

'I didn't call you back because we've had a problem with the cutting machine and I'm not sure we'll be able to harvest today. But hold on a minute. I'm just arriving at work so I'll see if he's been able to fix it.'

I grip the handset and hold my breath.

'He must have started early! He's done a couple of laps already. You best come over quickly before he's finished.'

I grab my camera and notebook and skid out of my driveway. Cambounet-sur-le-Sor is much closer to my home than either Lectoure or Montgeard. Under normal circumstances the journey would take twenty minutes, but I arrive in twelve.

After all the frustration, this is a truly beautiful sight. A tractor chugs up the hill towards me. Attached to the back is a Bonino AB

60 TR self-loading cutting wagon. The tractor draws closer, and I stand there grinning like an idiot and I even wave to the driver. Above the noise of the tractor, I can hear the whir of cutter blades and the rumble of conveyor belts inside the cutting wagon, and through its slatted sides I glimpse a mountain of freshly-cut green leaves. This is the type of machine they use to cut spinach and certain types of lettuce. It can also cut *pastel.*

It is a perfect morning. No wind, a clear blue sky, and the sun is already drying the morning dew. Below me lies a wide and fertile valley where the Sor flows into the Agout. Most of the fields are shades of yellowy-brown – wheat stubble, sunflower stubble or parched maize waiting to be cut. The field where I am standing is an exception. It is covered in squat green plants. There are no gaps between them and the dense vegetation rolls down into the valley like a carpet of lamb's lettuce. The smell of cut foliage floats in the air. It is not the pleasant scent of freshly mown grass; it is more like the odour of cut flowers when you take them out of the vase and throw them away.

I watch the cutting machine slice its way through plants that are no higher than my ankles, and my mood fluctuates between excitement, relief and indignation that it has taken me so long to find a field of *isatis tinctoria.* Why didn't I discover this place sooner? The Château de la Serre makes no attempt to hide its three hectares of *pastel.* The field sits beside the road for all to see, although no one would drive down this tiny lane by chance. The extraction unit is housed inside a steel-framed wood-clad building opposite the field. There are two large signs outside; one explains how they grow *pastel* and extract its pigment, and the other shows how they distil oil from their lavender fields. There is even a wooden shutter and a notice which invites the casual passer-by to slide it open and watch the factory at work.

This morning the shutter is already open and I peer inside. The building only has three walls. It is open on the far side and sunlight floods into the yard. A current of cool air drifts through the hatchway and I have no doubt I can take as many photos as I wish. Here, I sense a desire to share the history and future of *pastel* with as many people as possible.

The tractor rumbles noisily into the yard and the cutting machine bulges with foliage. Beyond the mechanical ensemble, I glimpse a wing of the château and a round tower with a pointed roof like a witch's hat. The history of the Château de la Serre is uncertain because its archives were destroyed in 1569 during the Wars of Religion. If you want to explore inside, you can book yourself in for dinner, bed and breakfast. This, and other buildings nearby, are the home of Sirius, a company originally founded in Paris by Gilles Berthoumieux to trade in essential oils. In 2009 he decided to repatriate his business to the area where he was born, and before long he branched out into *pastel*.

The tractor backs up to a large steel container that resembles the type of skip used by waste disposal companies, but this one is watertight and, perhaps inevitably, painted blue. An elevator belt at the rear of the cutting machine hums into life, and green leaves pour into the container. After a few moments, David Santandreu jumps inside and the elevator discharges tonne after tonne of foliage around his feet. He pushes it into the corners with a pitchfork, and the leaves glisten with their juices and the morning dew. The sky is a faultless blue and his shirt is the same colour. He dyed it himself, because David dyes all the fabrics at the Château de la Serre. He is the *maître pastelier* and even his hands are blue.

The scene is a confusing mixture of time and place: an American tractor, an Italian crop-cutting machine, a sixteenth-century French château, and a plant that has been cultivated since Neolithic times. Then there is the extraction unit itself: an assembly of galvanised steel pipework, steam generating plant, electric pumps and a lengthy array of thousand-litre polythene tanks. David designed this system himself based on a process developed under Napoleon to help thwart the British.

Napoleon didn't care much for *les anglais* (when Napoleon referred to *les anglais* he meant the British, like most French people today). Those treacherous islanders financed his enemies, set assassins on his trail and called him names: the Corsican Ogre when they were feeling charitable, and the Antichrist when they were not. In May 1806 they began a blockade of all French ports. Six months later, Napoleon retaliated by declaring his Continental Blockade which was intended to close every port in Europe to British merchants.

In practice, the Continental Blockade leaked like a sieve thanks to, among others, the Portuguese, Spanish, Danes, Swedes and Russians. Instead of damaging British commerce, it soon began to cause shortages of numerous products in France, and the search for alternatives began. Before long, chicory was being used instead of coffee; grape syrup or sugar beet instead of sugar; linen instead of cotton; madder instead of cochineal.

By this time, indigo had almost completely replaced *pastel*, and Napoleon began to run out of blue dye. Although he himself often wore the green uniform of the Imperial Guard's light cavalry regiment, he liked to see most of his boys dressed in blue. *Pastel* was an obvious solution, but Napoleon was a man of science and much too impatient to tolerate the lengthy medieval method, so he launched a competition to find a faster process. The search took longer than he would have wished, and it was not until 1813 that Professor Giovanni Antonio Giobert, director of Napoleon's Imperial School for the Manufacture of *Pastel* Pigment in Turin, was able to publish a book based on his evaluation of all the proposed solutions. His work included a section helpfully entitled, '*The method of extracting the pigment from pastel that is preferable to all the others*'. This cut the time between harvest and pigment down to a mere five days.

The Lamberts acquired a rare copy of this book early on in their research, but decided to invent an even faster process. David Santandreu chose to work with the Napoleonic method where the only chemical employed is lime.

The conveyor belt stops and there is silence. Six tonnes of *pastel* leaves fill the blue container, and David tells me it is time to make tea. How very English! But instead of filling up the kettle, a technician opens a valve and steaming hot water gushes into the container to make an infusion of *pastel.* David dangles precariously over the top of the container with a thermometer. He needs a temperature of around seventy degrees Celsius to make a good skip of *pastel* tea. After a few hours he will transfer the water to his precipitation chambers where, with the help of the lime, the pigment will oxidise and precipitate. After filtration and decantation, the precipitate will be removed in the form of a dark blue paste.

David tells me he will be working until midnight. He will sleep on site and rise at five in the morning to inspect his blue brew. He is a man dedicated to the traditions of *pastel*-dyeing. This year he made a couple of hundred *cocagnes* to sell in the Château de la Serre's shop, and next year he plans to make a larger quantity that he will turn into *agranat.* He wants to experiment with even greater historical authenticity.

I return to the field for a last look and I ask the boss's brother, Bruno Berthoumieux, what made them think of growing *pastel* in the first place.

'We are right in the heart of the area where *pastel* was once grown. It was a natural development.'

Bruno tells me that, like the Lamberts, the Château de la Serre obtained its first seeds from the museum at Milly-la-Forêt. Now they cultivate a separate area of *pastel* hidden in the woods where they hand-select the seed stock for the following year's crop.

While Bruno chats away, I pick one of the more mature leaves and take a bite. It tastes like rocket. I chew on a younger leaf and the after-taste is even stronger and it burns my throat.

'Ça pique, hein?'

Yes, it certainly has a bite to it. I cough and wish I had a bottle of water in my pocket.

Bruno smiles. 'We're talking to some local restaurants about creating *pastel*-based dishes. I can make a good gazpacho soup with the leaves.'

I'm still coughing and swallowing. 'It's not blue is it?'

He laughs. 'Only a little.'

To complete my research into the culinary properties of *isatis tinctoria*, I dip my fingers in David's vats of dye and taste them. Although not disagreeable, it is not a soup I would serve to my guests at dinner, not even at lunch come to that, and I trust Bruno's gazpacho tastes better.

I also learn how David keeps his potions fermenting for several months by feeding them with chopped-up henna, chestnut leaves and dates. Machine may have replaced man in the cultivation and harvesting of *pastel*, and pigment extraction is about a hundred times faster than in the days of Jean de Bernuy, but when it comes to dyeing the fabrics, little has changed since the fifteenth century. Learning the art of *pastel* dyeing is a true apprenticeship, and it requires the kind of dedication we usually associate with craftsmen of old. As Denise Lambert told me, 'With *pastel*, you can produce the most exquisite blues in the entire world, colours which are moments of pure grace, colours which make you forget all the hassles you had to obtain them. But there's one more thing: you know you will never reproduce exactly the same colour again.'

During the long weeks I have spent writing this chapter, I have worn a *pastel*-dyed shirt. Not the same one, I should add. Somehow I acquired a new garment with every visit I made, and although I was too late to see the *pastel* field in Roumens, I had no difficulty in finding Carré Bleu's tempting shop in the market square of Revel. At the Château de la Serre I even dyed my own tee-shirt.

From a personal perspective, pulling on one of these garments is a very different experience from wearing an ordinary blue shirt. I feel I am wearing a piece of history, the history of the Lauragais. Perhaps my views have been coloured by writing this chapter, and now *pastel* has got under my skin too.

Part VI

A Question of Religion

28

A Protestant Stronghold

There is no better way to resolve a problem than to take a quiet stroll through the lanes around my village. On these ribbons of tranquil tarmac I always encounter more creatures than cars, but many a time when my thoughts are roaming free among the woods and fields and distant mountains, something that is neither bird nor beast leaps out from behind a bush, or pops its head above the trees, or jumps unannounced into the saddle between a couple of hills. I know it is only Puylaurens, but still I stop and stare and lose my train of thought. Viewed from the north, the town scowls down from its hilltop at the approaching visitor, but if you catch sight of it from my direction, Puylaurens shines almost white in the midday sun and at dusk it sparkles as if sprinkled with gold. At any time of day the spire of Notre-Dame-du-Lac is a beacon for travellers who have lost their way in this part of the Lauragais.

On more intimate inspection a polite visitor might call Puylaurens an unassuming little town. A few years ago even its own *mairie* described it as impressive from afar, but disappointing up close. Maybe Puylaurens is exhausted by the weight of its long history because there is a lot more to its past than the water well in Jean-Pierre's cellar and half a grain silo in the western car park. Even the cannonball in Madame Colombié's front wall and the smaller one she keeps in her fireplace cannot do justice to the past glories of this quiet little town.

At the time the bottom was falling out of the *pastel* market in the second half of the sixteenth century, visitors approached Puylaurens with very different attitudes depending on their religion. For the Protestants, it was a place of refuge that resisted all attacks whether they were launched with military bravado or villainous treachery. For the Catholics, Puylaurens was an impregnable fortress whose warlike inhabitants hauled their cannons back and forth across the Lauragais to rescue other communities of heretics or to bombard those loyal to the pope.

This military role lasted throughout the Wars of Religion. When peace finally came, Puylaurens was exhausted by forty years of war, but a few decades later it was reborn as a brilliant centre of Protestant learning. Puylaurens encapsulates the history of French Protestantism, from Jean Calvin to the flight of the Huguenots.

A couple of years after Jean de Bernuy decided to build his extravagant mansion in Toulouse, Pope Julius II decided to develop the even more grandiose Saint Peter's Basilica in Rome. The first was built with the profits of *pastel*. The second was largely financed by the sale of a supposedly more spiritual commodity: indulgences.

Three centuries earlier, Simon de Montfort and his crusaders had been obliged to serve the church for forty days in return for their salvation, or pay someone else to suffer on their behalf. By the early sixteenth century things were more straightforward:

if you wanted an indulgence, you simply went out and bought one.

A Dominican friar called Johann Tetzel was the champion salesman with his slogan, '*As soon as the coin in the coffer rings, the soul into heaven springs*'. One of his compatriots, an Augustinian monk, objected to this crass commercialisation, and in 1517 he wrote to his bishop to tell him so. With his letter he enclosed a piece he had written called, '*Disputation of Martin Luther on the Power and Efficacy of Indulgences*' in which he insisted that forgiveness was God's alone to grant and that it could not be bought over the counter. From this theological clash, new and more austere varieties of Christianity spread across Europe like wildfire, closely followed by the flames of war. Nowhere did this conflict rage more bloodily than in France, and the Lauragais found itself in a particularly bad place. At its western end lay the Catholic city of Toulouse, and at its north-eastern extremity lay the Protestant hotbeds of Puylaurens and Castres. The countryside in between was a chequerboard of Catholic and Protestant communities which the two enemies systematically laid to waste during four decades of war. Almost every château, village and town I have mentioned in this book was scarred by the conflict, and many changed hands several times, always with deadly violence.

In France, it was a young lawyer called Jean Calvin who was the leading light of the reformist movement, and his followers were variously known as Calvinists, Reformists, Huguenots or Protestants. The new religion spread quickly. By 1560 there were two million Protestants in France – around twelve per cent of the population – and they prayed in 1,200 temples across the country (in French, the word *temple* is commonly used to describe a Protestant church).

Relations between Catholics and Protestants steadily worsened, and before long they descended into outright war. Historians generally divide the French Wars of Religion into eight, spanning the period 1562 to 1598. In theory, there were about eight years of peace between the various wars, but in the Lauragais the adversaries paid little attention to the truces and treaties signed in other parts of the kingdom. They never trusted each other, and they were constantly on their guard against a surprise attack, or watching out for the opportunity to launch one of their own. During these perilous times few towns remained as constant to one faith as Puylaurens.

Various theories have been proposed to explain why the new religion took such a strong hold in the Lauragais. Some choose to see a link between Protestantism and the anticlerical, anti-corruption spirit of the Cathars, and they seek to portray the south as a land of heretics. Theologically the two movements had little in common, and during both these periods of religious upheaval, the majority of the local population remained loyal to the teachings of Rome.

Others claim *pastel* was the key. The rich merchants learned about the new religion through their trading links with northern Europe. For the general population, the *pastel* mill was the perfect place for a secret assembly: people could travel there from the surrounding countryside at almost any time of year without arousing the suspicion of the authorities. It was in these mills that the pioneers of Protestantism first exposed their ideas to the people of the Lauragais, and hidden among the men criss-crossing the countryside to buy *cocagnes* and *agranat* were wandering booksellers who secretly sold Protestant works. Their greatest novelty was one of the oldest books of all – the Bible. Thanks to the technology of the printing press and the first translations of the Bible into French, the common people were able to buy the good book and read it for themselves without going through the intermediary of the clergy.

In the early 1530s, Protestantism established a foothold in Puylaurens and several of the town's consuls embraced the new faith. By 1561, around nine-tenths of the population had rejected Catholicism, and the consuls chose a Protestant – the Count of Caraman – to be their military governor. The following year the town gave asylum to its first religious refugees.

When Pierre Assézat and his fellow-Protestants failed to take control of Toulouse in 1562, they were eventually allowed to leave the city unarmed, but as soon as they were outside the walls the Catholics fell upon them. Those mounted on good horses fled to safety in Puylaurens and other Protestant towns. Many of the others were slaughtered.

A few weeks later, the Count of Caraman had second thoughts about his new faith and he imposed a Catholic garrison on Puylaurens. Their position in such a strongly Protestant town was precarious. Towards the end of the year, the townsfolk helped Protestant troops from Castres sneak over the walls during the night, and together they forced the unwelcome garrison to flee without loss of life. To celebrate their victory, the Protestants smashed all the statues in Notre-Dame-du-Lac and gave prayers of thanks amid the debris.

At the beginning of 1563 the consuls of Toulouse made their first attempt to capture their Protestant neighbour. They sent a detachment of troops with artillery, but the attackers were not strong enough to mount a proper siege and they soon withdrew. Rather than intimidate the people of Puylaurens, this aborted attack encouraged them to go on the offensive. Over the next few weeks they rampaged through the Lauragais as far as the outskirts of Toulouse, sometimes in the company of the Protestants from Castres. The first War of Religion officially ended on 19 March 1563 when Catherine de Medici signed the Edict of Amboise and guaranteed the Protestants a measure of religious freedom, but this was of no interest to the soldiers of Puylaurens. They continued their attacks, pillaged the homes of rich Catholics, vandalised the churches, and at Easter they cut off communications between Toulouse and Albi by capturing the town of Buzet. Hostilities eventually ground to a halt thanks to a common enemy rather than a treaty, a common enemy which made no distinction between Catholic and Protestant: the plague, probably brought to Puylaurens by refugees from Toulouse.

29

A One-Sided Siege

When the second War of Religion started in 1567, the troops of Puylaurens and Castres once again joined forces and resumed their raids on Catholic towns and villages throughout the Lauragais. They had a powerful army of 500 cavalry and 4,000 infantry, but many of the Protestant soldiers were soon called away by their leaders to fight in the north. The military governor of Toulouse, Pierre de Saint-Lary, saw that this was the moment to launch an attack. At the beginning of March 1568 he set off to besiege Puylaurens.

Pierre de Saint-Lary knew that even in the absence of its best soldiers Puylaurens remained a formidable enemy. He called for help. On the plain of Revel, he joined forces with the Count of Aubijoux and his troops from Albi and Lavaur; the governor and soldiers of Carcassonne; and many of the leading Catholic nobles from the Lauragais who were all keen to take part in the siege of such a redoubtable Protestant stronghold.

Perhaps as a warm up exercise, the Catholic army of 6,000 men with their eight cannons picked on a couple of softer targets. First, they recaptured Revel which the Protestants had seized a few months earlier. Second, they decided to besiege

Soual and cut off communications between Puylaurens and Castres. When the governor of Soual saw the might of his attackers, he dashed out to meet his enemy and offered to surrender the town without a fight. In response, the Count of Aubijoux made the memorable comment that he was fond of treachery but not of the traitor, and he promptly hanged the cowardly governor on the spot.

Now the Catholics were ready to attack Puylaurens, but when they arrived there on 7 April 1568 they discovered that even 6,000 men were not enough to encircle the town. They would have to leave the steep northern slopes unguarded.

The attackers installed some of their cannons by the windmills of the Quartier du Dretchenc. If you walk up the Rue des Moulins beside the retirement home on the western edge of town you can still see three of the windmill towers. It was a vantage point that gave the Catholic gunners an unobstructed line of fire onto the Porte de Foulimou and all along the southern ramparts. Their remaining artillery pieces were sited on a promontory to the south of the town. This offered a clear shot at Madame Colombié's front wall as you will see if you stand in the road outside number nine, Rue du Roc. The cannonball is clearly visible, even from a range of 200 metres.

The Catholics were now ready to begin their siege, but before giving the order to open fire, the Count of Aubijoux sent a herald to sound a trumpet and deliver an unambiguous message: his men would burn everything and kill everyone if the town refused to surrender.

The military governor of Puylaurens did not fear a siege. The town would not go thirsty because of all those water wells in people's cellars, and they would not starve even if the silos ran low because the town was not surrounded. '*Tell your master that before leaving this town I hope, with the help of God and the support of my friends, to make a bridge with the bodies of your dead that I shall cross to destroy your army.*'[15]

Bang! Crash! Disaster!

The Count of Aubijoux gave the order to open fire. The first salvo was unbelievably lucky. It smashed the drawbridge of the Porte de Foulimou and broke the chains holding it up. Before the attackers could profit from their sharpshooting, the defenders carried out frantic repairs and their governor decided it would be a good idea to ask his friends in Castres for some help. A hundred fresh men soon arrived, and over the next few days the defenders were strong enough to make the occasional sortie.

The siege dragged on and the consuls of Toulouse grew impatient. After five days, Pierre de Saint-Lary wrote to assure them his men were keeping up the bombardment, and as soon as they could make a wide enough breach in the walls he would order an assault and nothing inside the town would be spared. The consuls of Puylaurens noted in their records that the Catholic bombardment consisted of 357 cannonballs, and the precision of this figure leaves me wondering who did the counting.

Two days later more Protestant reinforcements arrived from Castres. A couple of hundred men crept into Puylaurens at one o'clock in the morning guided by a Catholic whose Protestant brother was one of the defenders. The two brothers embraced and resolved to make a fresh sortie against the enemy at daybreak.

One contemporary account says the Catholics learned of these reinforcements through their spies and retreated during the night. Another says the two brothers and their comrades launched their dawn raid and forced the Catholic troops to flee in such haste that they abandoned all manner of supplies including some of the cannons they had brought from Toulouse. Either way, the siege was broken after a week.

---

15 Translated from : Pradel, Charles (editor). *Mémoires de Jacques Gaches sur Les Guerres de Religion à Castres et dans le Languedoc 1555-1610.* Paris: Librairie Sandoz et Fischbacher, 1879 (page 70).

There are two curious aspects to the siege of Puylaurens. The first goes back to something I mentioned at the start of this book when I was admiring Madame Colombié's cannonball: the death toll was reported as six among the defenders and 600 in the Catholic camp. When the besieging army included hotshots who could hit the chains of a drawbridge from 200 metres, how could the fight have been so one-sided, even if one allows for a degree of exaggeration?

According to Charles Pradel, who published his '*Notes Historiques sur la Ville de Puylaurens*' in 1907, '*The besieged also had their artillery pieces. They could fire safely from behind their ramparts. Always on the alert, they looked out for the right moment to make a sortie and fall on the enemy without too much risk to themselves. In contrast, the soldiers outside were exposed, not only to enemy fire, but also to epidemics in their camps where the hygiene was deplorable. A mercenary army such as that which besieged Puylaurens used to drag in its wake a large number of filthy servants and prostitutes who took no part in the combat*'.[16]

Another factor was that the Protestants were fighting to preserve their homes, their livelihoods and their religion. Soon after the siege, the president of the parliament of Toulouse complained in a letter to the king, '*The Catholics do not have this ardour and affection which our enemies have, enemies who fight much better for no pay than our men do [for pay]*'.[17]

The second curiosity is that the siege was conducted in a time of peace. The second War of Religion ended when the Treaty

16 Translated from : Pradel, Charles. *Notes Historiques sur la Ville de Puylaurens*. 1907. Reprint & rev. ed. Puylaurens: Centre Archéologique du Puylaurentais, 2012 (page 117).

17 Translated from : Pradel, Charles. *Notes Historiques sur la Ville de Puylaurens* (page 118).

of Longjumeaux was signed on 23 March 1568. The news was certainly known in Toulouse at the start of April, but it had no effect on the plans of the city's consuls or its military governor. This was a private war between neighbours, and even the failed siege did not diminish Toulouse's appetite for revenge. A few weeks later its consuls offered the governor of the Languedoc 120,000 *livres* if he would rid the countryside of Protestants by capturing Castres, Montauban and Puylaurens. By my calculation that was about 1.7 tonnes of silver, or a million dollars in today's money.

Even the official peace was short-lived. Hostilities resumed in August, and the soldiers of Puylaurens soon overran several villages and presumably stocked up on copper cauldrons when they captured Durfort. The following October, Puylaurens welcomed another group of refugees.

This time the consuls of Toulouse had sent Pierre de Saint-Lary south to capture the bastide of Mazères. After being bombarded by 1,845 cannonballs and resisting two fierce assaults, the Protestant defenders negotiated an honourable surrender: they would be allowed to leave the town in the company of their pastor carrying all their arms and baggage, and proceed under armed escort to a safe place of their own choosing.

Given the spirit of the age, we can assume the Protestants of Mazères were rather nervous throughout their sixty kilometre journey to the north-east. How long would it be before the two companies of Catholic cavalry riding with them decided to cut the voyage short by massacring their charges? Unless they took a truly tortuous route, they would have marched through the centre of Auvezines. Under the circumstances it was fortunate that in those days there was no plaque to remind them of what had happened there in 1211.

Maybe the Protestants began to believe in their salvation as soon as they caught sight of the Promised Land shimmering on its hilltop, and when they reached the safety of the town's walls, I suspect neither they nor the people of Puylaurens could believe in such good fortune.

Pierre de Saint-Lary was not so lucky: he died the following year from a wound he received during the siege of Mazères.

30

An Uneasy Peace

The Saint Bartholomew's Day massacre which left 20,000 dead on the streets of Paris in 1572 had no immediate effect on Puylaurens or the Lauragais, but during the weeks that followed, people like Pierre Assézat took it as a cue to return to Catholicism while others, like the inhabitants of Puylaurens, began to plot ways of avenging their dead.

The rest of the decade was mostly consumed by four more wars, and the occasional periods of peace were too short and too uneasy to give either side much respite. Throughout this time Puylaurens was an important centre of Protestant military operations. Its military governor styled himself General of the Albigois and Lauragais, and his troops and their cannons launched attacks on a long list of Catholic communities and rushed to defend besieged Protestant towns such as Caraman and Mas-Saintes-Puelles.

In November 1580, yet another peace treaty was signed and the seventh War of Religion drew to a close. A notaire of Puylaurens called Monsieur Pelras described the celebrations and captured the mood of the moment. '*On Saturday 25 January 1581 the peace which it has pleased our good Lord to grant to this poor kingdom of France has been solemnly announced in Puylaurens to the great joy of the people and also in the market outside the town. After the announcement was made we lit a great celebratory fire on Les Ravelins later that same day. The cannons were fired from Les Ravelins and they filled the air with a great noise and terrible voice of thunder. Prayers were said in the square with great joy and ardent heart towards God by our pastor Monsieur de Campdomerc. Afterwards at nightfall we saw innumerable small fires stretching to infinity which the poor people had lit in the countryside to thank God for such a blessing. God by his grace wants this peace to be long lasting, and by this means, all this pillaging and cruelty which are practised daily by both sides will come to an end.'* [18]

This peace turned out to be the longest-lasting of the whole period, nearly five years. Life was able to resume a more normal rhythm, but it was not without its dangers. For a start, rather like in the days of *les Grandes Compagnies,* the countryside was infested with bandits. As the wars had gradually exhausted the Catholic and Protestant armies, both sides had abandoned many of the outlying châteaux and forts that were too difficult to defend, and unwelcome neighbours of no particular religious persuasion had moved into these vacant premises. From time to time, Catholics and Protestants collaborated in an attempt to rid the countryside of these organised gangs. For example, during a short truce in 1578 they evicted the bandits from Dourgne, Péchaudier and Saint-Germain-des-Prés. In 1582 the soldiers of Puylaurens used their cannons to attack another band of outlaws in a village down the road called Cambon-les-Lavaur. They handed over their captives to the Catholic courts in Lavaur and twenty-five were hanged.

Even the inhabitants of a well-defended place like Puylaurens could not sleep easily during these times of peace. There was always a danger their enemies would try to capture the town by subterfuge. One such plot failed in September 1581.

18 Translated from : Pradel, Charles. *Notes Historiques sur la Ville de Puylaurens* (pages 130-131).

Wednesday was market day in Puylaurens – and it still is – but 400 years ago it was a much more important event than it is today. It attracted scores of merchants and hundreds of peasants from the surrounding countryside. These people travelled during the night or before first light to reach the market, and it was this weekly exodus that provided the perfect cover for a Catholic conspiracy. Twelve hundred plotters arranged to meet beneath the walls of Puylaurens under cover of darkness, and with the help of traitors inside the town they would scale the walls and seize control.

Somehow, the Protestants of Caraman got wind of the plot and they lit their signal fire on Tuesday evening. In response, the people of Puylaurens lit their own fire on the roof of the bell tower and patrolled the ramparts throughout the night. At each changing of the guard the tocsin rang out its warning. It was a dark night and the defenders could see nothing beyond their walls. At one point, the Catholics fell upon a servant called Rouyre who was saving a place outside the walls for the market stall of his master. His cry of alarm attracted the attention of the sentries, but the Catholics forced him to reply, *'It's nothing! My donkey trod on me while I was sleeping!'*

Only in the morning did the townsfolk realise the extent of the danger they had escaped. Peasants arriving at the market reported that they had met armed groups of between two and three hundred men scattered around outside the town, and Rouyre recounted how he had eavesdropped while the attackers argued about who would pillage the finest houses, but in the end they had not dared to attack a town which had been put on its guard by the Protestants of Caraman.

31

A Chaotic Walk

I shall let you in on a secret: the sun doesn't always shine in the Lauragais. When the estate agent who is trying to sell you an ancient stone dwelling says there is no need for central heating in this part of the world, he – or she – is lying. Take today for example: my heating is set to maximum and any home with a hearth is puffing smoke out of its chimney. We have been drowning in freezing fog for the last three days, but I must venture out all the same. I am determined to visit the temple in Puylaurens, although I admit I am more interested in a relic locked up in its garden than in the service. The temple and its garden are only open now and again on a Sunday morning, and if I don't go today I'll have to wait another five weeks to see inside.

There are two dangers in making this visit. First, there are the obvious hazards of driving in fog so dense you have no idea where the road stops and the ditch begins. Second, it risks playing havoc with the chronology of this chapter because the temple stands in the Rue Foulimou. If I walk up this street, the house numbers will follow an orderly sequence, but the memories it evokes of former residents and past events are likely to be chaotic. Depending on your temperament, a stroll in a place like the Rue Foulimou can be exhilarating or deeply unsettling. This is one of the differences between exploring the past in a history book and discovering it live on location.

I drive up the hill towards town and experiment with closing my eyes. It makes no difference, and I turn the steering wheel more out of memory than in response to any visual clues. I park below the half-cut grain silo at the western end of town. The ramparts tower above me and I can barely make out the shape of the monstrous iron cross behind the parapet where once stood the church of Sainte-Marie. Visibility is even worse than it was on that dark night in 1581 when Catholic plotters gathered here to scale the walls.

I take a last deep breath of warm air and open the car door. Puylaurens is caught in an icy sweat and it feels as if someone has vaporised chilled water on my cheeks. I fasten the collar of my coat and pull my hat down over my ears. I'll leave my notebook in the car: it is too cold for the ink in my pen and the blood in my fingers. With luck, I should be able to work the buttons on my voice recorder while wearing gloves.

I climb a short, steep hill onto the bridge across the filled-in moat. On the far side, a street sign confirms I haven't taken a wrong turn in the fog. This was once the Porte de Foulimou, the Foulimou Gate, bombarded with such good fortune by the Catholics in 1568.

Today, the town's historians like to point out that until a century or so ago Puylaurens viewed from the air looked exactly like a submarine. This unusual urban shape is depicted on an ecclesiastical map from 1248, but the most striking image is an eighteenth-century town plan where the submarine is making an emergency dive to a safer depth. The western end where I have parked my car makes up the stern, Madame Colombié's cannonball-encrusted wall is the keel, the restaurant-hotel Cap de Castel at the far end of town is the bow, and a large promontory to the north of the church is the conning tower. Right through the middle runs the main deck – named the Rue Foulimou for much of its length – and this morning I can see about as much of it as if I really had dived to the bottom of the ocean. There is one upside to this awful weather: the wraiths of vapour drifting in the lifeless air are like ghosts from the past, and it won't need much imagination to conjure up memories of the people who have lived and died in this street during the last 800 years.

A few paces beyond the Porte de Foulimou an inscription on the stone lintel of number forty-six brings me to a halt. I start talking into my voice recorder. 'The inscription reads 1610, no that must be a seven, 1670, TRANSLATUM ANNO 1182 MF, then the stone has been broken and there's half an indecipherable character with the letters J, E, T below it…'

The shutters on the window above the inscription creak open and a lady looks out. I press the pause button and we stare at each other. I'm not sure who is more surprised. The Rue Foulimou is a narrow street with no pavements, and if we both stretched out an arm we could almost shake hands.

'*Bonjour Madame*. I was admiring your inscription.'

In some places I have lived she would already have reached for the phone to summon the police and be preparing to keep me at a safe distance with a stream of curses until they arrived. Instead, she smiles and says, *'Oui monsieur,* it is rather intriguing, isn't it? We assume the stone has been reused from an even older building.'

My visit to the *pastel* shop in Toulouse is still fresh in my mind and on this occasion I decide to seek authorisation. 'Would you mind if I were to take a photo?'

'Je vous en prie, monsieur!' 'You're welcome!' And she closes the window.

I take my photo and try to guess what the inscription signifies. The date 1182 brings to mind someone who was born twenty years later, either here or in Toulouse, no one is quite sure. What is more certain is that Guillaume de Puylaurens was the prior of Puylaurens after the Albigensian Crusade. Like Jourdain de Roquefort, he was another man who appears to have maintained good relations with both sides in the conflict. He was the senior Catholic priest of Puylaurens, a close associate of Bishop Foulque of Toulouse, and he served as an occasional member of the Inquisition. On the other hand, he also worked as notaire, secretary and chaplain to Count Raymond VII. In his spare time he wrote the third great chronicle of the Albigensian Crusade, a work which displays far greater impartiality than either '*The Song of the Crusade*' or the writings of Pierre des Vaux-de-Cernay.

I plunge deeper into the Rue Foulimou and deeper into the fog. The ecclesiastical map of 1248 shows a church at each end of the street and, as the town's prior, Guillaume was responsible for all of them. He would have been a regular traveller in the Rue Foulimou. I don't believe I'll bump into his ghost, but in this fog anything seems possible.

I resume talking into my machine and attempt to describe the variety of the architecture. Some houses have been renovated with coarse rendering and electric roller shutters as if in denial of their medieval past. Number forty-four looks abandoned and ready to collapse. Number forty-five is the first one I see that has been sympathetically restored, but number thirty-nine is even finer and I stop to take another photograph. It dates back to 1615 and was once the home of the town's pastor. The ground floor façade is made of thick vertical planks of wood bleached by the sun and pockmarked by the nails that once provided a key for the daub. On the first floor, the timber frame is filled in with slender pink bricks, some laid in a herringbone pattern, others diagonally.

As is often the case in towns of this age, I find the houses grow grander as I approach the centre. Numbers twenty-nine and thirty-one have been lovingly combined and restored by my old tennis partner, Philippe, and his wife, and turned into a bed-and-breakfast. Across the street at number twenty-eight is another bed-and-breakfast, this one with military connections. This imposing edifice with six windows on the first floor and six more on the second was the birthplace and deathbed of one of Napoleon's generals.

Brigadier-General Jean-Pierre Antoine Rey fought in dozens of battles across Europe, including Arcole Bridge, Austerlitz, Jena, Eylau and Vitoria. His last fight was down the road at the Battle of Toulouse in 1814, so he didn't have too far to travel home afterwards to lick his wounds and mourn the downfall of his emperor. In better weather, I have walked around the stretch of ramparts which makes up the submarine's conning tower and visited his grave. It lies in the Protestant cemetery opened in 1788 on a steeply sloping piece of land beyond the northernmost extremity of town. Despite this remote setting, General Rey's spirit is never lonely; he is surrounded by old comrades-in-arms and several of his high-ranking descendants. If it is rare to find three generals buried together in the same corner of a graveyard, it is perhaps unprecedented when they all come from the same family. Buried alongside this trio of General Reys are other relatives, including a Colonel Rey who was killed in May 1940 when he had the crazy idea of trying to stop German tanks with his cavalry regiment. '*Poor us with our horses,*' wrote one of the survivors.

My favourite tomb lies a couple of paces beyond the resting place of Jean-Pierre Antoine Rey's skull. Today, the proud obelisk marking the grave of Captain Pierre Rivière lies fallen and broken like the brave man underneath it. Luckily for the amateur historian, the obelisk has toppled inscription side up and we can learn that the good Captain was made a Chevalier de la Légion d'Honneur on the field of Austerlitz. The list of his campaigns reads like a grand tour of Europe: Italy, Naples, Austria, Prussia, Poland, Spain and France. He too fought at the Battle of Toulouse, under the command of his neighbour in the graveyard. These old soldiers perpetuated the military traditions of Puylaurens, and between them they fought in so many battles they will never run out of war stories. If you dare, visit the cemetery after dark and listen to the whisper of their memories in the cypress trees.

Their commander-in-chief and emperor, Napoleon, said an army marches on its stomach, but Captain Rivière and his infantrymen knew only too well that it also marches on its feet. They walked enormous distances to fight their enemies, and it is reasonable to assume that Captain Rivière made the acquaintance of a cobbler or two, including Puylaurens' most famous repairer of footwear.

Guillaume Lavabre was another Protestant and he lived at the cheaper end of the Rue Foulimou, but it was not his skill at the awl that made his name. Largely forgotten for over a century, he is recognised today as the father of Marianne, and he was a troubadour in the true Occitan tradition.

When I talk to people from other parts of France, I am surprised how few of them know that Marianne was born in Puylaurens. Today her image is everywhere: you will find her on the coins in your pocket, on the postage stamps on your letters, and on almost every official government document from the national budget to my annual tax return. You will also find her bust – usually draped in the *tricolore* – in most official buildings including the law courts and all 36,000 *mairies*. In more recent times, she has been modelled on French actresses including Brigitte Bardot, Catherine Deneuve and Sophie Marceau. Marianne is a constant presence, unlike the portrait of the President of the Republic which also graces most official buildings but risks being replaced each time there is a presidential election. Marianne is the symbol of the French Republic, an allegory for liberty, a young woman who wears the Phrygian cap once worn by the freed slaves of Rome. But where did she come from, people used to wonder.

In 1976, a professor from Albi called Christian Laux was working on a book about Occitan when he came across a brochure produced by the Puylaurens youth club. In it he found the songs of Guillaume Lavabre in their original Occitan, including a piece called *'La garisou de Marianno'*, *'The cure of Marianne'*, which relates how a young woman was cured of an illness in 1792 by the bloody events of the Revolution. It was not until three years later that historian Maurice Agulhon came to the conclusion that this song marked the first recorded use of Marianne to represent the Republic. Naturally the *mairie* of Puylaurens seized on this chance to add to the town's prestige, and it created the Association Marianna which organises a programme of events to celebrate her birth in the Rue Foulimou.

What I find odd about this forgotten song is that if someone had looked up 'Marianne' in Frédéric Mistral's 1878 Occitan dictionary, they would have found the following entry: *'The significance given by the people to the name Marianne has its origin in the first Revolution. After the arrest of the king on 10 August 1791, one sang throughout the Midi a detestable song, 'La Garisou de Mariano'.* In fact, Louis XVI was arrested on 10 August 1792, and perhaps it was this mistake that caused historians to stop mid-sentence and overlook such an obvious clue.

Guillaume Lavabre and his family were among the poorest residents of the Rue Foulimou. Unfilled by the daily grind of banging nails into the soles of other people's shoes, Guillaume took to the road like a true troubadour. He sang his songs and spread the fame of Marianne throughout the land, but life as a wandering minstrel was tougher in the nineteenth century than in the days of Raimon de Miraval. Before long, poverty and politics forced Guillaume to abandon his revolutionary principles: after 1814 he switched to writing pieces to celebrate the restoration of the monarchy. None of these compositions were money-spinners, and in 1820 the mayor of Puylaurens had this to say about Lavabre: '*One would be led to believe that he is suffering from mental illness and that he is not in possession of all his senses. Added to that, he is very fond of wine*'.[19] Nonetheless he survived until 1845 when, aged ninety, he died in hospital in Toulouse.

19 Translated from : Richard, Bernard. (2014) *Marianne, représentation féminine de la République en France.* Retrieved online from: bernard-richard-histoire.com.

32

INSIDE THE TEMPLE

General-Baron Rey must have been delighted when in 1818 work started on a new temple next door to his home. People of his faith had been yearning for somewhere of their own to pray since 1685. During most of this period, the Protestants had been forced to gather in secret to avoid persecution. Before 1685, there had been two other temples and both had suffered undignified ends.

During the first three decades of the Wars of Religion, the Protestants commandeered the Catholic church of Notre-Dame-du-Lac. In 1589 they laid the foundations of a true temple, but this was in the middle of the eighth and final War of Religion and no one found the time to build anything on top of the foundations for another three years. Then, still at war, the temple was built in a Christmas rush and the first service was held on 25 December 1594. Ten days later it collapsed. Presumably the Protestants did not take this as a sign of God's displeasure because the inauguration of a second temple took place a few years later. Although this one was solid enough to defy gravity, it could not resist the wishes of the king and it was destroyed eighty-seven years later.

There is some doubt about the precise location of the first two temples, but they probably stood next door to General-Baron Rey on the same site as the one I am about to enter. Wrought iron gates and spiked railings usually keep visitors firmly in the street, but today the gates are open and the service is about to begin.

I follow a gravel path between privet hedges towards the temple door, but before I go inside I turn to my right. This is the true reason I am here, to take a photo of an unusual gate that is invisible from the street. It is the only physical reminder of the final act in Puylaurens' days as a Protestant powerhouse, so in an attempt to recover from the chronological anarchy of my walk down the Rue Foulimou, I shall save its story for the end of this chapter.

I adjust my camera to allow for the fog and I take several pictures. While I'm here, I really should go inside and see where General-Baron Rey, Captain Rivière and Guillaume Lavabre once prayed, although I would prefer not to be obliged to stay for the entire service. There's much more history I plan to visit before lunchtime.

The collapsing temple of 1595 is still on my mind, and I duck when I sneak inside the building. The light is poor and I peer down a long hallway that is closed off from the main body of the church by heavy drapes. Perhaps I can slide in at the back and hide in the crowd. I poke my head through the curtains. All nine people chatting in the aisle stop in mid-sentence and stare at me. I toy with the idea of fleeing back to the Rue Foulimou, but a lady in a bobble hat smiles and comes to shake my hand. She looks vaguely familiar.

'Haven't we met before?' I ask.

'Yes. You were taking a photo of my inscription.'

This is too spooky. She couldn't slip past me in the street, not even in the fog. Perhaps there's a secret passage from the days when the faithful never knew when they would have to flee for their lives.

I decide I should justify my presence. 'I'm writing about Puylaurens and the Wars of Religion.'

We exchange a few words but everyone still stares at me. Maybe it is my accent, or perhaps they are unaccustomed to strangers dropping in for the Sunday service. They quickly establish I am English, and therefore probably Protestant, and a few more smiles begin to form. The owner of the inscription gives me an earnest look. 'Why don't you come and sit at the front?'

The service begins and I inspect my puritanical surroundings. The arched ceiling is plain white. The walls are off-white. The wooden pews, floorboards and wall panelling are unadorned. The glazing in the windows is clear. There are no paintings and no statues. The only extravagance is the enormous carved wooden pulpit attached to the wall behind the altar. It dominates the room, and I am disappointed the pastor does not use it. Instead, he preaches from a modern floor-standing lectern.

We sing the first hymn *a capella* and I try to identify what might have changed since the days when the old soldiers and poetic cobbler used to pray here. Very little, I conclude, apart from the addition of electric lights and wall heaters, both of which are woefully inadequate on a day such as this.

Towards the end of the service, the pastor reminds us that this year marks the 500th anniversary of Martin Luther's fateful letter about indulgences. This strikes me as a timely thought to take away with me, and I slip outside.

This end of the Rue Foulimou may boast the grandest homes, but their architectural style, construction materials and state of repair remain variable. The sympathetically restored stone façade of number four stands in stark contrast to its neighbour, number two, which is as large as a château. A sign on its dilapidated wooden gate tells me it is for sale, and I presume the crane rusting in the overgrown courtyard with its boom hanging pitifully over the roof is included in the price.

On the opposite corner stands number one, the start of the street and the place where my own story in the Lauragais began. Back then, it was occupied by a notaire, and it is where we signed the purchase papers for our house.

I turn and contemplate the Rue Foulimou. The fog makes it colourless, but my knowledge of its history has painted the street in vibrant hues. And I have yet to mention the bloody duel that took place here between the two aspiring pastors, or the academy around the corner where they were supposed to be learning about the grace of God rather than planning to kill each other. But first, if I am to restore any semblance of order to this chaotic narrative, I need to walk another twenty paces and stop outside the house where in 1585 a king went to bed without his supper. After five years of peace, the eighth and final War of Religion was about to start and the people of Puylaurens would once again take to the road with their cannons.

33

Too Many Henrys

In 1584 the kingdom of France ran into a problem. Henri III was king but he had no children. When his younger brother died of malaria, the next in line to the French throne was Henri, King of Navarre. The problem was that Henri de Navarre was a Protestant. The members of the Catholic League, created by another Henri, this one the Duke of Guise, objected and began plotting to ensure that their Catholic founder would be the next king. For a little over a year, the opposing parties sought to strengthen their positions while they prepared for war.

On 13 March 1585, Henri de Navarre rode into Puylaurens escorted by 600 cavalry and some of his most noble supporters. He was travelling to Castres for a meeting with the governor of the Languedoc, and with the hope of rallying moderate Catholics to his cause.

The townsfolk of Puylaurens had only a day's warning of the royal visit, but they made great efforts to put on a parade fit for a man who for them was more than a future king. They viewed him as their Saviour. For over twenty years they had fought for the right to worship as they pleased. Many had died in the struggle, and even in the brief periods of peace they had been unable to lower their guard. But with a Protestant on the throne, they would win lasting security and freedom of conscience.

The whole town turned out to greet Henri. The rich and important paraded in full dress on their finest horses, and the poor watched in awe. Five hundred soldiers fired their muskets, and on Les Ravelins the town's fearsome cannons saluted the royal visitor. Only one thing marred the welcome: the *vent d'autan*. It whipped away the heady fumes of burnt gunpowder, and it tried to snatch the ensigns from the hands of the standard bearers, but worst of all, Henri de Navarre was so unnerved by this terrible wind, he went to bed without his supper at what is now number four, Rue de la Mairie.

The next morning, he attended church with the town's dignitaries, strolled down past Madame Colombié's front door where perhaps someone pointed out the cannonball, and took a turn on Les Ravelins. He lunched early and continued on his way to Castres, but soon after his departure the *vent d'autan* gave way to rain. According to the same Monsieur Pelras who described so eloquently the peace celebrations in 1581, '*After the rain, heavy snow fell and there was much lightning and terrible thunder*'.[20] This is an unusual meteorological progression to experience in a single day, and perhaps the words of Monsieur Pelras were metaphorical. The political climate had been worsening ever since the death of Henri III's younger brother, and the storm clouds of war were about to burst over the kingdom of France.

Over the next four years, Henri III, Henri de Navarre and Henri de Guise fought one another in various combinations of two-against-one in a war sometimes referred to as the War of the Three Henrys, but which was also the first phase of the eighth War of Religion.

In the Lauragais, hostilities broke out in August 1585. A newly-recruited company of Protestant soldiers was making its

20 Translated from : Pradel, Charles. *Notes Historiques sur la Ville de Puylaurens* (page 134).

way to Revel and they paused in a tiny hamlet called Choples on a delightful backroad between Auriac-sur-Vendinelle and Saint-Julia. They were ambushed and cut to pieces, and only four out of 120 men escaped with their lives. In response, the soldiers of Puylaurens took to the road once again with their cannons, capturing Catholic villages and châteaux, burning others, and rushing to help besieged Protestant communities. Meanwhile, the Catholic governor of Lavaur carried out his own attacks and destroyed Appelle, Péchaudier and a dozen more châteaux around Puylaurens.

And so the war dragged on. Elsewhere in the kingdom there were major battles – Jarnac, Moncontour and Coutras for example – but the Lauragais suffered an endless succession of skirmishes and sieges which were never decisive and always bloody. There was no frontline, no geographic logic to which town, village or château was Catholic and which was Protestant. The Lauragais was in constant movement as the two sides burned and pillaged their way around the countryside.

34

WAR DIARY

When I read contemporary accounts of this period I am struck by the appalling monotony of the conflict. Consider, for example, the diary kept by a Protestant from Castres called Monsieur Faurin.[21] In addition to all the battles, skirmishes, ambushes and assassinations, he records 459 sieges of towns, villages or châteaux, the great majority of them in the Lauragais or its immediate surroundings.

Few places in the Lauragais were as fortunate as Puylaurens. Although many of its townsfolk died in the wars, most were killed fighting elsewhere; the town itself never suffered the destructive effects of an enforced change of faith. What happened to the neighbouring town of Sorèze shows how lucky Puylaurens was, and predictably it was the soldiers of Puylaurens who played a central role in this series of calamities.

Sorèze lies seventeen kilometres down the road from Puylaurens next door to Durfort, and it is a place with a long religious history. The Benedictines established an abbey here in 754, and Jourdain de Roquefort's cousin was its abbot during

21 Pradel, Charles (editor). *Journal de Faurin sur les guerres de Castres*. 1878. Reprint. Nîmes: Editions Lacour, 2002.

the Albigensian Crusade. In October 1571 – officially a time of peace – a Protestant army pillaged the town and set fire to the abbey's church and all its archives. There was no bloodshed, and the Protestants did not stay.

Two years later when war was official, the soldiers of Puylaurens decided to take permanent control of their Catholic neighbour. One night in June 1573 a raiding party scaled the walls and captured the town. They killed most of the garrison and some of the Catholic inhabitants – around a hundred souls in all – and they demolished parts of the abbey. They also stole all the stones from the parish church to repair the town ramparts, but they left the bell tower of Saint-Martin intact, probably because it provided an excellent lookout from which to spy on the Catholics who would inevitably try to recapture the town. To this day, the tower stands bereft of its church, rather like the Kaiser Wilhelm Memorial Church in Berlin.

I recount these events as an introduction. It is what happened to Sorèze during a six-month period in 1580 that gives a true flavour of the reality of the war. What follows below is an abbreviated version of a record kept by another Protestant from Castres. Jacques Gaches was born around 1555, took an active part in the conflict and wrote his memoirs twenty or so years after the wars were over. My earlier account of the siege of Puylaurens in 1568 was also based on his writings.

---

3 March 1580. Catholic troops drawn from Castelnaudary, Saint-Félix-Lauragais and Saint-Julia scale the walls of Sorèze and recapture the town. The more fortunate Protestants flee to Durfort or Revel. With a promise of safe conduct out of town, eighty others surrender, but they are beaten to death with mallets.

4 March 1580. The Protestants from Puylaurens and Revel rush to save the town but it is too late: Sorèze is lost.

May 1580. The Protestants decide to cut off the supply routes to Sorèze. With the help of the cannons of Puylaurens, they capture three nearby Catholic châteaux – Lastouzeilles, Garrevaques, Gasc – and install garrisons in several small forts closer to Sorèze. They try to draw the Catholics out for a fight, but the garrison refuses the bait.

June 1580. The Catholics conclude that Sorèze is too isolated to defend, and too vulnerable to attack due to the presence of Puylaurens and Revel on its doorstep. Their leaders resolve to destroy the town's fortifications and abandon the ruins to the Protestants. They call for reinforcements and two cannons to help with the demolition.

15 June 1580. The Protestants learn of this plan; they would prefer to capture the town intact and they prepare to intercept the Catholic convoy. The Protestant leader, the Viscount of Turenne, orders his military governors to concentrate their troops on Revel. In response, additional Catholic reinforcements attempt to converge on Sorèze. The countryside is swarming with men on the move, all with the same destination but not all on the same side. Near the tiny village of Puycalvel, the Catholic contingents from Lautrec and Montdragon have the misfortune to meet the Protestants from Briatexte and Réalmont. The captain of the Briatexte troops, *'makes such an extraordinary effort and catches a soldier with such a horrible sideways blow that he cuts the man's body clean in half'.*[22] There are no Catholic survivors.

17 June 1580. The Protestants send two companies to lie in ambush for the main Catholic convoy near the fort of La Balbauge, one-and-a-half kilometres north-east of Sorèze. The Viscount of Turenne promises to send reinforcements in the morning if necessary.

18 June 1580. The ambush party spots three companies of infantry approaching from Dourgne with their drums beating

22 Translated from : Pradel, Charles (editor). *Mémoires de Jacques Gaches sur Les Guerres de Religion à Castres et dans le Languedoc 1555-1610* (page 274).

and standards flying. The cavalry of Sorèze ride out to meet them from the other direction and the Protestants are caught in the middle. They break cover, and the ensuing fight continues until the Viscount of Turenne keeps his promise and gallops to the rescue. The supply convoy is forced to turn back, the Catholic cavalry retreat to Sorèze and the Protestants withdraw to Revel. At nightfall Turenne sends 300 fresh soldiers back to La Balbauge.

19 June 1580. At dawn the Protestant soldiers at La Balbauge see the supply convoy is already on the move in another attempt to reach its destination. A long battle ensues, first with arquebuses (a forerunner of the musket), then with swords. The Protestants are outnumbered and barricade themselves inside the fort. The Catholics make for Sorèze with their cannons and leave a hundred dead on the battlefield. As well as the human casualties, some of the oak trees in the surrounding forest are shattered by so many bullets, they subsequently die.

20 June 1580. The Catholics of Sorèze decide to attack Borioblanco, a fortified farmhouse a few hundred metres outside their walls to the west. They try to block the route to Revel with cavalry and infantry, but as soon as the Protestants hear the cannons they dash up the road to rescue the twenty-five men trapped inside the farmhouse. During the battle the defenders decide to blow up Borioblanco and retreat, but first they launch a furious assault on the Catholics who are forced to withdraw to Sorèze. The Protestants return to Revel, leaving Borioblanco in flames.

July 1580. The Protestants resume their blockade of Sorèze. It is harvest time, and they want to ensure that their supporters gather the crops and the Catholics go hungry. When the harvest is finished, the Protestant soldiers withdraw. They drop off the cannons in Puylaurens and return to Castres for a rest. Instead, almost everyone including the Viscount of Turenne catches a highly contagious new disease. In the north, the king and most of his court have already suffered from it. Whooping cough brings a month of peace to the area.

September 1580. The Protestants still have designs on Sorèze. With the help of spies inside the town they hatch a plot and wait for favourable weather.

13 September 1580. The night is dark and the *vent d'autan* is violent. An hour before dawn six Protestants sneak into Sorèze through a secret door and open the main gates for their accomplices. Once inside, the attackers separate and make for the various sentry posts so that they can kill the guards before the alarm is raised. When they creep into the guardhouse, the Catholic commander jumps out of bed and, in a move worthy of d'Artagnan, he throws his cloak over the fire and escapes in the ensuing darkness. Other members of the garrison are less fortunate: eighty Catholics are put to the sword.

Six months in the life of one small town – admittedly a particularly bad six months, even for those times – but similar stories were repeated in hundreds of places across the Lauragais and thousands more across France. Four decades of this type of warfare would eventually leave between two and four million dead, or between ten and twenty-five per cent of the population (if my maths seems odd, it is because the exact size of the population is unknown). But whereas nearly every French community has its *monument des morts* in memory of the 1.4 million soldiers who died in the Great War (3.5 percent of the population), I have found only one memorial to anyone who perished in the Wars of Religion. I made my discovery in unlikely circumstances one Saturday afternoon when I was in the midst of writing this chapter.

35

Disturbing Encounters

After a morning spent doing battle with the unfamiliar seventeenth-century spellings used by Jacques Gaches and Monsieur Faurin in their memoirs, I decide to brave the January weather and clear my head with a bike ride. It is windy as well as cold, and after the climb up to Puylaurens I decide to take an easy option and cruise ten kilometres downhill to Soual. On a back lane, I stop to take a photo of the Château de Farinières. Usually I fly past, but only this morning I have deleted a paragraph about the murder of the lord of Farinières. I reasoned that with so many miserable deaths to choose from, if I were to keep this particular one in my text I would need a better excuse than the fact my wife once played tennis here. But the story is still on my mind. I wheel my bicycle alongside the hedge towards the main entrance for another photo, and I remember that not one but four lords of Farinières were killed during the religious wars, and then their château disappeared too. The elegant country house before me with a tennis court but no towers was built on top of the original in 1805.

A few kilometres further and I enter Soual. The main street is always busy, particularly on a Saturday, and it has been narrowed by so-called traffic calming measures which do nothing to calm the nerves of a cyclist. I decide to take a back street, but I miss my usual turning and find myself surrounded by an unfamiliar jumble of ancient dwellings. On a bend in the Rue de Barry I spot a calvary. In front of it, a white plastic sign is attached to blue iron railings and I stop to read it. When I finish, I stare in disbelief at the figure of Christ on his iron cross. I am looking at my first memorial to someone who perished in the Wars of Religion. It was erected by the people of Soual in memory of Charles d'Alric, lord of Farinières, who was assassinated not far from this spot in 1575.

For a moment I think of Pierre Bouyssou and his suggestion that a human version of tropism pulled him towards the Château de Montgey when he was a boy. I don't believe in mysterious forces, but how else do I explain my discovery of the memorial to Charles d'Alric on this particular day? And the sign looks new. If I had come down this road a year ago I wouldn't have stopped. In this part of France you'll find a roadside crucifix every couple of kilometres, so there has to be a good reason to stop for one. I scratch my head and wonder if the ghost of Charles d'Alric is telling me to undelete those words I wrote about him this morning. No, he deserves better than that: I shall paraphrase the account of Jacques Gaches, and I'll include the untimely death of the murdered lord's son three weeks later.

The Protestants of Puylaurens knew that every Saturday Charles d'Alric was in the habit of making the journey from Labruguière, where he was governor, to Soual, where he kept a whore. On Sunday morning, 25 December 1575, they lay in ambush in a ruined mill on the outskirts of Soual and waited for him to emerge after his Christmas Eve of pleasure. Before long, Charles d'Alric rode out of town through a gate near the calvary-memorial accompanied by the governor of Soual and three soldiers who were armed only with swords. Under cover of thick fog, the assassins took the Catholic party by surprise and brought Alric to the ground with a pistol shot. He rose to his knees, and with sword in hand he defended himself courageously until one of the attackers ran him through with a Protestant blade. The governor of Soual and the escort were taken prisoner.

When news of the assassination reached Labruguière, Charles d'Alric's son was appointed governor in his place. He died soon afterwards in an unlikely scene which would be more at home in a movie.

On 17 January 1576, the young Alric decided to avenge his father's murder by attacking a passing troop of Protestant cavalry and musketeers. He and his men killed thirty of their enemies. The others fled except for their commander, Captain Daves, who was carried off to Labruguière a prisoner. For some unexplained reason, one of the Catholic soldiers then decided to take a sword swipe at the captive. Fearing he was mortally wounded, Daves decided to use his final moments on earth to further the Protestant cause. He still had his pistol, and the young Alric was standing right in front of him, so he shot him dead. Predictably this earned Daves a second sword strike which killed him instantly. Two more men lay dead on the ground and more blood soaked into the soil.

The War of the Three Henrys lasted three years. In September 1588, Henri de Guise was assassinated on the orders of Henri III, and the following August, Henri III was assassinated by a fanatical monk. As the last of the Three Henrys still standing, the one from Navarre claimed the crown, but the Catholic League now wanted Henri de Guise's son to be king. The eighth War of Religion would rumble on for nine more years while Henri de Navarre gradually took control of his kingdom. In the meantime, the Protestants of Puylaurens remained on their guard because they were still threatened by enemies from without and within. In 1589 a traitor inside the town plotted to let Catholic soldiers enter through a secret entrance near the Rue Foulimou. He was hung, drawn and quartered on market day in front of the consuls and other dignitaries. Shortly afterwards, another resident was caught trying to deliver both Puylaurens and Caraman to the Catholics. He was broken on the wheel.

In February 1591, the Catholic League held a meeting in Lavaur and decided to ask the king of Spain to send reinforcements to help their cause. In response, six thousand Spanish troops crossed the Pyrenees, and they soon captured numerous châteaux in the Lauragais, the Montagne Noire and around Carcassonne. Just in the short stretch of countryside between Puylaurens and Lavaur, they captured Cambon, Lacroisille, Magrin, Mouzens and Roquevidal. In response, around four hundred men from Puylaurens made the short journey down the road to Lacroisille, and with the help of their cannons they forced the Spanish to flee, but at the end of the fighting yet another château and its village lay in ruins.

In July 1593 Henri de Navarre converted to Catholicism, and the following February he was crowned Henri IV of France. In 1595, the pope lifted his excommunication and more and more Catholics rallied to his cause. Understandably many Protestants felt betrayed by their newly-converted king, although perhaps not surprised: Henri was a Catholic by birth and this was his sixth change of faith, although it is only fair to point out that most of these changes were forced upon him. Perhaps this made him the ideal man to reconcile the two sides. In the spring of 1598 he signed the Edict of Nantes which confirmed Catholicism as the established religion of France, but granted a wide range of rights and freedoms to the Protestants. The eighth and longest War of Religion was finally over.

As well as the tragic loss of human life, the kingdom was by now a physical wreck. Many of the towns, châteaux and churches were in ruins, and the roads and bridges were in a perilous state. Spare a thought also for the peasants: short of manpower; short of animals to pull the plough; always vulnerable to pillaging by soldiers and mercenaries from both sides, not to mention the bandits who infested the countryside. No wonder they had given up on labour-intensive crops such as *pastel.*

In the case of Sorèze, the war caused an unusual and irreparable loss: Revel stole its Saturday market. During the wars, people from the surrounding countryside became increasingly wary of entering Sorèze on market day, and for a large part of 1580 the siege made it impossible. The consuls of Revel came up with the bright idea of establishing their own Saturday market in addition to the one they already held on a Thursday in accordance with the charter of 1342. When the new vendors and customers discovered the square of Revel with its magnificent market hall and elegant arcades, they never looked back. Over the next couple of centuries the consuls of Sorèze tried in vain to reclaim their lost business, but even sending a letter of complaint to the king failed to produce the desired result.

Today, Revel's Saturday market is one of the busiest weekly events in the Lauragais, and it is the main reason the town has spent over a decade in the Michelin guide to '*Les 100 Plus Beaux Détours de France*', '*The 100 most Beautiful Detours of France*'. But few visitors, be they tourists or locals, know that this popular market was pinched from Sorèze.

There was another threat to daily life which the Edict of Nantes did nothing to address: the wolves. Given the general state of lawlessness and insecurity during the wars, it is understandable that after a fight the dead were not always buried promptly, and sometimes not at all. For much of this period my line about the Lauragais being a land soaked in blood was gorily true, and the corpses provided the wolves with a steady supply of carrion. But now the wars were over, and the ravenous beasts roamed further afield in search of food. In 1604, all those living in wild areas such as the Montagne Noire were authorised to carry arms and shoot the wolves, but this wasn't enough to rid the country of the fearsome creatures which, in the words of the Puylaurens historian Charles Pradel, '*ravaged the plains, gnawed at the doors and howled at the windows*'.[23] A few years later everyone living in the diocese of Lavaur was given permission to shoot them, but wolves continued to be a danger up until the time of the Revolution.

Despite these difficulties, the economy improved quickly and the Lauragais began to rebuild itself, but peace was not destined to last. In 1610, it was Henri IV's turn to be assassinated. Over the next few years the religious hatred which had been supressed but never eliminated festered away, and in 1621 it erupted into a Protestant rebellion led by yet another Henri, this one being the Duke of Rohan. Some of his troops were stationed in Puylaurens and the town was still perceived as a safe haven for Protestants. In June 1622, Caraman was captured by the Catholics, and its Protestants fled to Puylaurens for safety. A few days later it was the turn of the inhabitants of Cuq-Toulza to seek refuge within the walls of their stronger neighbour. Shortly afterwards, Louis XIII besieged the Protestant town of Briatexte twenty-five kilometres to the north. Five hundred soldiers set out from Puylaurens with fresh supplies and succeeded in breaking the siege, but a few weeks later the king and the Duke of Rohan signed a peace accord which obliged Puylaurens to dismantle its ramparts. In early 1623, two thousand men and women carried out the demolition works under the watchful eyes of representatives from both sides. It took them

23 Translated from : Pradel, Charles. *Notes Historiques sur la Ville de Puylaurens* (page 149).

six weeks. When the duke started another rebellion two years later, Puylaurens had finally exhausted its thirst for war and preferred instead to remain loyal to the king – even a Catholic one.

Over the next few decades the town underwent a slow drift towards Catholicism. One estimate gave the population in 1630 as 3,100 Protestants and 300 Catholics. By 1665 the total population was similar, but the split was fifty-fifty. This change was largely due to conversions, many of them bought for cash by the Catholic clergy, but the Protestants of Puylaurens were about to be woken from their slumbers by an unruly bunch of schoolchildren in Montauban and their even more badly-behaved parents.

36

SWORDS AND SCHOOLBOOKS

If you wanted to train as a pastor in seventeenth-century France, you could choose from five Protestant academies. One of them was founded shortly after the Edict of Nantes in the town of Montauban a hundred kilometres north-west of Puylaurens. Attached to the academy was a Protestant college for younger students.

Academic life in Montauban remained suitably scholarly until 1633 when the Protestants were forced to cede half their establishment to the Jesuits. It doesn't take an expert in inter-denominational affairs to realise that placing pupils of both faiths under the same roof was unlikely to result in peaceful cohabitation. Before long the children had started their own War of Religion. In 1659, the end-of-year prize giving ceremony turned particularly violent. Town consuls from both sides tried to calm the situation, but instead the conflict spread and Montauban found itself engulfed in a full-scale riot. Afterwards, some of the leaders were hanged or sent to the galleys, and others were birched or banished from the town forever.

When the pupils returned to their studies after the summer holidays, the tensions and the scuffles recommenced. A few weeks later, Louis XIV was down the road in Toulouse working on a treaty with Spain. When he heard about the troubles in Montauban he decided to act, and before long the consuls of Puylaurens received a staggering surprise in their postbox.

'To our dear and much loved consuls and inhabitants of our town of Puylaurens. On behalf of the king... having ordered the Academy and college of Montauban... to be transferred to our town of Puylaurens... we indeed wish to advise you of this with this letter, and give you the mandate and express order... to provide a place and facilities for the establishment of [the Academy and college] in Puylaurens. Do not fail to accomplish our intentions because such is our pleasure. Decreed in Toulouse, 12 December 1659.'[24]

Ever since the assassination of Henri IV, the Protestants had suffered a steady erosion of the rights they had struggled so long to obtain through those dark years of civil war. Did the king's letter mean this tide of misfortune was about to turn? I can almost hear the news passing from one disbelieving neighbour to another up and down the Rue Foulimou and along every other street in Puylaurens. 'The king wants us to do *what*?' The effect must have been similar to a small American town during Prohibition receiving a letter from the president instructing them to open a distillery and start selling whisky.

More thoughtful inhabitants may have wondered why Louis XIV had chosen Puylaurens of all places. Perhaps he assumed the town's gradual conversion to Catholicism was a sign of general apathy among its Protestant population, and therefore concluded the academy would wither and die if he relocated it there, offering a far smarter way of killing off Montauban's academy than outright closure. And one less academy would help his long-term aim of re-establishing Catholicism as the sole religion in his kingdom.

24 Translated from : Pradel, Charles. *Notes Historiques sur la Ville de Puylaurens* (page 171).

If this was the king's reasoning, he underestimated the people of Puylaurens. This was their chance to breathe new life into their town, and both teachers and students would bring new wealth.

The Protestants of Montauban were fully aware of the scale of their loss, and they promptly sent envoys to the king in an attempt to change his mind. This perhaps encouraged the people of Puylaurens to move quickly, and early the following year the new academy was ready to start teaching. Before long, so many students flocked to the academy and college that in 1662 the town ran out of bread and the bakers were fined for failing to foresee the growth in demand.

What did the students learn? The academy employed two professors of theology, two for philosophy and one for Hebrew. At the college, three teachers taught the younger students grammar, rhetoric and the humanities. There were activities outside the classroom too; the students elected their own captains, and on ceremonial occasions they paraded like a company of military cadets. Unfortunately for the town, this seems to have put martial ideas into their young heads.

During the reign of Louis XIV, duelling was so widespread that he issued eleven separate edicts to outlaw the practice. The penalties were harsh: the edict of 1679 prescribed death for the two principals and their seconds, along with confiscation of all their property. It was therefore in the interests of everyone involved in this popular pastime to keep matters private, and we can assume that only the most violent combats came to the attention of the authorities.

In his history of Puylaurens, Charles Pradel cites numerous bloody and often deadly confrontations, but I shall only report the most notorious. In 1632, Jacques Rivenc, from a good and ancient family of Puylaurens, killed Pierre Maury in a duel. He was condemned to death but he had already fled. In his absence his effigy was executed and his property confiscated. One summer's evening in 1673, Captain Du Puy and his orderly fought side by side against two local nobles – Pierre de Gineste and Jean de Vialate. The captain was injured in the arm and his orderly received Vialete's sword in the stomach and dropped dead on the pavement.

With their elders setting such a violent example it is perhaps unsurprising that the students of the academy followed suit. In 1665 two aspiring pastors, Bourdin and Harignan, drew their swords in the Rue Foulimou. Bourdin was injured and a warrant issued for Harignan's arrest. Their fathers, who were both pastors, concocted a cover story: Bourdin had been hurt during a scrap among a group of students and he didn't know who struck the blow. To seal the deal, the reverend Harignan paid the reverend Bourdin ninety pounds – more than two months' salary for a teacher at the academy, and more than enough to cover the wounded son's medical bills. A couple of years later one of the teachers prevented a duel between two of his students and persuaded them to sign a peace treaty in front of a notaire.

The final tragic example demonstrates that the students did not restrict their animosity to their classmates. One February evening in 1676, a young father-of-three called Marc-Antoine de Salvignol and one of his friends bumped into three students with whom they had already had a confrontation: Labarthe, Brusque and the son of Professor Martel. All five young men unsheathed their blades on Les Ravelins and the swordplay commenced. Before long, Salvignol lay dying and Labarthe and Martel fled. The case ended up before the parliament of Toulouse and Professor Martel found himself considerably out of pocket.

These stories make the academy of Puylaurens sound rougher than the toughest inner-city school, so it is only fair to mention three alumni who distinguished themselves in more scholarly ways. First there was Abel Boyer. He finished up in England teaching French to Queen Anne's son for whom he produced two hugely successful works: an English-French dictionary, and a text book called '*The Complete French-master for ladies and gentlemen*'. The second, David Martin, became a respected theologian, and while living in Holland he published numerous scholarly works. And lastly, in his day Pierre Bayle was one of the most widely-read philosophers and Voltaire described him as '*the greatest master of the art of reasoning that ever wrote*'. He composed his most famous work, '*Dictionnaire historique et critique*', in Holland.

As well as being educated in Puylaurens, these three old boys have something else in common: they all built their reputations overseas. The story of the academy's destruction explains why they fled.

Although the academy and college were thriving in Puylaurens, Protestants in the rest of France were coming under increasing legal, administrative and religious pressure. The Catholic clergy bought numerous conversions, but they soon realised that all too often the newly-converted members of their congregations simply pocketed the bribes and went straight back to the temple. As a result, the priests demanded and obtained from the king new laws against religious relapse. Those who had converted were forbidden from entering a temple and, if they did, the pastors would be held responsible. The Protestants were obliged to guard the doors of their own houses of worship.

In Puylaurens, matters came to a head towards the end of 1684 when the clergy of Lavaur claimed that the ten-year old son of a man who had converted to Catholicism had entered the temple of Puylaurens during a service. Arrest warrants were issued, and two pastors and two teachers from the academy – including Martel, the father of the duellist – gave themselves up and were imprisoned in Toulouse awaiting trial. Before they left, the pastors held an emotional service on 28 December 1684. They suspected correctly that the temple would never reopen, and while they were in prison Louis XIV ordered the closure of the academy.

On 16 October 1585 four companies of infantry arrived in Puylaurens. They were billeted for eight days in Protestant homes, and their mission was to demolish the temple and force their hosts to convert to Catholicism. A week later the king signed a new order that revoked all the provisions of the Edict of Nantes.

Whereas the Puylaurens philosopher Pierre Bayle wrote, '*It is tolerance that is the source of peace, and intolerance that is the source of disorder and squabbling*', Louis XIV believed the exact opposite: the best way to ensure peace and stability in his kingdom was to tolerate only one religion. In brief, his Edict of Fontainebleau decreed the destruction of all Protestant churches and academic establishments; outlawed all forms of Protestant worship; gave pastors a fortnight to choose between converting to Catholicism and going into exile; and banned all other Protestants from emigrating, on pain of the galleys for the men and prison for the women.

Despite the dangers of trying to flee the country, this triggered an exodus of biblical proportions, including the alumni of Puylaurens and many of the academy's teachers. How many people fled is uncertain: estimates range from 200,000 to a million. Most sought asylum in neighbouring countries including England, Holland, Prussia and Switzerland, and four thousand fugitives found sanctuary in New York and Virginia. The registers of Geneva report that on a single day, 18 April 1688, a captain and a lieutenant with forty-two soldiers reached safety in the city. They were all from Puylaurens.

For over a century, Puylaurens had been a stronghold of Protestantism, but now, stripped of its academy, robbed of its scholars, deserted by its soldiers, and with many of its leading families decimated by departures, Puylaurens lost its identity and sense of purpose.

For most of its existence, the academy occupied a private mansion on the northern side of Notre-Dame-du-Lac in what is now called the Place Pierre Bayle. The building was demolished at the end of the nineteenth century, and all that remains of it today is the gate which I photographed in the garden of the temple in the Rue Foulimou. It is a grand gateway with a stone arch and two ionic columns, and above the lintel is a frieze dominated by two winged mermaids. The gateway is sealed by two wooden doors which over the centuries have acquired the pallor of a corpse. All this has been slotted into a wall which divides the garden of the temple from the garden of its neighbour, and the ensemble looks mournfully out of place as if it had lost its way in the fog. Who thought of moving it to this place of safety is unknown.

For me, this gate is emblematic of Puylaurens, and like the old soldiers slumbering in the Protestant graveyard, it evokes an illustrious past where the town was a centre of military aggression, a beacon of hope, and a seat of learning. These reminders may crumble and decay, but they will always be there for anyone curious and patient enough to seek them out.

Part VII

From the Bottom of a Lake

37

A Walk in the Desert

I am in a depression, a depression of the geographic kind. My bare arms are covered in goosebumps, perhaps because of the cool morning air, perhaps because of excitement. To the west, barren outcrops of granite rise above a desert of gritty sand and rough pebbles. In the lowest-lying areas the parched land is deeply fissured, and the bright morning sun turns the cracks into dark shadows which make the surface look like crazy paving.

This desert is not entirely devoid of moisture: the crazy paving is covered by a thin duvet of delicate green, but on closer inspection the green is not the growth of new grass. It is composed of tiny algae which have found enough moisture to profit from the unaccustomed light. Through the middle of this alien landscape, the faintest trickle of a stream crawls westwards along a rusty channel. I go with the flow for nearly a kilometre until I reach the start of a gorge which the stream has carved out in more vigorous times.

I pause to take some photographs. Ahead of me, the gorge winds its way through granite cliffs until its progress is checked by a massive wall. A sign warns me to keep out, but that won't stop me. During the winter of 2016 and 2017, this has been the most popular tourist attraction in the Lauragais. The organisers of this rare spectacle could have cut their costs by dispensing with the 'Danger – Keep Out' signs which everyone ignores, and the security fencing which in many places has been brushed aside by the multitudes who have flocked to see something which no one has seen for twenty-two years and which few of us will ever see again. Many, like me, have been unable to resist making multiple visits, because every week this disappearing lake has revealed something even older.

I follow a treacherous path that clings to the rocky slope of the gorge. I find a new vantage point and sit down on a lump of fractured granite. Below me, the stream runs through mudflats and disappears into a brown puddle where a doleful drake and two ducks swim in ever-decreasing circles around a small blue raft. They are the last survivors of an unnatural winter drought.

Two stairways lead up from the puddle to the top of a stone wall where an obelisk gives the finger to a sky which it has not seen for a very long time. It is flanked by two stone bollards, and when I came here a few weeks ago, waves broke over the top of the steps and spattered the obelisk with spray. Today, the mudflats make the scene look more like a wharf in a creek at low tide. Beyond the obelisk, the ground rises steeply until it reaches the base of a gigantic stone wall nearly a kilometre wide which blocks my view. This is Saint-Ferréol and this is the oldest dam in France. This was the key that enabled man to achieve something he had dreamed of doing since the Roman era.

Three hundred and fifty years ago, at exactly the same time as the students of Puylaurens were studying their bibles and fighting duels on Les Ravelins, up to 12,000 of their neighbours were engaged in hard physical labour, up here in the Montagne Noire above Revel, and down on the plain all the way from Toulouse to the Mediterranean. They toiled away for fourteen years on what was the biggest, most audacious construction project of its day: a waterway to link the sea and the ocean. On a map, the fruit of their labour splits the Lauragais neatly in two. Back then it was called the Canal Royal de Languedoc, but today it is known as the Canal du Midi and it is the oldest working canal in the world.

History may be just below the surface in the Lauragais, but when it is submerged under thirty metres of water it is considerably more difficult to explore. Luckily for me, this winter the dam at Saint-Ferréol needs to be repaired from top to bottom and the reservoir has been completely drained. A few days ago, one of the historians from the Museum of the Canal du Midi whispered in my ear that the engineers responsible for the dam hope never to do this again. It is an expensive process: as well as the cost of erecting the disregarded warning signs and futile fencing, the outflow had to be constantly monitored and regulated during draining to avoid polluting watercourses downstream, and while the dam is empty electronic probes check for signs of alarming movement (five centimetres so far). Then there was the live aquatic show which entertained the spectators when the reservoir was nearly empty: the costly business of catching sixteen tonnes of fish and transporting them to a new home. In a few months' time more money will be spent on bringing some of them back to restock the reservoir.

According to my source, the dam's engineers hope modern technology will allow them to carry out future inspections and repairs without totally draining the lake. So, although 'never' is a long time in anyone's language, this winter may be the last time I and thousands of other visitors can get to the bottom of how a man named Pierre-Paul Riquet found enough water to fill the highest section of his canal where it passes through the driest parts of the Lauragais.

38

FROM SEA TO OCEAN

In times gone by, emperors of Rome and kings of France dreamed of creating a navigable waterway between the Atlantic and Mediterranean so their ships could avoid the long and hazardous voyage around the coast of Spain and Portugal.

From Toulouse, the Garonne flows west towards the ocean. All that was required to realise this dream was a canal to connect the Garonne to the rivers running east into the Mediterranean. Unfortunately there were two difficulties. First was the profile of this stretch of countryside: if you head out of Toulouse along the route followed by the Black Prince, the land rises gently for forty kilometres from an elevation of 132 metres to a highpoint of 189 metres at a place called the Col de Naurouze located almost exactly in the geographic centre of the Lauragais. From Naurouze it is downhill all the way to the seaside.

Leonardo da Vinci's perfection of the canal lock at the end of the fifteenth century provided a practical solution to cope with these changes of elevation, but that still left the second problem: there are no rivers close to the Col de Naurouze. If the most elevated section of the canal were to be anything more than a damp ditch, it would need a copious water supply at its highest point.

In 1662 Pierre-Paul Riquet thought he had found the solution. He was born in Béziers in 1609, but he made his fortune in and around the Lauragais by levying the king's taxes on salt and becoming involved in its production and transportation. For a while he based himself in Revel, and it was perhaps this proximity to the Montagne Noire that inspired him to come up with an idea which he unveiled in a letter to Louis XIV's controller of finances, Jean-Baptiste Colbert, the same Colbert who would later become preoccupied by thirteen shades of blue.

In his letter, Riquet first summarised the problem. *'The thing which has caused all project plans to fail up until today is the difficulty of lifting water to the height of the stones of Naurouze. In twelve leagues [thirty-eight kilometres] of countryside one finds neither stream nor river which can provide enough water for a canal.'*

Canals are thirsty: they leak, however well they may be built; water evaporates, particularly in the hot summers of the Lauragais; and every time a barge passes through a lock, water drains away. A canal through the Lauragais would need thirty million cubic metres of water a year delivered to its highest point.

Riquet then unveiled his three-part solution. First, he planned to dig a seventeen kilometre channel high up in the Montagne Noire where the rainfall is twice what it is on the plain. This would allow him to divert water from the rivers Alzeau and Lampy into the Sor, the river which flows through the valley below the ruins of Roquefort and once powered the hydraulic hammers of Durfort. Just outside Durfort there was already an artificial channel which the consuls of Revel had built in the fourteenth century to take water from the Sor and supply their bastide. The second part of Riquet's solution was to extend this channel by forty-five kilometres across the plain from Revel to Naurouze. These two new channels would later become known as the Rigole de la Montagne and the

Rigole de la Plaine, and I shall henceforth adopt the word 'rigole' because it is far more pleasing to the ear than 'water channel', and the rigoles are delightful stretches of water.

The third part of Riquet's plan was to build fifteen or sixteen small reservoirs in the mountain. These would store enough water to keep the canal full when the rivers ran low during the driest months of the year.

When he received Riquet's letter, Colbert had been in post for eighteen months. He realised this was exactly the sort of grandiose project which would appeal to the Sun King, but he also knew Riquet was a tax collector with no engineering or scientific background. What could a man like that know about hydrography and canal building? Nevertheless, Colbert obtained Louis XIV's support, and towards the end of 1664 he sent a group of commissioners to Revel to study the feasibility of Riquet's project.

After a month of research, the commissioners delivered a report in January 1665 that was generally favourable, but concluded it would be unwise to rely on theory for a project of such considerable importance and expense. They proposed that someone should dig a miniature test rigole two feet wide to prove that water could flow all the way from the Alzeau to Naurouze.

At this point Riquet bet his own money on the project: he offered to pay for the test rigole and said he would only expect recompense from the state if the experiment was successful. In May, he received authorisation from the king and set to work in the Montagne Noire. His first task was to mark out a route for the test rigole with the help of his surveyors.

The western section of the Montagne Noire is not particularly high – the Rigole de la Montagne starts at around 680 metres – but the land is cut by steep-sided valleys and riddled with ravines. It was no mean feat to plot a gently-sloping course through this type of terrain armed only with a compass and a primitive levelling tool. There were no large-scale maps to help them, and Riquet and his team must have spent a long, long time tramping through the forest to gain such a detailed knowledge of its topography.

By July, Riquet was ready to start digging, and multiple teams of 200 men apiece set to work. Because this rigole was experimental and he would end up footing the bill if it failed, Riquet marked out a route in the mountain that was very different from that proposed by the commissioners, and from that which he would eventually adopt. He went out of his way – quite literally – to avoid building any dams, aqueducts or tunnels, but the project still cost him 200,000 *livres* (to put this in context, he later paid his canal builders a monthly salary of ten *livres*).

By the end of October the mini-rigole was finished. The official test took place on 9 November 1665 and, to the amazement of Riquet's many sceptics, water flowed from the Alzeau all the way to Naurouze. A couple of months later Colbert instructed the king's senior military engineer, Louis Nicolas de Clerville, to draw up detailed plans and costings for the whole project. On 7 October 1666 Louis XIV signed an edict authorising the building of the canal, and a week later Riquet was awarded the contract to carry out all the water supply works in the Montagne Noire and to build the first 120 kilometres of canal between Toulouse and Trèbes.

By now Riquet was nearly fifty-eight, an age when most men of his day were either thinking of retiring, dying or were already dead. Instead, he would seek the glory of linking the sea and the ocean, of realising the dream he and others had shared for so long. It was an ambitious retirement project and he would not live to see its completion, but the canal would secure his place in history.

The project kicked off early in the New Year of 1667 when work started on the Rigole de la Montagne and the Rigole de la Plaine. Then came something new, one of the most important changes Riquet made to his original plans. He dropped the idea of scattering small reservoirs across the Montagne Noire. Instead, he would erect one enormous dam of a size no one had ever seen.

On Sunday 17 April 1667, the first stone was laid at Saint-Ferréol.

39

The Eighth Wonder of the World

In more recent times, Saint-Ferréol has become the summer playground of Revel. The wooded slopes of the Montagne Noire rise from the lake's southern and eastern shores. The northern side is lined with Scots pines, and their trunks are so tall and bare, they remind me of coconut palms. Behind them stands a strip of hotels and restaurants, and together with the tennis and sailing clubs they create the ambiance of a quiet lakeside resort.

I swam here last summer in five million cubic metres of water and the lake was a hive of activity. Flotillas of ducks patrolled the waves between pedalos and dinghies and the more adventurous swimmers; matchstick people strolled or jogged along the distant shore; and the green grass near the dam was dotted with picnics and pushchairs. I had no concept of what lay thirty metres below me because the water was so clouded by suspended particles, when I waded in from the shore my feet disappeared long before my swimming trunks were wet.

Today I am discovering what lies beneath the waves and I can even stand here with dry feet. It is an odd experience to gaze up at the dam wall from the bed of its empty reservoir, but it won't be empty of life for long. Already the morning sun is beginning to warm the air and attract other visitors. By lunchtime they will swell into a crowd considerably larger than the one that assembled here in April 1667.

On that inaugural day almost exactly 350 years ago, a very different group of people gathered in a very different valley. The slopes were covered with real grass, not the green algae I can see today, and through the middle of this pastureland ran a quiet little river called the Laudot and on it stood a modest mill. There is no official account of the ceremony, but in a letter Riquet wrote to Colbert a couple of days later, he reports that the Archbishop of Toulouse, the Bishop of Saint-Papoul, the Baron of Lanta and other local dignitaries all took part in the ceremonial placing of the dam's first stone.

However hard I look, I shall not be able to identify that initial block of granite even in the lake's current state. Below the paddling feet of the obstinate ducks, six metres of mud ooze around the base of the dam and no dredging is planned this year. Also, this wall was refaced with harder granite in 1750; Riquet's first stone lies buried somewhere inside the dam and beneath the mud.

After the pomp and ceremony the serious work began. The first task was to build a stone tunnel in the bed of the river through which the Laudot could flow during and after the construction of the dam. This was later christened *la voûte d'enfer*, the tunnel of hell. With the river safely contained, work began on the construction of three walls which would make up the dam. The upstream wall – the one closest to me and the ducks – was the smallest: sixty metres wide and twenty metres high. In the centre, the main wall rose twenty-seven metres above the stream bed and would eventually stretch 780 metres across the valley. A little further downstream, a third wall completed the structure. All three ran in perfect straight lines, and the space between them was filled with rocks, stones and soil to create an enormous solid mass a hundred metres thick that everyone hoped would be enough to resist the water pressure generated by the lake. At that time, Pascal's experiments with hydrostatic pressure were a new development and no one was entirely sure how to apply his ideas to an undertaking on this scale.

A few months after the first stone was laid at Saint-Ferréol, a similar ceremony took place in Toulouse when work began on the lock that would connect the future canal to the Garonne.

During the next five years Riquet managed an extraordinary number of construction sites. By the end of 1672, he had completed the Rigole de la Montagne and the Rigole de la Plaine, and the dam at Saint-Ferréol was sufficiently advanced to start preparing for its first wet tests. Riquet's navvies had also dug 120 kilometres of the main canal from Toulouse to Trèbes and had even started work on the next section linking Trèbes to the sea.

To achieve so much so quickly, he employed platoons of stonemasons, carpenters and blacksmiths, and an army of navvies. His workforce reportedly peaked at 12,000 – although 6,000 is probably a more accurate estimate – and the bulk of it was made up of peasants from the surrounding countryside. A significant proportion were women – perhaps as much as a third – and Riquet even expressed a preference for female workers in a letter he wrote to Colbert in 1669: '*All the women who come to me, I shall hire them in the knowledge that these women working under contract will do as much work as men who are paid by the day.*'

To attract such a large labour force, Riquet offered innovative terms of employment. In a notice he signed on 8 December 1669 he made the following offer to any man or woman between the ages of twenty and fifty who was fit for work: '*In the name of the king we wish to make it known to all labourers who would like to sign up to work on the canal...that each person will be given ten livres a month without any deductions for public holidays or Sundays, or rainy days which will be had as rest days, and in addition he will be provided with a lodging for an average of two pennies a day… even those who fall ill will be paid during their illness as if they were working.*'

Sick pay, holiday pay, monthly pay, equal pay. These were revolutionary concepts in 1669, and the last one remains more of an aspiration than a reality even today.

Someone starts a generator and a pump bubbles away in the muddy puddle at the base of the dam. The ducks are unperturbed. Above them, a mechanical digger plays with a mound of sandy soil, and behind it four workmen climb onto scaffolding that stretches halfway across the main wall. It is a paltry workforce compared with Riquet's regiments, but in a few more weeks they will finish recoating the wall with the same type of lime-based rendering that was used 350 years ago, and then the lake will refill over a period of two or three months, depending on the rainfall.

Riquet carried out his first wet tests at Saint-Ferréol in 1673. The enormous brass taps he had placed inside the dam were opened for the first time and water flowed down the mountain to join the Rigole de la Plaine. These taps were located in a gallery immediately above the tunnel of hell, and the rush of water was so loud that the upper tunnel was christened *la voûte du tambour*, the tunnel of the drum. This winter while the lake is empty, both these tunnels are being cleaned and inspected, and the giant valves have been sent away for servicing. They are not the originals: after a hundred years of service, Riquet's valves were replaced, and his system was further modernised in 1994.

Those first tests did not mark the completion of the dam. Work continued right up until Riquet's death on 1 October 1680. Seven months later the canal was finished, and the king's engineer, La Feuille, began a long series of inspections to verify that all parts of this colossal system were working correctly. The official opening took place in Toulouse on 15 May 1682, and a ceremonial barge loaded with dignitaries set out on a nine-day, 240-kilometre voyage to Sète on the Mediterranean. They did not visit Saint-Ferréol. Perhaps if they had been privy to another of Riquet's many letters to Colbert, they would have made the detour. In this letter Riquet reports a comment made to him by La Feuille: *'He said to me that this reservoir was a monument without precedent and which will be passed down to posterity as the eighth wonder of the world.'*

40

SAND IN THE WORKS

In 1685, a few weeks after Louis XIV sent his troops to tear down the temple of Puylaurens, he sent another military contingent to the Lauragais. This one was led by his best military engineer, Sébastien Le Prestre de Vauban. His mission? Fix the Canal du Midi.

Three short years after its opening, the whole project had run into the sand, or more precisely, too much sand had run into the whole project. There was even talk of abandoning the canal when it had barely entered service.

Over the next thirteen years Vauban directed a programme of alterations and improvements to Riquet's creation. To reduce the accumulation of silt, he built aqueducts so that many of the streams and rivers bypassed the canal, but this in turn meant a greater volume of water had to come from other sources. To this end, Vauban added nearly eight metres to the height of the main wall at Saint-Ferréol, and this increased the storage capacity of the reservoir by fifty per cent. It also created two new challenges which I am about to investigate.

This morning, from the bottom of my empty lake it is easy to see the join in the main wall. At the top of the newly applied rendering is a ledge. Below it – and usually under water – lies the work of Riquet; above it stands the wall built by Vauban using massive blocks of granite.

Before I leave my depression I take some photos of the most striking object in my field of view, something which has nothing to do with Riquet or Vauban: a strange obelisk that was erected on the upstream dam wall in 1770. In the future I may glimpse its tip in times of drought, but I have no idea if I shall see its full height again.

For some inexplicable reason, local people call it 'the pyramid'; to me it looks far more like a stubby pencil that badly needs sharpening. The blunted tip is on the same level as the bottom of the main wall, so it is usually submerged and therefore useless because its true purpose is to gauge the depth of the lake at the glance of an eye. Five marker stones continue the scale up the main dam wall and provide a more useful means of measurement. All this was put in place thirty years before anyone started using the metric system, and the main gradations are at intervals of nine feet. The highest marker stone, just below the top of Vauban's wall extension, is ninety-nine feet above the original stream bed.

Further to the right, two modern water level indicators hang on the wall. They provide a more accurate reading using a scale marked in centimetres, but they lack the romance of the stones. They look as if a builder has sprayed his metal rule with bright blue paint and attached it to the dam wall with bright blue brackets.

On the other side of the dam, a steep grassy bank leads me down towards what used to be the home of the chief engineer but now houses the Museum of the Canal du Midi. Beside it is a wall built by Vauban, eighty metres long and thirty high.

As well as creating a larger reservoir, Vauban's heightened dam created a deeper lake which in turn increased the pressure exerted by the water. In response, he fattened the whole structure by thirty-eight metres, and this obliged him to lengthen Riquet's tunnels, bury the original downstream wall under more tonnes of soil, and build a new wall to create a hulking monster 140 metres thick. Compare this with the world's largest dam, the Three Gorges Project in China, which is a mere 115 metres thick at its base. (I should perhaps add an observation: the technology of dam-building has progressed in three-and-a-half centuries, and although the Chinese dam is thinner, it is six-and-a-half times taller and three times as wide.)

It hurts my back to think that the cavernous spaces between these four walls of stone were filled with earth and other material dug and carried by hand. Louis de Froidour, a dignitary who visited the construction site in 1671, wrote, '*I can confirm that there were as many as six or seven hundred people employed in this work when I visited, and above all I observed a highly practical method of moving and transporting the earth with baskets; there is a turnstile through which all those carrying it [the earth etc] must pass and for each journey they make they are paid one penny.*'

He also observed that the peasants were so motivated by profit, many of them earned as much as ten *sous* a day. There were twelve pennies or *deniers* to the *sous*, so this meant they had filled 120 backbreaking basketloads and lugged then to the dam. If they worked a ten-hour day, that was one full basket every five minutes. This calculation prompts me to touch my toes and share in their pain, if only for a few seconds.

Before I head higher into the Montagne Noire and visit Vauban's solution to the other problem created by his enlarged dam, I decide to trot down into the gardens below the museum in search of a president. This time I am referring to one of the true greats, a man who visited this spot in 1787.

In the nineteenth century Riquet's descendants – who still owned and ran the canal – turned the area below the dam into their idea of a romanticised park. They planted exotic trees and shrubs, built waterfalls and pools, and created streams and stepping stones. It is an idyllic spot for a stroll in summer, and the overheated visitor is soothed by mist from a water jet powered to a height of thirty metres by the depth of the lake. But on this February morning most of the trees are bare, and because there is no water in the dam, all the hydrological ornamentation is temporarily out of service.

I hop across a line of stepping stones which have been left high and dry by a barren stream, and I head deeper into the gardens. In a shady corner, mounted on a natural wall of granite beside the dried-out Laudot, is a cast-iron plaque which proclaims itself to be a symbol of Franco-American friendship. A pint-sized bust of a man juts from its surface and the text reminds us that twelve years before his visit, Thomas Jefferson was the principal author of the American Declaration of Independence, and fourteen years later, he became the third president of the United States. I squint at the bust from a shallow angle and conclude it looks more imposing in profile. It's still not Mount Rushmore, I grant you, but in those days Jefferson was only an ambassador on holiday, and he came to Saint-Ferréol by accident, or perhaps I should say, because of an accident.

In September 1786, he fell over in Paris and dislocated his wrist. The pain persisted, and early the following year he decided to follow the advice of his doctors and try a cure at the thermal springs of Aix-en-Provence. Afterwards he intended to examine the whole length of the Canal du Midi because in his home state of Virginia there was great interest in the idea of making the Potomac navigable.

Over the centuries Saint-Ferréol and the Canal du Midi have welcomed numerous illustrious visitors, so why does Jefferson merit a plaque when there is nothing to remind us of royal visits by Louis XVI's daughter, his brother who later became Louis XVIII, or Louis Philippe's eldest son? The difference between them is that when Jefferson spent eight days on the canal he recorded his impressions in notes and letters written while he was travelling, and he made observations on aspects of daily life which the locals took for granted and in which royalty took little interest. His writings covered agriculture, architecture, the price of goods and labour, the condition of the people, technical aspects of the canal, and where he could find the best wine.

Jefferson travelled down from Paris in his own carriage and when he reached the mouth of the canal near Agde he saw no reason to abandon it. He hired a barge to take him to Toulouse and loaded his carriage on deck.

'I dismounted my carriage from its wheels, placed it on the deck of a light bark, and was thus towed on the canal instead of the post road. That I might be perfectly master of all the delays necessary, I hired a bark to myself by the day, and have made from 20 to 35 miles a day, according to circumstances, always sleeping ashore. Of all the methods of travelling I have ever tried this is the pleasantest. I walk the greater part of the way along the banks of the canal, level, and lined with a double row of trees which furnish shade. When fatigued I take seat in my carriage where, as much at ease as if in my study, I read, write, or observe. My carriage being of glass all round, admits a full view of all the varying scenes thro' which I am shifted, olives, figs, mulberries, vines, corn and pasture, villages and farms.'[25]

According to Jefferson, most of the 240 barges operating on the canal were between seventy and eighty feet long and seventeen

25 Jefferson, Thomas. *Notes of a Tour into the Southern Parts of France, &c., 3 March–10 June 1787.* Retrieved from: Founders Online, National Archives, last modified April 12, 2018, http://founders.archives.gov/documents/Jefferson/01-11-02-0389. [Original source: The Papers of Thomas Jefferson, vol. 11, 1 January–6 August 1787, ed. Julian P. Boyd. Princeton: Princeton University Press, 1955, pp. 415–464.]

or eighteen feet wide. His own vessel was half that length and was drawn by a lone horse. When his barge floated into Castelnaudary on 18 May 1787, Jefferson's inquisitive nature prompted him to set out the next morning on a sixty-five kilometre round trip on horseback to visit Saint-Ferréol and the alterations Vauban had made to the hydrography higher up in the Montagne Noire at Les Cammazes and Lampy.

The second problem created by Vauban's enlarged reservoir at Saint-Ferréol was this: the Laudot was too feeble a river to fill it. His solution was to extend the Rigole de la Montagne by seven kilometres so that, instead of discharging into the Sor which ran straight down the mountain to supply the Rigole de la Plaine, it would discharge into the Laudot and supply the lake at Saint-Ferréol where the water could be stored and released when needed. This had always been in Riquet's plans, and he had even dug the first 1,400 metres of the extension before an obstruction that stood in his way prompted him to shelve the project until after the canal was opened. What barred the path of the new rigole was an inconveniently solid piece of rocky mountain nearly 300 metres thick just before the source of the Laudot in Les Cammazes.

Today, the main road through Les Cammazes passes over this obstruction and I park right on top of it. As soon as I open the car door I feel a change of temperature. It will be even colder underground, so I slip on a jacket and check my headtorch. A path leads me down the gentle slope of a cutting to the banks of the rigole. I double back on myself and follow the water into the cutting. The path is shaded by conifers and my feet move silently across a carpet of needles towards a black hole in the hillside. Ahead of me, the rigole takes a deep breath to squeeze into a tunnel, and this constriction makes it flow twice as fast until it breathes a sigh of relief at the far end.

This was Vauban's work. He excavated a cutting on each side of the barrier and dug a tunnel through the remaining 122 metres of rock. He had his workers attack the problem from several angles: they dug three vertical shafts from above which allowed two teams in each shaft to pick away at the rock in opposite directions, and two other teams excavated the soil and rock from each extremity. The tunnel was finished after two years and then the vertical shafts were sealed up.

When Thomas Jefferson came here he noted the tunnel was 135 yards long, a measurement which suggests he jumped off his horse and walked through it himself. How could he resist? The tunnel is three metres wide, but a third of that width is taken up by two narrow walkways – one on each side – which tempt the traveller into the darkness.

With the help of my headtorch, I stumble along the uneven paving stones above the rushing water. At the halfway point I stop and turn off my torch. From the far end of the tunnel, a keyhole of light paints the water silver. The babble of the rigole echoes off the walls, and I remember the six workers who died here on 15 April 1687, three men and three women buried by a rockfall. Three other young women had the good fortune to crawl out badly bruised but still breathing.

I lean my shoulder against the smooth wall of rock and reflect. If six out of nine casualties were women, it is reasonable to assume Vauban continued Riquet's habit of employing a significant number of female workers, even for the toughest and most dangerous tasks. During the century that followed the accident, the ladies of the Lauragais took on more and more jobs, although Riquet's enlightened policy of equal pay seems to have died out with him; Thomas Jefferson noted repeatedly throughout his journey that the women were paid half as much as the men. After his first few days on the canal, he also observed that most of the barges were worked by two hands, one of whom was usually a woman, and that most of the locks were kept by women. He then added: '*The encroachments by the men on the offices proper for the women is a great derangement in the order of things. Men are shoemakers, tailors, upholsterers, staymakers, mantua makers, cooks, door-keepers, housekeepers, housecleaners, bedmakers. The women therefore, to live are obliged to undertake the offices which they abandon. They become porters, carters, reapers, wood cutters, sailors, lock keepers, smiters on the anvil, cultivators of the earth etc. Can we wonder if such of them as have a little beauty prefer easier courses to get their livelihood, as long as that beauty lasts?*'[26]

With a curious leap of logic, Jefferson concludes that for every man who took a woman's job in this way, some poor girl was driven to whoredom.

I put my torch in my pocket and feel my way along the tunnel. When I emerge through the keyhole at the far end, I briefly toy with the idea of following Jefferson deeper into the mountain to Lampy Neuf, a reservoir which really was new at the time of his visit. It was built in 1782 to replace Lampy Vieux, constructed by Vauban to store even more water but which had always suffered badly from silt. It is a dozen or so kilometres to Lampy, a shady route alongside the rigole in the depths of the forest, and the earth track alongside the water is perfect for non-mechanised transport, be it two legs, four legs or two wheels. In many places, the stone sides and tiled bed of the rigole are clearly visible. In summer, it provides relief from the heat of the plain, and the cool waters of the lake at Lampy are always less crowded than those of Saint-Ferréol. There is even a café-restaurant to refresh the traveller before he embarks on the final stretch alongside the Rigole de la Montagne to the point where it draws its water from the Alzeau at La Galaube.

Regrettably, we are still in February and a chilly mountain breeze has taken all the warmth out of the sunshine. I am more

26 Jefferson, Thomas. *Notes of a Tour into the Southern Parts of France, &c., 3 March–10 June 1787.*

tempted by the thought of Le Salon de Vauban, a café conveniently located above the tunnel where I can warm myself up with a cup of coffee. I'll catch up with Jefferson when he resumes his stately cruise to Toulouse.

41

Legends and Broken Dreams

It takes each drop of water around fourteen hours to make the journey from Les Cammazes to Naurouze. It takes me considerably longer. After coffee and a few slices of *pain d'épices* in the comfort of Le Salon de Vauban, I was too lazy to continue my exploration the same day. I now realise this was a mistake because the weather has taken a turn for the worse. Tonight it will snow on the Montagne Noire, and down on the plain the *vent d'autan* is at its most ferocious. I abandon any idea of cycling along the Rigole de la Plaine from Revel to Naurouze. Even in my sturdy car I can sense the wind's strength, and I grip the steering wheel tighter and remember the train that left the tracks in 1916.

After the occasional swerve to miss fallen branches and errant dustbins, I reach Naurouze without mishap and park near what was once the home of the engineer responsible for this crucial part of the Canal du Midi. I zip up my coat, decide a hat is a bad idea unless I want to lose it, and heave the car door open. A sign on the corner of the engineer's house directs me onto the Chemin des Légendes, the Road of Legends, which leads towards a mound.

Over the millennia, Naurouze has attracted more than its fair share of legends. Pierre-Paul Riquet added one more. In a nineteenth-century engraving, he waves a rolled parchment at his astonished companions and points at the fountain of La Grave which bubbles from a rock and divides into two separate streams, one flowing towards the ocean, the other towards the sea. This was the moment when Riquet realised he would have to bring the canal's water supply to Naurouze. Unfortunately, this story is as fanciful as the engraving's depiction of the surrounding countryside. It had long been known that Naurouze was a watershed, although what first attracted man's attention to this place was a mysterious rock formation known as the stones of Naurouze.

Two thousand years ago, the Via Aquitania passed through here a few paces to the north, and the Roman town of Elusio grew up alongside it. In the twelfth century, the church of Saint Pierre d'Alzonne was built on the Roman remains, and its name is believed to be a corruption of Elusio. This explains why the rocks on their mound are sometimes called the stones of Alzonne, something which can confuse the visitor because there is also a village called Alzonne thirty kilometres further along the canal towards Carcassonne. As for Naurouze, the name first appeared in fifteenth-century Occitan as *la rocha de Nau Rosa*, which translates as the stones of Lady Rose. Another theory claims the name is a corruption of *la rocha d'en Aurosa*, which alludes to the rocks as a windy place. On a day such as today, I favour the second hypothesis.

I catch my first glimpse of the stones through bare winter branches. They stand in a line, maybe thirty metres long, three giant boulders divided by deep fissures into seven segments. In French, this type of rock is called *poudingue*, but in English it is known rather more poetically as puddingstone, or even better, plum-pudding stone, because it is made of dark pebbles cemented into a lighter-coloured, finer-grained rock. According to geologists, these stones are the hardy survivors after millions of years of erosion have swept away the land around them, but our less-scientific ancestors invented legends to explain their presence. My favourite – mainly because it translates so neatly – recounts a conversation between a giant called Naurouze and a local inhabitant.

'Where are you going, Naurouze?'

'I'm going to build Toulouse.'

'Go home, Naurouze, they've already built Toulouse.'

'Ah! If they've built Toulouse, my stones I can't use.'

In a rage Naurouze pulled the giant stones from his pocket and threw them on the ground with a curse. 'When the stones join together, girls and women will lose all restraint.'

My favourite troubadour, Raimon de Miraval, referred to this legend in '*A song written in despondency*', a composition which bemoans the faithless Azalaïs de Boissézon and her easy surrender to King Pedro. '*Madame has become quite the lioness; I know now that the stones of Alzonne have joined together since the one who offers most can be the first to enter.*'

In many people's opinion – but presumably not Pedro's – this type of sluttish behaviour signified the end of the world. Three centuries later, Nostradamus was allegedly referring to these same stones when he predicted that when the cracks between them closed, the end would be nigh.

With these legends in mind, I study the rocks with greater respect, but from afar. They are protected by a circular stone wall nearly three metres high and 150 metres in circumference. There is only one entrance and it is sealed by heavy iron gates. Today I find them locked, and they remain closed to the general public for at least 360 days of the year (try the third weekend in June or the second weekend in September). This measure has been taken to protect the future of mankind. In former times, visitors used to throw pebbles into the cracks between the rocks in the hope of putting off the Day of Judgement. How could the stones come together if they were wedged apart with pebbles? But the authorities in their wisdom realised that, over time, too many pebbles would entirely fill the cracks and bring the prophecy true. The gates must be kept locked!

Even here in a place so rich in legends, Riquet is a towering presence. In 1825, his family decided these ancient stones would make a perfect pedestal for a monument, but whereas the so-called pyramid at Saint-Ferréol gauges the depth of Riquet's lake, the obelisk at Naurouze was erected to show the height of his genius. At twenty metres, it is twice the height of the depth gauge, and it stands right on top of the central puddingstone of Naurouze.

Riquet's family also built the wall. On the day of the official opening in 1827, they took the risk of leaving the gates wide open, and ten thousand people gathered here and admired the bas-reliefs around the base of the monument. A series of classical allegorical scenes depicts the building of the canal, and the one facing west includes the words, '*To Pierre-Paul de Riquet*', followed by the names of the two engineers who oversaw the project. One of them was Jean-Polycarpe Maguès, the man whose town plans helped Jean-Paul Calvet rediscover the ramparts of Revel.

The dams and aqueducts, tunnels and rigoles, spillways and sluice gates built by Riquet, Vauban and others in the Montagne Noire are not exhibits in some enormous outdoor museum. They still function, every second of every day, and they supply water to the Canal du Midi in much the same way as they did more than three centuries ago. The canal itself is the oldest working canal in the world, although the boats that drift along it today are almost exclusively laden with tourists rather than merchandise, and the locks open and close at the touch of a button and are fitted with traffic lights.

Naurouze is a different matter. When I leave the obelisk and return to my car, I enter a sort of no man's land inhabited by discarded or obsolete projects. At the same time as they were building the dam at Saint-Ferréol, Riquet's men and women dug an octagonal basin at Naurouze to store more water for the canal. It was about 400 metres from side to side, and Riquet dreamed of making it the centrepiece of a new town and lining the shore with opulent houses modelled on the Palais Royale in Paris. In the centre of the lake he planned to erect a statue of Louis XIV riding in a chariot pulled by seahorses, and all the barges would salute the king as they floated through the basin.

This dream was one of the first victims of the silt that blighted the canal in its early years. When Vauban came here for his initial survey, he decided the basin was already doomed. He altered the course of the canal to bypass it, and he built a rigole that flowed both ways around the edge of the octagon and then joined up again for the final hundred metre dash into the deviated canal. Today, this divided rigole flows around a grassy meadow which is all that remains of Riquet's grandiose urban dream.

A few metres upstream from the basin, Riquet built two flour mills on the Rigole de la Plaine. The smaller one disappeared in the 1930s and its larger sibling closed in 1986. Viewed from the octagon thirty years later, the big old mill presents a forlorn face to the world; its jaundiced walls are tinged with green at the edges, and the wind whistles through broken windows. Around the corner there is more sign of life. Two outsiders, Andrew and Annie Spark, rescued this piece of Lauragais heritage from squatters in 1997 and are gradually putting it to new use. So far they have opened a snack bar, a hostel for travelling pilgrims, a bed-and-breakfast and a restaurant.

I turn away from the mill and go in search of the canal. Straight across the middle of the former basin runs a path leading to the Ecluse de l'Océan, Ocean Lock. The wind buffets me from behind and forces me to choose between breaking into a trot and falling flat on my face. After a couple of hundred paces, I dive into the lee of one of the plane trees lining the route. I lean against its trunk and catch my breath, and I remember the words Thomas Jefferson wrote to his daughter the evening after he passed through Naurouze.

'I write to you, my dear Patsy, from the Canal of Languedoc, on which I am at present sailing, as I have been for a week past, cloudless skies above, limpid waters below, and on each hand a row of nightingales in full chorus.' [27]

Lucky man! Jefferson came here in May and never once mentions the *vent d'autan*.

I give my tree a friendly pat. The two rows of monsters towering forty-five metres above my head have survived two centuries of the *vent d'autan*, but they and the other 140,000 plane trees lining the Canal du Midi and its tributaries are threatened by a less welcome visitor from America. Like Thomas Jefferson, it too started its journey along the canal from Sète, but unlike Jefferson who travelled down from Paris in a carriage, this one landed with the US Army in 1945.

Today, the classic image of the Canal du Midi shows a tranquil waterway guarded by columns of plane trees. Their reflections colour the scene with lazy shades of green, and sometimes their branches are so broad, the canal seems to be cruising through a leafy tunnel.

---

27 Jefferson, Thomas. *From Thomas Jefferson to Martha Jefferson, 21 May 1787.* Retrieved from: Founders Online, National Archives, last modified April 12, 2018, http://founders.archives.gov/documents/Jefferson/01-11-02-0350. [Original source: The Papers of Thomas Jefferson, vol. 11, 1 January–6 August 1787, ed. Julian P. Boyd. Princeton: Princeton University Press, 1955, pp. 369–370.]

When it first opened in 1682, the banks were bare. Seventy years later Riquet's descendants realised they were missing an opportunity to derive more profit from their canal. They planted elms for timber, white willows to protect the banks, and olives and mulberries for agriculture (at that time there was a thriving silk industry in the south of France and the mulberry leaves were destined to feed the silkworms).

Plane trees first appeared in small numbers in 1776, but widespread planting started fifty years later at the time when Riquet's descendants were building their obelisk on the stones of Naurouze. Today a microscopic fungus is killing them. Once infected, a tree is dead within five years. The most widely accepted theory is that the disease came over to France from the United States in 1945 in ammunition boxes made from American sycamore, a variety of plane tree which is itself relatively resistant to *ceratocystis platani.*

Today, ailing trees have been identified in numerous pockets of infection between Castelnaudary and the sea, but at present the disease does not appear to be spreading further west. Fourteen thousand trees have already had the chop, and many more are being monitored. It is feared that at least twice that number will have to be destroyed. Their last hope is a vaccine which was injected into a number of healthy trees in 2016, but it is too early to know the results.

The ravaged banks of the canal will not be left bare. Four thousand resistant specimens have already been replanted, but the glorious plane trees bordering my path to Ocean Lock went into the ground in 1809. Tourists in some areas will have to wait a long time for the canal to recover its picture-postcard image.

Between the upstairs windows of the lock keeper's house at the Ecluse de l'Océan, a sign announces the distance to the next lock to the east, 5,190 metres. This stretch of water is the highest section of the Canal du Midi. Down at eye level, Thomas Jefferson has been awarded another memorial plaque. Apart from the colour, it is identical to the one at Saint-Ferréol.

This souvenir prompts me to wonder why Jefferson didn't comment on the stones of Naurouze. He mentioned unusual rock formations in Burgundy and the Rhône Valley. Perhaps in the absence of Riquet's obelisk he failed to notice them, or maybe he was too rational a man to interest himself in silly legends. Instead, he concerned himself with lock design and observed that the lock gates were opened using laborious wooden screws.

'I calculate that five minutes are lost at every basin by this screw, which on the whole number of basins is one eighth of the time necessary to navigate the canal: and of course, if a method of lifting the gate at one stroke could be found, it would reduce the passage from eight to seven days.'[28]

Jefferson then sketches out an alternative design which, he says, he has suggested to Monsieur Pin who has promised to test it out and inform him of its success.

I look westwards and picture Jefferson's carriage floating down the canal on its barge while its owner strides along the towpath with his mind occupied by thoughts of a quadrantal lock gate turning on a pivot. That evening, he reached Ayguesvives where he spent his last night alongside the canal, and the next day he reached Toulouse and put the wheels back on his carriage. In a geographical sense, I shall catch up with him in the next chapter when I go in search of a French army fleeing along the Canal du Midi pursued by the Duke of Wellington.

---

28 Jefferson, *Thomas. Notes of a Tour into the Southern Parts of France, &c., 3 March–10 June 1787.*

A few weeks later, I return to Saint-Ferréol on a hot and lazy Sunday afternoon. Tomorrow is the first day of spring, but the weather thinks it is already summer, and all the car parks bulge in a way that leaves me feeling smug about travelling by bicycle. Since my last visit, the winter desert has acquired a generous waterhole, and children frolic at the water's edge like young wildebeest. The upstream dam wall has sunk out of sight and only the tip of the obelisk is visible, yet it still bears no resemblance to a pyramid. Instead, it reminds me of a marker buoy warning mariners of a wreck beneath the waves.

The main dam wall is still a couple of metres above the waterline, and I try to estimate how much drying time the new rendering has before it too disappears. I conclude the calculation is beyond me, so I pedal off in search of a drink on the northern shore. Any establishment that is open is packed, and I question the commercial sense of those which remain closed. I make a couple of runs along the strip before I spot a suitable table at La Mallaury. I claim a seat in a sunny corner by the barbecue, and for once I catch the waiter's eye at the first attempt.

'Dites-moi!' he says with a familiarity which suggests we have met before.

'A glass of rosé, *s'il vous plaît.*'

This is not my habitual drink during a bicycle ride, but today I am bidding farewell to Riquet's dam and all but the top of Vauban's extension. From my seat I spy tiny sections of dam wall through vertical slits in the palisade of Scots pines. In a few weeks' time, even these glimpses will disappear beneath the rising waters of the lake.

My drink arrives with a smile and an ice cube. I toast my good fortune to have come here so often while the lake was empty, and to have enjoyed the rare privilege of getting to the bottom of what makes this timeless piece of engineering tick. With care, the waterworks in the Montagne Noire will supply the Canal du Midi for another 350 years.

I raise my glass to the memory of Riquet and Vauban; but for some reason the words of Thomas Jefferson come to mind, words he wrote to his secretary back in dreary Paris when he first reached the south of France in the spring of 1787.

'I am now in the land of corn, wine, oil, and sunshine. What more can man ask of heaven?' [29]

29 Jefferson, Thomas. *From Thomas Jefferson to William Short, 27 March 1787.* Retrieved from: Founders Online, National Archives, last modified April 12, 2018, http://founders.archives.gov/documents/Jefferson/01-11-02-0242. [Original source: The Papers of Thomas Jefferson, vol. 11, 1 January–6 August 1787, ed. Julian P. Boyd. Princeton: Princeton University Press, 1955, pp. 246–248.]

PART VIII

THE ENGLISH CEMETERY

42

The Mystery of the Dead

I discovered the English Cemetery thanks to a local walking group soon after I settled in the Lauragais. We dropped down from the ramparts of Saint-Félix into a valley and climbed steeply onto the next ridge to the south. After a brisk march along a flat grassy track, we paused for breath beside a rough triangle of scrubland bordered by cypress trees. One of my companions gave me a sideways glance. 'This,' he said, 'is *le cimetière des anglais*.'

I knew there were a lot of us in the Lauragais, but I was surprised to find we had our own cemetery, and why choose such a lonely, windswept spot? Here and there a few rough stones poked out of the undergrowth, and larger boulders were piled up beneath the bushes alongside the track. They looked as if they had been discarded by the ploughman rather than erected to mark the graves of my countrymen, and the unkempt state of the place suggested no one had been buried here for a very long time.

'Why would there be an English cemetery up here?'

'I think it was something to do with the Black Prince,' said someone.

'I heard some soldiers lost their way during the Napoleonic Wars,' said another.

'I thought it was a legend,' said a cynic.

By the end of our walk I was still none the wiser, but the image of a mysterious and forgotten cemetery had lodged itself in my memory.

I forgot all about it for a couple of years until we brought some friends to Saint-Félix-Lauragais for lunch and a view. Like Puylaurens, the town is built on a hill and boasts numerous water wells. The one by the church is forty-two metres deep, exactly the same height as the spire, and those with a bent for engineering may deduce that this was no coincidence but was in fact a clever design that allowed the use of a counterweight to hoist building materials to the highest point of the edifice. The well in the château is two metres shallower, but perhaps even more interesting. Local legend claims an angry Simon de Montfort threw his sword to the bottom, and there it has remained to this day. Between these two wells lies a medieval square with a covered market which is a century older than the one in Revel, but for me the outstanding feature of Saint-Félix-Lauragais, even in this land of imposing vistas, is the view.

After lunch, we led our visitors into a walled garden beside the château, and up a flight of steps onto a section of the town's ramparts. On the remains of a tower in the south-east corner, a painted orientation table explained the local geography. On the exposed plateau to the north, wind turbines played with the *vent d'autan*, and behind them Puylaurens shimmered on its hilltop. To the east, the Montagne Noire stretched across the horizon, and Dourgne, Sorèze, Durfort and Revel nestled at its feet. To the south-east, the Pyrenees appeared from behind the Montagne Noire and marched across the southern skyline towards the distant ocean.

On this particular day, the sky was a flawless blue and the visibility was perfect. I ran my eyes along the mountain peaks and identified the ones I have climbed, and then something nearer to hand caught my attention: a platoon of cypress trees standing guard on the next ridge. I glanced at the orientation table to confirm my memory.

'How about walking off our lunch? I'll show you the English Cemetery.' To my surprise, our visitors agreed, and we left town by the Porte de Roqueville.

Viewed from the heights of the ramparts, the terrain to the south of Saint-Félix reminds me of corrugated iron. The land rises from the edge of the plain and then a succession of ridges and valleys runs north-west towards Toulouse. Farmhouses hide in the furrows where the soil is fertile, and the high ground is thinly-grassed or covered in brushwood and oak. One ridge looks much like the next and I missed our turn, but we soon doubled back and within minutes we stood among the whispering sentinels of the cemetery.

The site had been transformed since my last visit, both by the hand of man and the coming of spring. Someone had cleared the brush, a neat triangle of emerald-green grass was speckled with yellow by cowslips and dandelions, and the borders were marked out by orderly lines of stones. The first butterflies were out, and so were the first leaves on the broom and hawthorn, but more importantly from my point of view, someone had erected a granite stele with a memorial plaque etched with letters of gold. *'Ici reposent des soldats Anglais. Bataille de Toulouse 10 avril 1814. Les Amis du Patrimoine Napoléonien' ('Here rest some English soldiers. Battle of Toulouse 10 April 1814. Friends of Napoleonic Heritage').*

'Isn't Toulouse miles away?' asked one of our friends.

He was right: we were forty kilometres from *la ville rose*. Why would they bury anyone out here? And the phrase, '*some English soldiers*', was tantalisingly imprecise. Perhaps they were stragglers who died in a skirmish before or after the battle. I wasn't even sure who had won. I vaguely recalled reading something in French which claimed the home side was victorious, but my memory of Napoleonic history suggested April 1814 was rather close to Napoleon's first abdication, so surely they must have lost.

The inscription raised more questions than it answered, but despite many subsequent walks through the cemetery, it was only when I began work on this book several years later that I made any serious attempt to satisfy my curiosity. Before long, I was immersed in the story of a pointless battle fought by 100,000 men after the war was over, the fighting that took place after the battle was won (or lost), and finally I returned to the mystery of who, if anyone, may be buried in the English Cemetery at Saint-Félix-Lauragais.

43

A City at War

Over the centuries, Toulouse and the Lauragais have witnessed the rise and fall of proud kingdoms and mighty empires. Five centuries of Romanisation passed by in comparative peace, but then Germanic tribes swept south and Rome fell. First to appear were the Vandals, who unsuccessfully besieged Toulouse in 407. Six years later the Visigoths captured the city, and in 418 they made it their capital. For the next hundred years, Toulouse prospered at the political and geographic centre of a kingdom which at its height encompassed most of Spain and a large part of southern France. At that time the territories to the north were held by the Franks, and in 507 their king, Clovis, defeated the Visigoths at the Battle of Vouillé near Poitiers. A year later Clovis sacked Toulouse, and the regal capital was downgraded to the lowly status of a garrison town on the southern border of an enlarged Frankish kingdom.

In the second half of the seventh century Islam spread along the coast of North Africa, and in 711 the Moors crossed the Straits of Gibraltar. Over the next eight years they conquered Portugal and Spain, and then they crossed the Pyrenees and captured Narbonne. Two years later they marched through the Lauragais and mounted a siege of Toulouse. After three months, Christian reinforcements arrived from the north and the Moors found themselves trapped between the new arrivals and the battered walls of the besieged city. Although other battles followed and Narbonne remained in the hands of the Moors for a further forty years, the Battle of Toulouse in 721 marked the turning point of Islamic expansion into Western Europe.

During the next thousand years Toulouse and the Lauragais were caught up in a succession of conflicts including those covered in the preceding chapters of this book. Then, in the summer of 1799, the last major royalist rebellion of the French Revolution broke out in the countryside around Toulouse. In the Lauragais, the royalists took control of towns including Baziège, Caraman, Lanta, Montgiscard and Muret. Their army numbered perhaps 40,000 men, but very few were armed, so they planned to sneak into Toulouse with the help of sympathisers inside the city, capture the arsenal and steal its weapons. Their plan failed. During the days that followed, the local republicans called in reinforcements from Albi, Carcassonne and even Perpignan, and they pursued the rebels south towards Spain, eventually defeating them at the Battle of Montréjeau.

In 1804, the French Republic became the French Empire and the First Consul became the Emperor Napoleon. A decade later, Toulouse was the setting for the final battle before Napoleon was exiled to Elba and France became a kingdom once again. The fighting began at first light on Easter Sunday 1814 and it dragged on until dusk, but the decisive action was all over by ten in the morning. In the thick of it, desperately trying to extricate his men from the calamitous mess his divisional general had landed him in, was Jean-Pierre Rey of number twenty-eight, Rue Foulimou, Puylaurens.

It had been a long and bloody road to Toulouse for Brigadier-General Rey and the French army, and for the British, German, Portuguese and Spanish troops who were pursuing them.

Napoleon first sent an army to Portugal towards the end of 1807 in an attempt to enforce his continental blockade, but before long the French found themselves embroiled in a conflict that engulfed most of Portugal and Spain. In April 1809 a British army landed in Lisbon, and three weeks later it defeated the French outside Porto. This was the first confrontation between Arthur Wellesley and Jean-le-Dieu Soult. Over the next five years their armies waged war across the Iberian Peninsula. Wellesley won most of his battles and was rewarded with a succession of titles: Viscount Wellington, Earl of Wellington, and by the time he chased his enemies back into France in December 1813, he was the Marquess of Wellington. On 3 May 1814 he would be made a duke, but first he had to win the Battle of Toulouse.

Thanks to Napoleon, Jean-le-Dieu Soult was already a duke, of Dalmatia. He was a local boy from a village in the shadows of the Montagne Noire and he had been fighting for his country since the first days of the Revolution. In March 1813 he was recalled to Germany, and in his absence Wellington inflicted a crushing defeat on the French army at the Battle of Vitoria. Soult was immediately sent back to Spain to rescue the demoralised survivors. Outnumbered by the allied army, he had no option but to retreat north across the frontier.

In February 1814, the two armies clashed again at the Battle of Orthez near Pau and Soult was forced to continue his retreat. By now his dwindling army was short of men, low on supplies and drained of hope. In a letter to the minister of war a few days later, he complained that two or three thousand of his troops were marching barefoot. Their only salvation lay a couple of hundred kilometres up the road, a long march for men with no shoes, but *la ville rose* offered everything an exhausted army could wish for. In Toulouse, Soult and his soldiers would find food, shelter, munitions, an arsenal, the National Guard, and comparative security inside a fortified city where they would be able to snatch some rest before the next battle, but only if they could get there before Wellington.

From Tarbes, Soult chose the longer, flatter and better-maintained roads which ran near today's A64 *autoroute*. Wellington opted for a shorter, hillier course which he hoped would be faster, but heavy rains made bad roads worse, and Soult beat him to the city by nearly two days.

On 24 March Soult marched into Toulouse at the head of his troops. It was pouring with rain, but thousands of spectators turned out to watch the drenched regiments march by in perfect order. During the preceding days, pitiful convoys of sick and wounded men had stumbled into the city, men who at best were filthy, feverish and starving. The people of Toulouse had begun to fear that Soult's entire army was in a similar state, and what, they wondered, would 35,000 men like that do to a city of 50,000 inhabitants. Soult's martial air and the discipline of his regiments reassured them. Nevertheless, the finer shops closed their shutters and locked their doors, the ordinary citizens hid everything of value, and the rich fled to their country houses.

During the first four days most of the army camped outside the city walls, but that did not stop them foraging for food and other supplies. To the consternation of the townsfolk, the officers struggled, or made little effort, to discipline their starving, thieving men.

Soult and his generals had other concerns: they had precious little time to reorganise their miserable army and strengthen the defences of the city against the attack that was sure to come. As soon as they arrived in the city, the military engineers set about transforming Toulouse into one enormous fortified camp. The fine trees lining the avenues were chopped down and turned into planks to reinforce the city gates and earthworks. Gun emplacements sprang up at key points around the city, and barricades blocked the streets. Soldiers, horses and artillery rushed hither and thither in a frenzy of activity.

Relations between the citizens and the army were strained, a mixture of mutual suspicion and fear of what would happen when Wellington attacked. Sometimes the civilians were filled with pity, both for the steady trickle of wounded stragglers who continued to crawl into the city, and for the fit and healthy men who were working like slaves on the construction of new earthworks. One of these sympathetic residents was the Count of Montbel, and in his memoirs he recalls seeing a squad of poor soldiers who were being forced to work so hard that passers-by tried to intervene. *'An officer jumped out of the trenches and shouted, "We know how hostile you lot are towards the emperor. The first person who says another word will be shot right here in this trench".'*[30]

The following day, press-gangs were on the street, and the Count of Montbel was marched to the trenches, given a shovel and told to start digging. This, he observed, was a task for which he had as little inclination as aptitude. He was an aristocrat whose father had been guillotined during the Revolution, and like many people in Toulouse he longed for Napoleon's downfall and the return of the king.

On 2 April Soult issued a new instruction. *'The inhabitants of the city are ordered to work on the defences…each in his quarter, particularly on the city gates, advance positions and the ramparts…*

30 Translated from : Montbel, Guy de. *1787-1861, Souvenirs du comte de Montbel.* Paris: Plon-Nourrit, 1913 (page 87).

[we will] impose fines on those who refuse to participate.'[31]

These efforts to bolster the city's defences may have given the soldiers more confidence, but they had the opposite effect on the townsfolk. They began to fear that Soult would defend Toulouse to the last man and that the streets of their wrecked city would run red with blood.

Jean-Pierre Rey and his men knew little of these preparations. They were stationed to the west of the city in an area now buried beneath the runway of Blagnac Airport. Along with the bulk of the French army, they were waiting for Wellington. Soult did not intend to abandon the countryside around Toulouse without a struggle, and he needed time to prepare his defences. The allied army's vanguard came into view on 25 March and promptly launched an attack. The next two weeks were filled with a succession of skirmishes and troop movements as Wellington manoeuvred his army into position to encircle the French and prepare for an assault on Toulouse. By the end of March, Rey and his men had retreated inside the fortified quarter of Saint-Cyprien just across the river from the main city.

At the start of April, Wellington ordered General Hill and 13,000 men to cross the Garonne south of Toulouse and head into the Lauragais. Their mission was to prevent a possible junction between Soult's troops and another French army of 10,000 men which was camped out near Narbonne under the command of Marshal Suchet.

At this stage in my research, I find myself wondering excitedly if Hill's men made it as far as Saint-Félix-Lauragais, if their casualties are buried in *le cimetière des anglais*. I obtain the typescript of a detailed account of this incursion written by the president of the Ayguesvives history society in the 1970s. Unfortunately I learn

31 Translated from : Geschwind, Henri and François de Gélis. *La Bataille de Toulouse (10 avril 1814) d'après les documents les plus récents.* 1914. Reprint. Cresse: Editions des Régionalismes, 2015 (page 93).

that Hill's corps didn't even cross the Canal du Midi. One of the allied cavalry patrols came within a couple of kilometres of the canal at Ayguesvives and clashed with its French counterparts, but the bulk of Hill's men were stuck in the glutinous mud of the southern Lauragais, and they were forced to hire local peasants and their oxen to drag the artillery out of the quagmire. After that, Hill and his army decided to retreat the way they had come. When they reached the western outskirts of Toulouse, they blockaded all the roads into Saint-Cyprien. This ensured that Jean-Pierre Rey and his comrades would not be able to escape to the west, but the defenders remained in a strong position. If the allies stormed their defences, they would simply retreat across the Pont Neuf and blow up the bridge, and in 1814 this was the only link between Saint-Cyprien and the main city. In search of a weaker point to attack, Wellington and the rest of his army crossed the Garonne fifteen kilometres further north on 5 April.

Over the next few days, the rain continued to fall in torrents, and the allies captured a bridge here, a hamlet there, and prepared for battle. On 8 April the Count of Montbel watched one of these skirmishes through a telescope. *'Our thirteenth light cavalry were defending a water course. The enemy hussars advanced in their direction. It was raining, the English officers were on horseback with an umbrella in hand, something which seemed eminently ridiculous to us. Suddenly the English hussars closed their umbrellas, attached them to the pommels of their saddles, unsheathed their sabres and threw themselves on our cavalry who defended themselves valiantly, but their mounts were not as strong as the enemy horses. Our soldiers were therefore overcome and their colonel seriously wounded.'* [32]

Despite his royalist convictions and desire for Napoleon's downfall, the count was overcome with sympathy for his compatriots. *'This spectacle made the most painful impression on me. Nothing is more frightful than a scene of carnage in which one does*

32 Translated from : Montbel, Guy de (pages 89-90).

not share the danger.' [33]

That same day, the count received news that another allied army had entered Paris, but his sources could not tell him anything about the fate of Napoleon. The following morning he and his royalist friends discussed what course of action they should take, but their deliberations were disturbed by the sound of explosions. *'From time to time, detonations seemed to announce the start of the battle. I roamed along the ramparts…they were bristling with mortars and cannons of all calibres. Beside them stood the gunners with their fuses lit; they waited with perfect calm for the signal to fire.'* [34]

The signal came early the following morning.

It is not my intention to describe the battle in detail. A whole library has already been written on the subject, by soldiers and civilians of both sides who were there, and by an army of historians who were not. Instead, I shall join Brigadier-General Rey and retrace his long and disastrous day.

33 Translated from : Montbel, Guy de (page 90).
34 Translated from : Montbel, Guy de (page 90).

44

Night Manoeuvres

At three in the morning, Jean-Pierre Rey was on the move. He commanded a brigade of three regiments, and he had 3,039 men ready for action. Two thousand others were injured or sick, the cumulative effect of the long retreat from Spain.

Rey's troops had gone to sleep expecting to defend Saint-Cyprien, but during the previous evening Soult had reconnoitred the countryside to the east of the city and observed the disposition of Wellington's troops. He concluded that the most determined attacks would come from the east, against a ridge of high ground that dominated the city. He needed more men below that ridge, men he could throw into the fray wherever it was most desperate.

Rey's brigade formed one half of the fourth division commanded by General Taupin, and they all set out together from Saint-Cyprien and marched in the dark towards the river. Attached to Taupin's division were a hundred artillerymen with cannons and horses commanded by Captain Edouard Lapène. In 1822, Lapène wrote the first book devoted to the Battle of Toulouse, and his work is the main source that allows me to follow Rey's painful progress.

My dedication to history is not quite strong enough to bring me to Saint-Cyprien at three in the morning, although I do arrive in the dark. When I climb the stairs leading up from the metro, I am welcomed by an empty blue sky and warm walls of pink brick. Like Rey, I head east towards the Pont Neuf, and shortly before the bridge I pass the Hôtel-Dieu Saint-Jacques. Some of its buildings date back to the twelfth century when they provided lodgings and medical care for pilgrims walking to Saint-Jacques de Compostelle. By 1814, the pilgrims were expected to sleep elsewhere and this had become the city's largest hospital. When Rey marched past, many of its four hundred beds were already occupied by the sick and wounded from earlier battles. By the end of the day the hospital would be overflowing with new casualties, and after the battle its medical staff cared for soldiers from both armies.

I reach the right bank of the river and my mind is already swimming in history. To my left is the Quai de la Daurade where Jean de Bernuy and Pierre Assézat once loaded their *pastel* onto barges bound for Bordeaux. Also on my left, and nearer to hand, is my favourite riverside café. From a low comfortable chair on the mezzanine floor of the Café Cerise I survey the bridge, the hospital and the river, and I study my notes and maps of the battle.

While General Taupin and Brigadier-General Rey march past with their men, and Captain Lapène trundles past with his artillery, I shall explain the defences of Toulouse in 1814. Otherwise, the disaster that is about to engulf our gallant general from Puylaurens will be hard to comprehend.

Soult knew Wellington's army was larger, better-equipped and better-supplied: 53,000 men compared with 42,000, and it boasted three times as many cavalry. Even worse, around 7,000 of Soult's men were inexperienced conscripts. He was counting on a combination of natural and man-made barriers to even up the odds.

During the couple of centuries that have passed since the day of the battle, Toulouse has grown into a sprawling metropolis of 1.3 million inhabitants, but in 1814 most of the population still lived within the confines of the ancient city walls. These ramparts and their fifty towers were reinforced with earthworks, and they provided Soult's inner line of defence.

Next came the wet barriers, part man-made, part natural. If you think of Toulouse as a clock, the Garonne protects its west flank between seven and ten, and I am drinking coffee at nine o'clock, both literally and figuratively. At ten, the Canal du Midi branches off from the river and turns clockwise around the city to about five o'clock. The area to the south between the canal (five o'clock) and the river (seven o'clock) was, in theory, the weak spot in this second line of defence, but it mainly consisted of marshland made still wetter by unusually heavy rains. It would be hard going for men and almost impossible for horses or artillery.

The land beyond this second line of defence was predominantly countryside, dotted with farms and hamlets and the occasional rich man's home or château.

The key to controlling Toulouse was a ridge running down the east flank of the city, from the old Albi road in the north, to the Revel road in the south. This high ground is squeezed between the Canal du Midi and a feeble river called the Hers, which today lies forgotten alongside the six lanes of the *périphérique*. Whoever held this high ground would have Toulouse at his mercy because it offered a clear line of fire down onto all parts of the city, and it also controlled all routes east. During the first days of April, the French engineers frantically dug a row of seven redoubts all along this ridge to help them resist allied attacks.

I drain my cup and fold away my maps. I have a lot of ground to cover today, and I march rather than stroll along the Rue de Metz. Nevertheless, I take a moment to slip inside the gates of the Hôtel d'Assézat and glance up at its tower. Captain Lapène will explain later how vantage points such as this were turned into grandstands on the day of the battle.

Further down the road I resist the temptation to linger too long outside the Musée des Augustins. This is one of the oldest museums in France, and it first opened its doors twenty years before Jean-Pierre Rey marched past. In its former life as an Augustinian convent, its orchard hosted the first Floral Games in 1324.

A few minutes later I reach the cathedral of Saint-Etienne. Rey and his men paused here and waited. With the first light of dawn they would march through the Porte Saint-Etienne and complete the last kilometre to their designated position near the road to Castres.

I stare at the disturbingly asymmetric cathedral and wonder what the soldiers were thinking while they waited to go into battle. According to Captain Lapène, they had received the news of the fall of Paris with the cold indifference of men hardened by two years of defeats and disasters. Officers and men were determined to make a final effort, more to preserve the independence of France than prolong the reign of Napoleon. *'A decisive battle could no longer be postponed. Inhabitants, leaders, soldiers, everyone ardently desired an end to the state of crisis which had already lasted too long.'*[35]

At dawn the church bells began to ring. In those drowsy moments between sleep and wakefulness, some citizens may have thought they were hearing the tocsin, but then they remembered this was Easter Sunday. At six o'clock, the Count of Montbel and

35 Translated from : Lapène, Edouard. *Evènements Militaires devant Toulouse en 1814.* Paris: Chez Ridan, 1822 (page 54).

his family were in the cathedral of Saint-Etienne celebrating the Resurrection. I follow them inside and take a pew near the tomb of Pierre-Paul Riquet. I suspect the count and his fellow-worshippers prayed more fervently than usual that morning, for a swift end to the battle, for lasting peace, and above all – according to Lapène – for the safety of their property.

After prayers, the count and his family came out to a joyous spring morning: the rain had finally stopped, the trees were in flower and the leaves were coming out. '*Suddenly*,' recalls the count, '*a distant explosion tore me away from enjoying this gentle sight [of spring]. The artillery thundered, shots crackled, the battle had commenced.*'[36]

I leave the cathedral and march towards the canal. Within a couple of hundred paces I encounter another distraction: an obelisk erected in memory of Brigadier-General Dupuy who was murdered in Cairo in 1798. What catches my eye is the fact that he commanded the thirty-second infantry regiment (or *demi-brigade* as it was called at the time). On 10 April 1814, this regiment was under the command of Jean-Pierre Rey, and among its officers was Captain Rivière, the man who now keeps him company in the graveyard at Puylaurens.

Twenty paces on the Pont Guilhemery take me across the Canal du Midi, but if Wellington's soldiers came this close to the city, they wouldn't find the canal so easy to cross because Soult's engineers had mined all the bridges, ready to blow them up if the battle went badly. On the other side of the canal, Rey marched his men up the hill to a crossroads flanked by two houses belonging to the Bataille and Cambon families (today this is near the junction of Rue Marancin and Rue Lucien Cassagne). The surrounding area had been fortified with earthworks, and this is where Taupin, Rey, Lapène, Rivière and five-and-a-half thousand men took up their positions at around six o'clock.

36 Translated from : Montbel, Guy de (page 90)

45

A Long and Disastrous Day

I am standing at the foot of a brick obelisk equal to the combined height of Riquet's depth gauge and his monument at Naurouze. It was erected twenty-five years after the battle as a memorial to the seven thousand men killed or injured on 10 April 1814. At six o'clock in the morning Soult stood on this spot and watched Wellington's troops launch their first attacks from the west and the north. Back then it was called Mont Calvinet, but today it is Mont Jolimont, a peaceful park on a hilltop with an observatory, magnificent trees, and tantalising glimpses of the urban landscape to the west and the countryside to the east. The whole area is unashamedly suburban, and this morning the only sounds are birdsong, children playing, and the distant hum of traffic from the city below.

Near the obelisk is a large map which shows the disposition of both armies and explains how the battle unfolded. I study it for a moment to check I have correctly understood Captain Lapène's description of the frantic marches Taupin and Rey are about to make.

At seven, Soult looked to the north and spotted three divisions of infantry and two brigades of cavalry massing around the bridge over the Hers at La Croix-Daurade. If he had taken the time to count them all, he would have come up with figures of 20,000 men and 2,000 horses. There was no doubt they would attack the redoubts of Mont Calvinet. Now was the moment to call for reinforcements. He dispatched a messenger to Taupin.

My walk to Mont Calvinet has taken me through the cemetery of Terre-Cabade, a place so vast and with paths so twisty, I had to pause several times to check my position using GPS. It first opened its gates in 1840; at the time of the battle Taupin's division struggled through fields of mud rather than a maze of tombs. When they reached Mont Calvinet they waited for further orders, and Soult waited for an allied attack.

The first assault came from two columns of Spanish troops. One started to climb the northern slopes of Mont Calvinet while the second marched towards what is now the Gare de Matabieu. In the ensuing fighting, both columns were badly mauled and their losses accounted for half the total allied casualties in the battle.

While the Spanish were occupying the attention of the French defenders, the rest of the allied infantry and all the cavalry Soult had spotted earlier at La Croix-Daurade marched southwards alongside the Hers in search of an easier route onto the ridge. Soult knew the weakest point was his most southerly redoubt at La Sipière. That's where he needed to be, and he ordered Taupin's division to follow him.

I make the journey myself, but it is an unrewarding couple of kilometres which I would recommend to no one except, perhaps, the most devoted battlefield enthusiast. It may be easy to step back in time in the market square of Revel or the Rue Foulimou in Puylaurens, but my path to La Sipière takes me through an endless succession of suburban streets lined with smart villas and neat gardens where the only signs of life are the clatter of a builder's drill or the chatter of an electric hedge trimmer. I am sure it is a pleasant environment in which to live, but I find it disorientating when I try to picture Taupin and Rey leading their men in a forced march across sunken roads and through fields of ploughed mud. Lapène didn't even attempt the journey with his artillery; he stayed at Mont Calvinet from where he witnessed the subsequent fiasco.

Down by the Hers, three columns of allied soldiers made slow progress through even worse terrain. Wellington's orders looked simple on paper: '*The fourth and sixth divisions of infantry... will proceed in a direction which has been pointed out to Marshal Beresford, until they are far enough advanced to be enabled to act against the right flank of the French position; they are then to ascend the heights and to attack the enemy*'.[37]

The fourth division had been on the move since midnight, and the sixth, like Taupin's, since three. Now they found themselves struggling through the marshy ground between the river and the ridge, up to their waists in water and mud. They were mostly out of range of the French artillery, but it was still a long, unnerving march across the enemy field of fire.

Soult watched their progress from his new vantage point at La Sipière, and Taupin and Rey soon joined him. The allied columns drew level with the redoubt and abruptly wheeled into line. Twelve thousand men began to labour up the muddy slopes. They were a colourful sight: a blend of English, Irish and Welsh regiments in their scarlet tunics; the Scottish in their kilts; the menacing black uniforms of a company of Brunswickers; the Portuguese infantry in blue and their elite light infantry – the *caçadores* – wisely dressed in dark brown.

Soult foresaw his opportunity. If he waited for the leading brigades to come close enough and then attacked them from the

---

37 Gurwood, John. *The Dispatches of Field Marshal the Duke of Wellington during his various campaigns in India, Denmark, Portugal, Spain, The Low Countries, and France. Volume the Seventh.* London: William Clowes and Sons, 1845 (page 422).

flanks, he could cut them off and destroy over four thousand men. He ordered Taupin to take Rey's brigade to the right of the redoubt and wait out of sight just below the ridge. When he gave the signal, they were to attack from that direction. Meanwhile, the other half of Taupin's division prepared for a similar move from the left, and six squadrons of cavalry joined the two ambush parties. When the trap was sprung, the leading allied brigades would be caught between the guns of the redoubt above them, Taupin's infantry on each flank, and then the cavalry would finish them off.

Today, the site of La Sipière is occupied by the bland buildings of the Jean Macé primary school, but I find a better spot from which to appreciate the imminent action when I walk a hundred paces down the Avenue Raymond Naves. All my previous visits to the city have left me with the impression that Toulouse is flat, but here the road drops sharply. With a cyclist's sensitivity to gradients, I estimate the slope at about twelve per cent, or one-in-eight. On the northern and eastern boundary of the school playground a retaining wall rises nearly as high as the ramparts of Revel. It is easy to picture the place as a redoubt from which Soult patiently observed the progress of the allied soldiers. They were struggling further up the steep hill and deeper into danger. It was nearly time!

Soult turned to Taupin and cried, *'Here they are, General Taupin! Here they are! I'll leave them to you; they're ours!'* [38] All the troops within earshot echoed his words. *'They're ours!'* This would be an easy victory. Thousands of allied soldiers would soon be dead, wounded or taken prisoner.

Presumably Soult expected Taupin to follow the plan. Perhaps he forgot the man's reputation for being brave to the point of reckless, a general who led from the front in a charge and was last man in the rearguard during a retreat.

---

38 Translated from : Lapène, Edouard. *Evènements Militaires devant Toulouse en 1814* (page 74)

'They're ours!' The men's excitement was too much for General Taupin, and waiting a little longer to attack the enemy's flank would delay the action. Instead, he charged down the centre of the hill straight towards the allied lines, and Jean-Pierre Rey and his three thousand men slid down the slope behind him, a swirling torrent of blue and white uniforms and bobbing black helmets.

The French guns on La Sipière fell silent; they could no longer fire without risk of hitting their own men. Why hadn't Taupin attacked from the flank? Even taking account of the man's character, this was a shocking error of judgement for an old soldier who had survived Marengo, Austerlitz, Jena and more than a dozen other Napoleonic battles. It was an error of judgement which meant he would not survive this one.

The allied infantry halted, stunned by Taupin's mad charge centre stage and perturbed by the sight of French cavalry prowling in the wings. The Cameron Highlanders swiftly formed a defensive square against the threat of the mounted troops to their right, and the other regiments prepared to repulse Taupin and his foot soldiers with lead ball or steel bayonet.

Suddenly, a couple of Congreve artillery rockets exploded among Rey's charging brigade. This was a frightening new weapon few of them had seen before, and they hesitated. The allied soldiers took heart and opened fire.

How close were the combatants at this point? The effective range of the smoothbore muskets used by both sides was about a hundred metres, and Captain Lapène laments that none of the allied shots missed their target. In contrast, only the men in Rey's leading battalion could fire back. When the front ranks fell, the excitement of those further down the line turned to dismay and panic, and they began to scatter. This was not the easy victory they were expecting.

Taupin knew he had bungled. He tried to rally his troops and restore their confidence by doing what he always did: he put himself in the most perilous position possible – at the head of the front rank.

Unfortunately for Taupin, the allied divisions included several rifle companies, and rifles were much more accurate than muskets. In a letter to his minister of war, Soult once complained that in battle the allied marksmen were expressly ordered to aim for officers and generals. Exposed at the head of his men, Taupin was an obvious target for rifle or musket. Three bullets brought him to the ground, and Rey's brigade fled back up the hill carrying the injured Taupin with them. If only they could reach the safety of the redoubt, they would be able to draw breath and regroup without someone trying to shoot them in the back. Behind them, the allies broke their formation and gave chase.

We can only guess what General Rey was thinking about his foolhardy superior officer during his scrabble up the hill, but we can assume he shared the reaction of the rest of the army to the calamity that followed. In the words of Captain Lapène, '*a deplorable weakness, impossible to predict, took hold of the troops defending La Sipière*'.[39]

The redoubt was defended by a battalion of the ninth infantry regiment, an elite unit which had proved its courage many times during the Peninsular War, but their depleted ranks had been bolstered by conscripts who were facing enemy fire for the first time. These raw recruits watched with horror as the allies chased Rey's three thousand men up the hill. It was too much for them to bear. They fled.

The terror of the conscripts was just as infectious as the earlier excitement which had caused Taupin to lose his head and launch his crazy attack. All the defenders bolted and they paid no heed to General Dauture who yelled at them to come back. By the time Rey and his brigade struggled to the top of La Sipière, Soult had

39 Translated from : Lapène, Edouard. *Evènements Militaires devant Toulouse en 1814* (page 77).

no choice but to order a general retreat towards his next line of defence down towards the Canal du Midi.

Left on Mont Calvinet without orders, Captain Lapène decided to take his battery down to the rallying point near the Cambon's house and cover the retreat with his cannons. He recalls the bitterness of the moment. *'This irreparable loss was for us like a bolt of lightning, and we refused to believe in a misfortune which was only too real; we were forced therefore to see all our hopes vanish in an instant, and to abandon thoughts of a victory which seemed assured. This sacrifice, as cruel as it was unexpected, caused the whole army the most bitter regret.'*[40]

Captain Lapène was not the only person keeping a close eye on the retreat from La Sipière. By now the Battle of Toulouse had become a grotesque spectator sport, and the reaction of the home crowd was, perhaps, even more demoralising for the French army than the loss of the redoubt.

'At the first sound of cannons,' writes Lapène, *'the citizens of Toulouse hid themselves away in their homes... Before long the only movement in the streets came from the wounded trying to drag themselves towards the hospitals, or ambulances sited in the squares... Fear and anxiety mounted with each passing minute...but when the inhabitants had recovered from their initial fright they risked satisfying their curiosity...they rushed into the streets and squares; several climbed onto the ramparts; and a few even began to explore the battlefield. But most of them perched on roofs or church towers, silent spectators waiting impatiently for the outcome of this terrifying struggle.*

'At the moment when the allies, masters of La Sipière, appeared on the heels of Taupin's division, at this moment a portion of the inhabitants, whose views and characters disposed them towards the enemy, revealed sympathies which until then they had kept to

40 Translated from : Lapène, Edouard. *Evènements Militaires devant Toulouse en 1814* (page 77).

themselves...when the English...appeared on the heights of La Sipière, these unworthy French people gave a joyful shout.' [41]

Out of fairness to the people of Toulouse, Captain Lapène adds that this reaction was limited to a very small number of onlookers. Others, who longed for peace but not one dictated by the allies, watched the enemy's progress in gloomy silence. As for the bulk of the crowd, which was made up of the poor with nothing to lose whatever the outcome, they turned the battle into a show and noisily speculated about what would happen next.

Amid the noise of the battle and preoccupied by their retreat, Rey and his brigade may not have heard the reaction of the spectators, although Captain Lapène was so incensed he probably told them as soon as they joined him at the Cambon's house. I can picture Jean-Pierre Rey contemplating the crowd on the ramparts with an expression similar to the one he wears in the only portrait I have found of him: it shows a thin-faced man with curly black hair cut short, and the arch of his eyebrows and set of his mouth lend him a look of disdain.

As for Taupin, he didn't have much time to think about anything. He and La Sipière had fallen at around nine-thirty. By ten, Rey's brigade had stretchered him back to the Cambon's house. By eleven, he was dead.

Another spectator rejoiced when he saw the fall of La Sipière. Wellington watched it through his spyglass, and once his men were in control he galloped up to the redoubt with his general staff. It was the first time he had beheld Toulouse from on high and he gave a cry of admiration. He may also have blessed his good fortune: thanks to General Taupin the allies had captured La

41 Translated from : Lapène, Edouard. *Campagne de 1813 et de 1814 sur l'Ebre, les Pyrénées et la Garonne.* Paris: Chez Ridan, 1823 (pages 405-406).

Sipière with extraordinary ease, and now they could bring up their artillery and fire onto the redoubts of Mont Calvinet to the north.

According to Captain Lapène this was the turning point of the battle. Until now, the French had resisted allied attacks on other points around the city, and they had almost destroyed the Spanish divisions below Mont Calvinet. If Taupin had followed Soult's plan, the battle may have reached a stalemate before lunchtime. Of course such conjecture is academic and, as we shall see, the outcome of the battle proved to be irrelevant to the political futures of both Britain and France.

After the fall of La Sipière, both sides paused for a couple of hours to regroup. At midday, fresh fighting broke out all around the city. From La Sipière the British artillery covered a succession of attacks on Mont Calvinet, and this was the deadliest area of the whole battle for the French army. At around four o'clock Soult realised that sooner or later Mont Calvinet would fall, and to prevent its defenders and their artillery falling into enemy hands, he ordered them to abandon all five redoubts and retreat towards the Canal du Midi.

Soon afterwards, the allied guns fell silent and the battle came to a virtual standstill. Beresford's fourth division had received orders to capture the area defended by Rey and his brigade, but they made no move. They were exhausted after sixteen hours on the move and the assault on La Sipière. A tacit truce reigned over the city, and without the stupidity of some of Rey's men, that may have been the end of the battle. Instead, hotheads in his forty-third infantry regiment fired off a few extra rounds despite orders to the contrary, and this brought the allied guns back to life. Fusillades and cannonades continued until nightfall and, according to one source, the last shot was fired at nine o'clock in the evening. Jean-Pierre Rey's eighteen-hour day of battle was over.

Despite the fall of the redoubts, the first day of fighting had been indecisive. The French army was weakened, but intact.

Wellington had gained ground, but he had captured no cannons and seized no standards. Toulouse remained a formidable fortress protected by its ramparts, river and canal.

When Wellington received his casualty figures that evening, he learned that 593 of his men were dead and 4,046 were wounded. Later he would learn that French losses were 321 dead and 2,369 wounded, figures that would one day be used by some French historians to support their contention that Soult had won the battle.

As for Jean-Pierre Rey, he had been injured in other battles – Arcole Bridge, Castricum and Talavera – but as far as we know, he came through 10 April 1814 unscathed apart from his wounded pride. The question was, would he and his men survive a second day of battle, or would they finish up as dead as Taupin? The lives of nearly a hundred thousand soldiers, and the future of Toulouse and the safety of all its citizens, depended on what Wellington and Soult chose to do next.

46

Retreat into the Lauragais

As soon as the guns fell silent, Soult began a four-hour council of war with his high command. The French army was strong enough to defend Toulouse for months, but there were also 50,000 civilians to take into account, many of whom would prefer to see their city surrendered intact to the allies rather than destroyed by a lengthy siege.

Soult and his generals voted unanimously to do what they had been doing for months: continue their retreat and preserve an army which might still serve the empire, or a new kingdom, because by now they too had heard the rumours. In a letter Soult had addressed to Suchet in Narbonne on 7 April, he mentioned the disturbing news that the allies had entered Paris.

There was only one escape route still open to Soult's army: down the Canal du Midi and through the Lauragais, but for the first few kilometres they would have to pass right beneath the noses of the enemy up on the heights of Mont Calvinet and La Sipière. Retreat required subterfuge, and only Soult's inner circle knew what was planned.

At four o'clock in the morning on 11 April, Jean-Pierre Rey and most of the French army were ready and waiting for the signal to go into action for a second day. At first light they could see the allies were also ready for battle. Both armies waited, either for the order to attack, or for the other side to make the first move. They carried on waiting.

The citizens of Toulouse woke to an eerie silence, and it continued throughout the day. They watched the immobilised armies from the same viewpoints they had used the day before, and the more adventurous strayed as far as the front lines.

This stillness was deceptive, and behind the scenes there was frantic activity on the French side. Before dawn, Soult had begun to evacuate his wounded by barge down the Canal du Midi towards Castelnaudary. The arsenal and magazines and supply depots inside the city were stripped bare, and the troops given what new clothing could be found. Late in the evening of the 11 April, thirty thousand men slipped out of town along the south-west bank of the Canal du Midi.

In the dark hours before dawn, the allies watched the bivouac fires in the French lines go out one by one. At sunrise they sent out reconnaissance parties, fearful of an ambush, but the French positions were deserted.

Later that morning, Wellington and his troops entered the city to cries of *'Vivent les anglais!'*, *'Vive Louis XVIII!'* and *'Vivent les Bourbons!'* In the Place du Capitole the crowds tore down the bust of Napoleon and dragged it towards the river. Ladies distributed white royalist cockades from their baskets, and inside the Capitole building even the city officials wore the royalist symbol when they welcomed the allied commander-in-chief. Inside the Salle des Illustres, Wellington was visibly perturbed. He warned the assembled dignitaries that their royalist zeal was premature, and perhaps dangerous to their persons; he was still waiting for news from Paris, and a peace treaty with Napoleon remained a possibility; the return of the king was by no means certain.

Wellington's own behaviour was more prudent. He cannot have been blind to Soult's preparations for departure, but if the rumours of Napoleon's downfall and the imminent return of an anglophile monarch proved to be true, then a destructive siege of one of the new kingdom's largest cities would be a poor start to a promising new relationship. On the other hand, if the rumours proved to be false, the allies would soon catch up with Soult in a less well-defended position where they could make more effective use of their numerical superiority and crush the French army once and for all.

This state of uncertainty was ended within a matter of hours by the arrival of two colonels – one English and one French. They carried dispatches and newspapers from Paris: Napoleon had abdicated unconditionally on 6 April, Louis XVIII had been declared king, and the provisional government had ordered all the armies of France to suspend hostilities. The messengers had left Paris on 7 April, but they reached Toulouse too late to prevent the battle. Even now their arrival did not mark the end of hostilities. Soult's army remained a danger until or unless its leader signed an armistice and swore allegiance to the new regime. If Soult and other leading generals refused to obey their new orders, there was a risk France would descend into civil war.

By now, Wellington's troops were scouting the roads towards Baziège, Revel and Caraman in search of the enemy. Both armies were heading deeper into the Lauragais, and when I start to retrace their steps, I soon discover another English Cemetery closer to Toulouse than the one in Saint-Félix.

Baziège, you may recall, lies on the route followed by the Black Prince, and its church shelters the stone that marked the fifteenth

Roman mile from Toulouse. It was a vital point on Soult's road to safety, because this was where he was most likely to find his way blocked by the allies.

From Toulouse, the French army marched along the southern bank of the Canal du Midi while the allies patrolled the hills on the other side of the canal and the Hers. Along the way, Soult's engineers blew up the bridges to keep the allies at a safe distance, but at Baziège they planned to cross the canal and the river, and then follow the old Roman road towards Castelnaudary. To protect this crossing point, Soult posted infantry and cavalry units in the hills above Baziège to stop the allies attacking the long column of his retreating army.

One wet and windy morning I take up a similar position in the chapel of Sainte-Colombe, two kilometres north-east of Baziège. It is a squat brick building with a modest bell-gable at one end, and it also has a porch which shelters me from the inclement weather. On the wall of the porch is a brief account of a cavalry clash that took place in the surrounding fields on 12 April 1814, and I am also carrying a more detailed version which was written by a local historian, Yvan Rousselet, to mark the bicentenary of the two bloody skirmishes which some locals refer to as the Battle of Baziège.

Unlike the mounted men two centuries ago, my only weapons are a pair of binoculars and a camera, and I use them to study and record my surroundings. The chapel is encircled by green fields of wheat. Looking towards Baziège, I can just make out the Château de La Motte and its farm buildings hiding among the trees of the park. On 12 April 1814, that is where a detachment of men from Soult's seventy-fifth infantry regiment was stationed. It was lunchtime, and they were enjoying a couple of barrels of good wine and waiting for the chickens they had requisitioned to finish roasting over the fire.

I turn my binoculars north-west. Steep slopes of wheat and

brushwood climb towards tree-lined hilltops, and that's where two squadrons of Wellington's cavalry rode into sight, around three hundred men and horses. Below them they could see the dust raised by Soult's army as it marched along the old Roman road. Nearer to hand – perhaps a kilometre away – they spotted the French infantry and maybe smelled their lunch. What they failed to see were the four hundred men of the tenth light cavalry hiding in a wood a kilometre further east.

The allied cavalrymen began to pick their way down the slope. At the château, the lookouts raised the alarm. Wine and chicken were forgotten and the soldiers grabbed what they could from the farm buildings and threw up a barricade. The allied horsemen crossed a stream and formed into two lines. They trotted past the chapel and then broke into a gallop and thundered across the field towards the château.

At a hundred paces the infantry opened fire, and the next moment the French cavalry attacked the allies from the flank and the rear. The allies beat a swift retreat back up the hill, where more squadrons of their own cavalry had just arrived. Overkeen to avenge their fleeing comrades, these fresh cavalrymen followed the same route down the hill without waiting for the retreating squadrons to reform. Another skirmish followed, this time nearer the chapel. The allies were forced to retreat for a second time, carrying their injured and abandoning their dead. As for the French, they found themselves masters of a blood-soaked field and, presumably, of some badly-burned chicken.

Twenty-five French cavalrymen died in the two skirmishes and about the same number were wounded, six of whom died later. Fifty-two allied cavalrymen perished, a figure which may or may not include eight men who succumbed to their injuries after the battle. The number of allied wounded is not known.

The next day – 13 April – the mayor of Baziège mobilised the local population to clear the battlefield. They buried their own dead in a communal trench in the graveyard of Sainte-Colombe. As for their enemies, the local priest refused to have them interred in the grounds of his chapel. This was reportedly on the orders of his bishop, and it is unclear if the objection was due to the nationality of the dead, or because they might be Protestants. Instead, the allied corpses were buried in their own communal grave near the site of the first skirmish by the château's farm. Ever since it has been known as *le cimetière des anglais*, and for around a hundred years the British Army paid the landowner to leave it fallow. The practice became a habit and the land remains untilled to this day. I have heard that the current owners are unwelcoming to visitors so I have no intention of knocking on their door. This is no great loss because I have already seen from photos that the cemetery is every bit as disappointing up close as it is through my binoculars from afar. If it were not for the two cypress trees, I would mistake it for a rubbish dump: a couple of yellow skips, numerous piles of logs, the occasional tree trunk, a mound of asphalt, a mound of uncertain composition overgrown with green grass, great lumps of broken concrete, unidentifiable bits of metal, and what may be the carcase of a portacabin or a railway carriage.

It is a sorry sight, disrespectful perhaps, the burial ground of some of the last allied soldiers to die fighting in the Lauragais. But who were they?

The information board in the chapel's porch claims they were from the fifth dragoons, a British regiment. The longer account I have brought with me adds in a squadron of the eighteenth hussars for the second skirmish. But Wellington's orders issued on 11 April 1814 and repeated the following morning instructed Ponsonby's brigade, which normally included the fifth dragoons, to stay near Toulouse. Two other cavalry brigades were to gallop into the Lauragais: Lord Somerset and his men were to ride towards Caraman and Albi; Vivian's brigade was ordered to '*move upon Labastide-Beauvoir, and to endeavour to disturb the enemy line of communication in the direction of Baziège and Villefranche*'.[42]

I check the position of these towns on my map. Labastide-Beauvoir lies three kilometres to the north of Sainte-Colombe, the direction from which the allied cavalry appeared. Both local geography and Wellington's orders suggest they were from Colonel Vivian's brigade, so who was in it? For a start, not the colonel because he had been injured in a skirmish at La Croix-Daurade on 8 April. There was a new man in charge at Sainte-Colombe: Lieutenant-Colonel Friedrich von Arentschildt who, as his name suggests, was German. He had two regiments under his command: an anglo-irish unit called the eighteenth hussars; and the first hussars of the King's German Legion. The latter was one of three German regiments in Wellington's army, all of them cavalry and all of them filled with men who had abandoned their homes for England after Napoleon had occupied the Electorate of Hanover in 1803.

I stare at the battlefield from the shelter of the chapel and ask myself if the English Cemetery of Sainte-Colombe deserves its name. I cannot rid my mind of a conversation from long ago, an exchange overheard by the Count of Montbel on the streets of Toulouse shortly after Soult's army retreated into the Lauragais. The count was standing beside a husband and wife, and they were watching a highland regiment march past in their kilts.

'Aren't they handsome?' said the wife. 'I would be so proud if our Alfred could enlist in their regiment. It would give him such a fine air.'

'Impossible,' said her husband.

'Why's that?'

'To join a Scottish regiment you definitely have to be Irish.'[43]

I have a hunch that the worldly count may have been mocking his less-cosmopolitan compatriots. I have another hunch that

42 Gurwood, John (page 423).
43 Translated from : Montbel, Guy de (page 99).

whoever gave this dump of a burial ground its name may have been as confused as Alfred's parents about the nationalities serving in Wellington's army. Worst of all, these hunches set off nagging doubts about *le cimetière des anglais* at Saint-Félix-Lauragais.

During the weeks that follow, I meet or correspond with several local historians. For reasons which will become apparent, I shall not identify them.

The information I glean is often contradictory and rarely matches my English-language texts. One of my first correspondents assures me he has documents to hand which prove the fifth dragoons fought at Sainte-Colombe, but when I suggest that perhaps we could meet to compare our sources, his documents suddenly go missing: he has lent them to someone but cannot remember to whom. Then someone tells me the British military authorities carried out excavations at Sainte-Colombe in the 1960s or 1970s, but unfortunately left no trace of their findings. Confusingly, this same person then adds that among the objects found at Sainte-Colombe were fragments of a type of sabre called the Blücher, a model used by the British hussars, light dragoons and the King's German Legion. When I repeat this story to another contact, he asserts that the only excavations ever carried out in *le cimetière des anglais* at Sainte-Colombe were clandestine and illegal, and that whatever was found undoubtedly disappeared into private collections. He also explains that the dead of Sainte-Colombe were unusual for battlefield casualties of the time. When an army buried its dead during long campaigns, the corpses were stripped of uniforms, footwear, insignia, and anything else that could be reused. But at Sainte-Colombe, the people of Baziège interred the allied corpses in the uniforms they were wearing when they died, so there would almost certainly have been something for the grave-robbers to discover.

When I mull over the various articles, emails, notes and recordings of my research into Sainte-Colombe, it occurs to me that the elusive evidence which supposedly proves these fallen men were from the fifth dragoons may have been among the artefacts unearthed during those illicit excavations. If so, I for one will never see them.

Is any of this relevant to the other English cemetery, the one closer to my home? Maybe, because after the two rounds of bloody fighting in the field by the chapel of Sainte-Colombe, the allied cavalry rode off to Saint-Félix-Lauragais carrying their injured with them. Later that day there was another skirmish down in Baziège between the French tenth light cavalry and, unquestionably this time, the first hussars of the King's German Legion. This was probably the last clash between the two armies, and the Germans captured twenty-seven men and twenty-five horses and chased the enemy down the Roman road as far as Villenouvelle. I have no casualty figures, but if some of the German troopers were injured in this action, they too may have been carried to Saint-Félix.

The story of Sainte-Colombe leaves me restless and dissatisfied. Perhaps I shall find peace in the engineer's house at Naurouze.

47

THE LAST BATTLE

When I came to Naurouze to see Riquet's monument a couple of months ago, the weather was cold and windy. How sunshine and the first days of summer can transform a place! Naurouze is unrecognisable. Hikers and bikers, cyclists and car drivers, they have all stopped for a break or a visit, and I even spot a bemused coachload of tourists wondering why the gates to the stones of Naurouze are locked. I resist the temptation to offer a facetious explanation involving the end of the world; instead, I make for the engineer's house and Spark's terrace where I grab a table in the shade of a giant plane tree and order a drink.

It is a soothing spot. The Rigole de la Plaine drowns out all other background noise, and the waiter's returning footsteps are inaudible, even on gravel. He startles me when he sets down a glass of beer brewed in Carcassonne. I take a mouthful and idly wonder what Soult drank when he paused here on 13 April 1814, the same day the people of Baziège were burying the dead troopers at Sainte-Colombe. Captain Lapène recalls how, that morning, news of an impending peace had begun to spread among the retreating troops. '*Little by little these rumours gathered credibility and they were passed from mouth to mouth through the ranks bringing with them an overdue ray of hope. Colonel Gordon, Wellington's first aide-de-camp, appeared moments later; he was escorting a French officer (Colonel Saint-Simon), sent by the provisional government, and he carried documents of the highest importance.*'[44]

The two officers crossed the French lines and were brought to meet Soult somewhere near where I am sitting. They handed over dispatches from the new minister of war, and Parisian newspapers covering events in the capital since 31 March.

Soult and his staff held an immediate council-of-war. I picture them sitting over there at the long table outside the engineer's front door, poring over the documents and passing them from hand to hand. Were they fakes? They studied them more closely and their decision was unanimous: there was no proof these documents were genuine; they could be the work of the allies.

'*Go and tell Lord Wellington,*' Soult told Colonel Gordon, '*that I can give no credence to news of peace if that news is given to me by the commander of the army I am fighting. You can add that I'm ready to give him ten more battles, all on the same scale as Toulouse, and at the end of them, if our losses continue in the same proportion as in the past, he and I will both end up as generals without an army.*'[45]

Soult's actions were more reasonable than his words. He immediately dispatched an aide-de-camp to Paris to find out what was really going on, and then he sat down and wrote, or dictated, a less bellicose message to Wellington. He proposed a temporary truce until he had received something official directly from his emperor's government.

Somehow these events have given rise to another Naurouze legend, the idea that Soult and Wellington met in this idyllic spot

---

44 Translated from : Lapène, Edouard. *Evènements Militaires devant Toulouse en 1814* (page 117).

45 Translated from : Lapène, Edouard. *Evènements Militaires devant Toulouse en 1814* (page 118).

where I am drinking cold beer and signed their armistice. It is, I regret, as unlikely as all the other Naurouze myths.

Wellington's response arrived the next day: no truce until Soult swore allegiance to the new government. Despite this stand-off, neither side made a move to attack, and the Rigole de la Plaine remained an unofficial demarcation line separating the two armies. By now, Soult and most of his troops had moved further east to Castelnaudary, and there they waited for the return of their messenger. It was a drole state of affairs, but it would not be so funny if the two armies fought a second pointless battle, this time amid the rolling hills of the Lauragais.

Wellington began to lose patience. In a letter to a correspondent in Paris dated 15 April, he wrote: '*I wait only to give the troops some shoes, of which they are in much want, to continue my movement forward; and I propose to do everything in my power to make the officers and troops of Soult's army acquainted with the real situation of affairs*'.[46]

Presumably the new footwear arrived quickly, because the next day he gave his generals new orders: the two infantry divisions that had captured La Sipière would encamp around Saint-Félix-Lauragais where they would find themselves in the company of Arentschildt's cavalry brigade; Somerset's hussars would move upon Puylaurens and send out patrols towards Castres and Revel; Ponsonby's dragoons (which included the fifth) would move to Caraman; other divisions would take up positions around the new headquarters at Baziège; and the Spanish division would march on Labastide-Beauvoir.

On 17 April, the peaceful countryside of the Lauragais was disturbed by the sounds of an army on the move, men who were preparing for one last battle against Soult somewhere in the fields to the north of Castelnaudary. By evening they were all in position. Lieutenant George Woodberry – a young officer in

46 Gurwood, John (page 443).

the eighteenth hussars – recorded in his journal that evening: *'Everyone believes there will be a battle tomorrow because Lord Wellington is not prepared to negotiate any longer with Soult... We think several [French] regiments will desert this evening : orders have been given to allow them through our lines. People say that the French cavalry wish to have a personal encounter with the English cavalry on these fine plains so well-suited to such manoeuvres. I don't know if that is still their inclination, but, for my part, I ask for only one thing, that the eighteenth should come to blows with two of their finest regiments, and I promise they will be thoroughly thrashed'.*[47] (Woodberry's journal has been available in French for 130 years, but at the time of writing it has never been published in English. This extract and others that follow are my re-translations of the French translations, and therefore will match the sense of Woodberry's original text but not his exact words.)

George Woodberry and the French cavalry did not have their longed-for clash, and the less belligerent on both sides did not suffer the battle they were dreading. For once, the soil of the Lauragais escaped being soaked in more blood. Instead, on the evening of 18 April Woodberry opened his journal and wrote these words. '*Soult concluded an armistice this morning with Lord Wellington and we have been over to the French lines and chatted with their officers.*'[48]

Soult had finally got hold of a copy of orders issued by Napoleon's chief-of-staff on 9 April, and they left him in no doubt about the true situation in his country. On 19 and 20 April, copies of the armistice were shuttled back and forth along the Canal du Midi between Toulouse and Narbonne for signature by Wellington, Soult and Suchet, and the two French generals pledged their allegiance to the new government.

---

47 Translated from : Hélie, Georges (editor, translator). *Journal de Lieutenant Woodberry: Campagnes de Portugal et d'Espagne, de France, de Belgique et de France (1813-1815).* Paris: Librairie Plon, 1896 (page 201).

48 Translated from : Hélie, Georges (page 203).

It was nearly time for everyone to go home. Wellington's army stayed in Toulouse and the Lauragais for a few more weeks. It was a peaceful occupation, and the most notable incident was the murder of an Irish soldier in Ayguesvives during an argument over wine and women. By mid-May, the infantry regiments were on the road to Bordeaux for a sea passage, and George Woodberry set off with 9,000 other cavalrymen for a leisurely two-month ride to the Channel Ports. The only allied troops left behind in the Lauragais were the dead.

A week after the armistice, Soult was back at home in Saint-Amans-la-Bastide, a town which would later change its name to Saint-Amans-Soult in his honour. He was soon caught up in controversy. On 15 May 1814, Woodberry noted in his journal, '*It seems Marshal Soult is under arrest in Paris; they say he knew of Bonaparte's abdication and the state of affairs in Paris three days before the Battle of Toulouse and he could have avoided it*'.[49] Woodberry then expresses the hope that such a brave and capable general would know how to justify himself in the eyes of France and Europe. Woodberry's wish came true: instead of being punished, Soult was appointed minister of war and decorated by the new king, Louis XVIII.

As for Jean-Pierre Rey, he made an even smoother transition from serving an emperor to supporting a king. He was given a knighthood and appointed military commander for the department of Basses-Pyrénées (now called Pyrénées-Atlantique). He remained in post during Napoleon's Hundred Days, but after Waterloo he was placed on the reserve list and there he stayed for ten years. This left him at home in the Rue Foulimou with plenty of time on his hands, time to keep an eye on the builders when

49 Translated from : Hélie, Georges (page 217).

they started work on the new temple in 1818, time to relive those dreadful moments on La Sipière, time to wonder if, despite his personal disasters, he had been on the winning side on 10 April 1814.

The dispute over the outcome of the battle reached its height in 1837 when a French military engineer, Pierre-Marie Théodore Choumara, wrote a book in which he argued that because the allies lost more men, and because Soult remained in control of Toulouse and merely lost some defensive positions outside the city, the French army was victorious. When Wellington was shown the book, he predictably wrote a long and indignant rebuttal.

At first sight this argument may seem as pointless as the battle, but at the time Choumara was writing his book, the symbolic importance of the Battle of Toulouse was steadily growing with every passing year of peace between the two nations. When Queen Elizabeth visited *la ville rose* in 2004, it was not because of an overwhelming desire to meet the Lamberts and learn about *pastel*. She came to Toulouse because the city has come to represent the past and the present of the often tempestuous relationship between Britain and France.

To explain why, I shall go back to 1066 when William the Conqueror muddied the waters separating the kingdom of England from the realm of France. As Duke of Normandy, he was a vassal of the French king; as King of England, he became his equal. Matters worsened ninety years later when Eleanor of Aquitaine left her husband, Louis VII of France, married Henry II of England, and took all her domains with her to create a situation where the English king ruled the greater part of France. For nearly eight centuries the two nations were usually at war, and occasionally in a state of uneasy peace, as they vied for control of France and other parts of Europe. The twenty-six years between the start of the French Revolution and the downfall of Napoleon was one of the most intense periods of this long conflict.

In 1815, the two countries fought their last ever battle near an insignificant village in Belgium, but the Battle of Toulouse in 1814 was the last time they fought each other on French soil. There was no doubt about the outcome of Waterloo, and no immediate prospect of avenging defeat on the battlefield, and this perhaps encouraged some French veterans to salvage national pride by claiming victory in that last battle on home soil against the hereditary enemy. Fortunately, this dispute did nothing to prevent a gradual improvement in relations between the two countries throughout the remainder of the nineteenth century, and the transition from enemies to allies was cemented in 1904 when they signed a series of agreements known as the Entente Cordiale, the friendly understanding. It was to celebrate the centenary of this alliance that Queen Elizabeth made a three-day state visit to France in 2004. Toulouse was an obvious destination, the city where the two countries fought their last battle on French soil, and where today they build passenger jets with the help of their German and Spanish friends.

In the height of summer I return to the English Cemetery at Saint-Félix-Lauragais. The land is parched and overcooked, and the triangle of grass between the cypress trees has lost its colour. I sit down and lean back in the shade of the stoutest trunk. My eyelids droop and I breathe in an air of tranquillity. This is a place to reflect or remember without the intervention of man-made distractions. Compared with a traditional cemetery, such as the one across the valley on the edge of Saint-Félix, this one is puritanical in the extreme. There are no funerary monuments, no stone or iron crosses, no photographs or silk flowers, no laments engraved by the living to mourn the dead. Apart from the cypress trees, the only clue to its sombre status is the granite stele erected by the Friends of Napoleonic Heritage.

I open my eyes and re-read the words on the plaque and mentally check my translation. '*Here lie some English soldiers.*' Or perhaps not. I recite what in recent days has become my favourite quote, words said about the Duke of Wellington by the Irish nationalist Daniel O'Connell: '*The poor old Duke! What shall I say of him? To be sure he was born in Ireland, but being born in a stable does not make a man a horse.*'

By the same token, I have come to realise, being buried in *le cimetière des anglais* does not make a man English, neither here nor at Sainte-Colombe. According to what seems to be no more than oral tradition, around forty cavalrymen wounded in the various skirmishes near Baziège were cared for in a makeshift hospital in a barn below Saint-Félix, and eight of them subsequently died. They have always been referred to as *les anglais*, but in truth they may have been English, German, Irish, or perhaps a mixture of all three. To add to the confusion, there was also the fortieth foot, a regiment raised in Somerset and part of Cole's fourth division that had fought on the slopes of La Sipière. When Wellington moved his troops into the Lauragais on 17 April 1814, the fortieth bivouacked on the ridge near the English Cemetery and stayed around Saint-Félix for several weeks. Maybe some of these infantrymen succumbed to wounds or sickness and were buried here.

I look beyond the memorial plaque to the main cemetery on the other side of the valley. Why weren't they buried over there? Presumably because Sainte-Colombe and Saint-Félix were in the same diocese, so both priests would have received the same instructions from the same bishop about refusing to inter the enemy dead among the graves of French Catholics.

A few days ago I visited Pierre-Alain Buvry, the man who reclaimed this simple cemetery from an overgrown and forgotten corner of the Lauragais. He also erected the stele and organised a ceremony in honour of the dead, complete with a squad of enthusiasts dressed in Napoleonic uniforms. One of them was

Monsieur Buvry himself, and photographs of the event illustrate the astonishing weight of gold braid that adorned a general's uniform in those days.

Monsieur Buvry's château in Vallègue was once the home of a genuine Napoleonic general, Count Jean-Dominique Compans, making it a fitting residence for the current owner who is the departmental representative of the Amis du Patrimoine Napoléonien, an association dedicated to preserving Napoleonic heritage. It is also another historic home where you can rent a room for the night.

When we first met at the gates of his château, I was disappointed to find Monsieur Buvry dressed in his gardening clothes. I was also taken aback by his greeting. *'Je n'aime pas les anglais.'* I was there on a mission so I smiled and soon established that the reason he does not like the English had nothing to do with me personally. Monsieur Buvry is among those who believe that Napoleon is not buried inside Les Invalides, Paris, but is in fact hidden underneath an anonymous slab somewhere in the floor of Westminster Abbey, London. Oh perfidious Albion!

Once inside the château, I discovered a treasure-trove of Napoleonic books, paintings and other memorabilia which more than compensated for my host's casual attire, and he talked with an enthusiasm that soon made me forget those dubious words of welcome. He regaled me with numerous tales of skulduggery involving bits, or in some cases large chunks, of Napoleonic heritage, and eventually we reached the subject of Saint-Félix-Lauragais.

I related what I had heard from one source: excavations were carried out there by volunteers thirty or forty years ago; each cypress tree marked the resting place of two English soldiers; the remains of equipment unearthed with the skeletons proved all the dead were cavalrymen.

There were three parts to Monsieur Buvry's rebuttal. First, to his knowledge no excavations have ever been carried out in *le cimetière des anglais* at Saint-Félix, officially or unofficially. Second, when he and his team were clearing the cemetery and preparing the stele, they probed the topsoil and found that in most areas it was only ten or twenty centimetres thick; there may however be a communal grave somewhere in the south-east corner where the bedrock lies deeper. Third, he reminded me of something I already knew: any corpses would have been buried with virtually nothing, making it extremely difficult to identify their regiment or nationality.

After I had bid a cordial farewell to Monsieur Buvry, it struck me as ironic that a man who professes a dislike of the English has done more than anyone to preserve *le cimetière des anglais* at Saint-Félix-Lauragais. He told me he would do the same at Sainte-Colombe if it were not on private ground.

These thoughts bring me back to the present, and I stand up and pace among the cypress trees. Usually I find their presence benevolent and protective, but today they are like prison guards hemming me in. So much uncertainty, too few facts, so much fake news. I kick the dusty soil in the centre of the triangle of dead grass. Is the rock really that close to the surface? The conclusive means of solving the mystery of *le cimetière des anglais* is obvious: a bulldozer would soon determine if there were any bones, and DNA testing might be able to identify their origin. Unfortunately, there are two problems. First, this kind of excavation requires authorisation from the Regional Director of Cultural Affairs, and permits are only granted to professional archaeologists such as those investigating the ruins of Roquefort. Second, this type of intervention is expensive, and in an area blessed with so much history, archaeologists and budget holders are spoilt for choice. Why would the possible presence of a few dead *anglais* be of interest to the French authorities?

I stand up and prepare to leave because there is nothing more I can do here today, or tomorrow. The truth will remain hidden, and on reflection I prefer it that way. Over the years, I have come here so many times I have acquired a sense of ownership. I am English and this is my cemetery. I want my graveyard to keep its air of mystery and romance. I want it to guard the identity of those unknown soldiers. If someone digs them up, I risk being dispossessed. This peaceful graveyard might become *le cimetière des allemands.*

Part IX

A Deadly Occupation

48

AT HOME IN THE CHÂTEAU

It is two o'clock in the morning and we are celebrating Claude's seventieth birthday. We are in Le Salon des Ancêtres where portraits of his wife's family hang on the walls. The air is filled with disco music from – appropriately enough – the seventies, and the parquet creaks under dozens of pairs of dancing feet. I keep half an eye on the dangerously gyrating limbs, but mostly my attention strays to an enormous mirror on the wall, not out of narcissism, but because I keep thinking of the portrait of Hitler that once hung in its place and watched over the men of the eleventh panzer division while they ate their meals in this room. In the mirror I see a forest of raised arms, and momentarily I imagine they are raised in Nazi salutes. Of course I know they are semaphoring the letters Y-M-C-A.

For a moment these celebrations strike me as anachronistic and incongruous, but they also remind me that history in this part of the world is not locked away inside a glass cabinet in the bowels of a dead museum. It is alive through the people and their homes, and my hostess Marie-Christine is the seventeenth generation of the same family to reside in the Château de Garrevaques. Her grandchildren are running around somewhere too.

The music fades and the dancers lower their weary arms. Their respite is brief, and one ever-popular, eternally-irritating song is followed by another tune from the days of glitterballs and feverish Saturday nights. I escape through giant French windows onto the terrace for some air and a look at the grounds. A few hours ago we stood here in the evening sunlight and drank champagne. Now I lean on the balustrade with a glass of red, and from behind me, light spills out through the open doors across the terrace, down the steps and into the park, far enough to reveal the ancient oak tree planted at a time when Columbus was still learning to sail.

Beyond the giant oak, the park is filled with long shadows from an even longer past. The Château de Garrevaques has had a troubled history: first established by Jourdain de Roquefort's descendants as a defensive home in dangerous times; besieged during the Wars of Religion; destroyed during the Revolution; rebuilt in the nineteenth century with the comforts of central heating and running water; requisitioned during the second world war; and finally, steered towards tourism at the end of the twentieth century.

I am partying in a place that epitomises the history of the Lauragais.

I turn away from the park and look up at one of the towers. Above its dark slate roof the sky is luminescent with stars, and I offer up a prayer of thanks to Jules the gardener.

At the time of the Albigensian Crusade, the Roqueforts were the most powerful family in my part of the Lauragais. From the Castrum de Roquefort and the Château de Montgey, they dominated or owned most of the territory around them. In 1470, one of Jourdain's descendants built a new château between these two centres of family power. Garrevaques lies on the plain, four kilometres from Montgey and around ten from the Montagne Noire.

Many years ago, I caught my first glimpse of the Château de Garrevaques towards the end of a long bike ride on a hot dusty day. I crossed a bridge over the Sor and something caught my eye through the trees. I propped my bicycle against a wall and peered through wrought iron gates. Although my view was partly obscured by bushes, I could see pink bricks, dark grey roof tiles, and tall windows flanked by bright white shutters. By repeatedly adjusting my position, I managed to piece these fragments together into the shape of an elegantly symmetrical façade. The central body of the château was flanked by two octagonal towers each crowned by a pointed roof, and a decorative outline of creamy stucco marked the intersection between slate and brick. Balustraded ramps led up from the foot of each tower to meet on a wide central terrace in front of three lofty pairs of French windows. Below the terrace, three glazed arches each the size of a double garage door illuminated what I guessed would be the kitchens and store rooms in the *sous-sol* or basement.

The park was peaceful and there was no sign of human activity. I gave free rein to my imagination, and I populated the terrace with distinguished guests gathered for a birthday party or a wedding. Of course they were drinking champagne, and when the moon came up, the countess or her daughter would play Debussy on the piano.

Riding a road bike on a hot day is fine as long as you keep moving, but without the artificial wind of my forward motion my body began to glow like a furnace. My jersey clung to my flesh and I remembered that men in sweaty cycle clothing acquire an odour which others may find unpleasant. This château was no place for me. I belonged with the unwashed rabble outside the gates of Versailles.

My eyebrows failed to cope with the sweat running down from under my helmet. My eyes stung from the salt, and I turned away and retrieved my bicycle. I pedalled down an avenue lined with plane trees beside the railings of the park. At the far end was a bridge over an abandoned moat, and a little further away I saw a sign: 'Le Pavillon du Château. Hôtel, Spa & Restaurant', but the château itself appeared to be private. I paused and leaned on my handlebars and tried to guess what it was like inside, but this time my imagination ran as dry as the moat. This was more than a dozen years before I started writing this book, and although I had paid a fee to visit many a tourist château, I had never entered one which was someone's home. I shook my head and continued on my way, but I couldn't stop my mind trying to conjure up images of life inside the Château de Garrevaques.

I have visited dozens of countries and I am ashamed how little I know of them. I have photographed their historical highlights, tracked their wildlife and climbed their mountains, but you cannot even begin to know a place unless you know its people. Of course I have met local inhabitants during the course of my travels, but mainly those involved in the tourist industry, and I would not judge New York by its taxi drivers or London by the baristas working in its cafés. This is one of the reasons I was attracted by the idea of settling in France, of staying somewhere long enough to get under its skin and discover what it is really like.

Now for another opinion: it is almost impossible to know a people and their country unless you live there, permanently. And how can you get to know anyone unless you speak their language? When I first moved to the Lauragais, my conversational French was a work in progress and I was still attuning my ear to the accent of the south-west, but when I met an old lady at a picnic, I was competent enough to understand a good half of what she told me. Ours was a rambling conversation to which I contributed little apart from my ears. I listened carefully in between mouthfuls – hers as well as my own – and it gradually dawned on me that Madame Marguerite-Andrée Barande lived in a château which had been in her family for more than four centuries. It was in a village called Garrevaques.

'Garrevaques?' I repeated, and I remembered how I had spied on her home through the bushes like a hot and bothered Peeping Tom. Madame Barande ignored my interruption and I tried to keep up.

The original Château de Garrevaques built by the Roquefort family was a true castle, and its towers, defensive walls and ditches were designed to protect its owners and the population of the village in times of conflict. During the Wars of Religion the lord of the château was Catholic, and his castle's defences were tested to breaking point. Since my picnic with Madame Barande, I have learned a lot more about that period from contemporary sources, and I shall rely on the memoirs of Monsieur Faurin rather than my own hazy recollections to explain how everyone inside her château came to be killed.

It was May 1580 and the Protestants were trying to cut off the supply routes to Sorèze. After they had captured Lastouzeilles on 20 May, they marched a couple of kilometres down the road and laid siege to the next Catholic château on their list. They had a particular grudge against Antoine de Vesins, lord of Garrevaques: they accused him of mutilating a pastor who was returning to Puylaurens after a service during what was officially a time of peace. The poor pastor made it home alive but without his ears, and presumably short of blood.

At nine in the morning the Protestants started their bombardment, using the inevitable cannons of Puylaurens. They soon made a breach in the walls and rushed inside where they killed ten soldiers, twenty peasants and four priests. To their chagrin, the ear-lopping lord was absent, so they marched off to attack other Catholic forts nearby. Eighteen months later the Château de Garrevaques was ransacked by brigands, and when the Wars of Religion finally drew to a close, one of Madame Barande's ancestors became its lord. The château has remained in the hands of the Gineste family ever since (Madame Barande's grandfather was Count Félix de Gineste, but he and his wife produced only daughters so the family name and title disappeared).

The next catastrophe arrived two centuries later: the Revolution reached the Lauragais in 1790 and the Château de Garrevaques was burned to the ground. Reconstruction began a decade later, and the new building incorporated two of the original towers and a stone staircase which had survived the fire.

Madame Barande talked on and on, and paused occasionally to take mouthfuls of a foil-wrapped sandwich which looked surprisingly English. I lost the thread of her story long before we had reached the twenty-first century and the end of our lunch.

This picnic was part of a visit organised by a cultural association I had recently joined. Madame Barande had been a member for decades, and a few months later she invited us to tea. I immediately added my name to the list because I hoped her story would make more sense on a second hearing, and since the picnic I had read somewhere that the Germans tried to blow her up in 1944.

I arrived at Garrevaques on a grey November afternoon, this time by car, and I parked under the plane trees. Their branches were silent and bare, but I was buzzing with excitement. Today I had permission to cross the dried up moat and walk across the park to Madame Barande's front door and step right inside.

A few minutes later our group was seated in a semicircle around our hostess. She presided regally over the assembly from a red and gold brocaded chair in the centre of a room which she told us was called Le Salon Rouge. She repeated her account of the early history of the château, and I half-listened and allowed my eyes to roam. Bookshelves rose to the ceiling, filled with leather-bound tomes; the piano in the corner was fitted with brass candlesticks to light the pianist's passage across the keys; either side of the French windows, gold curtains with a red motif shone in the bright light of a crystal chandelier whose candles had long since been replaced by electric light bulbs.

'This building was ultra-modern for its day,' said Madame Barande, and I realised she had reached the start of the nineteenth century and the reconstruction of the château after the Revolution. 'There was a boiler in the *sous-sol* which provided hot water and hot air central heating. Look!' She tapped the floor with her foot. 'You can see the air grilles in the parquet. And the whole château was exquisitely decorated, particularly this room where we have twelve panels of woodblock printed wallpaper in the style "grisaille de Zuber". It is rare for the full set of panels to have survived.'

I was familiar with the word *grisaille* from watching the weather forecast. It was perfect to describe the gloomy November sky above the trees of the park, and even under the bright electric lights of the chandelier the wallpaper lived up to its name. I could make out classical scenes in shades of grey, but I was hoping for something more colourful than monochrome wallpaper, however historically significant it might be.

'Let's talk about alcohol,' she said, and I paid attention again. 'I imagine you will all have heard of *phylloxera*?'

Everyone nodded. These were the tiny sap-sucking insects that destroyed most of Europe's vineyards in the second half of the nineteenth century, accidentally brought over from the Americas by careless British botanists.

'Not only was it a catastrophe for the wine growers, but in those days there were three liqueur producers in Revel. The most famous is still made to this day: Get 27. All three were based on eau de vie which was mainly distilled from grapes, so the death of the vines threatened the future of Revel's liqueur industry. My great-grandfather, Count Henri de Gineste, spotted an opportunity. He planted sugar beet on the farms around the château and built a distillery in the pavilion where we now have the hotel.'

Before Count Henri, sugar beet was relatively unknown in the Lauragais, and using it to produce alcohol was an innovation. By the standards of its day, the distillery was a modern factory with modern production techniques, and it produced industrial quantities of alcohol. From an annual harvest of 800 tonnes of sugar beet, Count Henri produced 72,000 litres of eau de vie. The liqueur producers of Revel sent their horse-drawn carts to collect the spirit from an enormous vat beside the château.

'The drivers were often tempted to sample the product, and more than one ended up in the ditch on the return journey. No doubt they swore to the boss that they hadn't touched a drop and their mishap was due to the fumes they had inhaled while the eau de vie was being transferred from the vat to their containers.'

Madame Barande paused, and thirty people in the room laughed politely and shuffled in their seats. The room was warming up and I sensed her story was too.

'Now we come to the story of my own life and what happened when the château was occupied by the Germans in the second world war. But first, I must tell you about our gardener, Jules Gasc.'

Why? I wondered. I had already heard enough about vegetables. I wanted Madame Barande to tell us about the Germans.

'Jules had fought in the Great War and he had been injured in the head by a shell splinter. He was our gardener and he drove my father's car, the first motor car in the village. His wife Sidonie was our cook, and Jules saved the château.'

49

Resistance is Not Useless

The first three years of the second world war left the Lauragais relatively untouched. After the defeat of 1940 it found itself in Vichy France, the so-called *zone libre* governed by Marshal Pétain under the watchful eyes of the Germans. This situation changed dramatically in the space of a few days towards the end of 1942. On 8 November, American and British forces invaded France's North African colonies, governed by the Vichy regime. On 10 November, Admiral Darlan signed a peace deal with the Allies and the fighting stopped almost immediately. As soon as Hitler learned of Darlan's surrender, he ordered his troops to occupy Vichy France. They crossed the demarcation line on 11 November, and the first troops arrived in Castres, Toulouse and many other towns the following day. All of France was now under direct German control.

To start with, the occupiers were met with a mixture of feigned indifference, bitterness and open hostility, but little violence. Most people simply got on with their lives as best they could. Roger Jullia was a child at the time, and he and his sister lived at

Saint-Ferréol with their mother. His father had been a prisoner-of-war since 1940. Roger remembers that during the early days of the occupation, the only Germans he saw were the physically wounded and mentally scarred. Most of them were survivors of the Eastern Front, and several hundred were lodged in the college and hospital of Revel, and in vacant holiday homes around the lake of Saint-Ferréol. Roger's mother washed the commandant's laundry, and the commandant's orderly brought her chocolates. Roger and his sister spent a lot of time with the soldiers during the day because they gave them bread, and down on the tiny beach below the Hôtel du Lac some of the Germans taught his sister to swim, but Roger was too scared of the water. For him, the greatest excitement came from the six planes that used to fly up the valley below the dam and skim the surface of the lake making waves and throwing up spray.

Life was far less relaxed in cities such as Toulouse with its spies and informants, and the dreaded Gestapo headquarters. Small Resistance groups began to form, and at first they mainly concerned themselves with anti-German propaganda. Their activities evolved into more active resistance when the occupiers stepped up their demands for forced labour. Most of the two million French prisoners-of-war captured in 1940 had already been deported to Germany. Men such as Roger Jullia's father first worked on farms and later in munitions factories, but the German economy was still short of labour. In May 1942 they recruited 250,000 French volunteers to join the prisoners-of-war. In January 1943, they demanded a further 250,000 workers, but by now volunteers were thin on the ground, and to meet this target the French authorities created an organisation called the *Service du Travail Obligatoire* (STO), obligatory national service. Those called up faced three unwelcome choices: take the train to Germany; face up to five years in prison and a hefty fine; or go into hiding.

In March 1943 there were violent protests by families in Mazamet, a town huddled against the northern slopes of the Montagne Noire, when the train carrying 116 unwilling workers was about to leave. Similar events occurred in Albi and many other towns. Before long, a growing proportion of those called up chose the third option: some sheltered with relatives in remote parts of the countryside; others hid in the mountains and worked with the foresters; a few joined the Resistance. By June 1943 the prefect of the Tarn estimated that between 400 and 800 young men were hiding in the forests of the Montagne Noire.

Over the next few months the French authorities made increasing efforts to track down these fugitives, and in February 1944 the Germans launched their own operation in the Montagne Noire. They made several arrests in Dourgne and Arfons, and in Durfort they arrested and deported thirteen people including the mayor and the schoolteacher.

On 20 April 1944, a meeting took place in Castres between seven leaders of the local Resistance groups, and a new organisation was born: the Corps Franc de la Montagne Noire (CFMN). One of its founders was Roger Mompezat, a forty-five year old accountant from Toulouse who had been involved in the Resistance from its earliest days in 1940. He became the commandant of the CFMN, and for the next six months he kept a journal which provides much of my information about the activities of the Resistance in my neighbourhood.

Towards the end of May the various groups that would make up the CFMN converged on the Montagne Noire, initially around its highest point, the Pic de Nore. In the beginning they numbered perhaps 200 men, but within a week they were inundated with volunteers because, on 6 June 1944, the Allies landed in Normandy, and two days later the rumour circulated that the Germans were about to intern all able-bodied Frenchmen, every single one of them. The ranks of the CFMN swelled to around 800 and they turned away hundreds more because there was a limit to how many men they could train, equip and feed in the mountains.

Two weeks later the CFMN moved west and settled into three main camps on the edge of the mountain around Arfons. This was an ideal place from which to disrupt enemy communications and movements. To the north ran the Castres-Mazamet-Béziers road; to the south lay the ancient route connecting Toulouse to the Mediterranean; at the foot of the western slopes was Revel and the Lauragais. It was less than twenty kilometres from the CFMN camps to any of these points, and the mountainous terrain would give those with local knowledge a great advantage over their enemies when it came to setting an ambush or making an escape. These were some of the same considerations that had attracted one of *les Grandes Compagnies* to occupy the Castrum de Roquefort six centuries earlier.

Enthused by the Allied landings in the north and excited by talk of an imminent invasion in Provence, Mompezat and his men stepped up their activity in a bid to inflict as much damage as possible on their enemy.

At around the same time, the mayor of Garrevaques received a telegram. The German army was commandeering the château, and the mayor was instructed to evacuate all the inhabitants but none of the furniture. The German troops would move into their new quarters the next morning. The young Marguerite-Andrée was about to move house.

'At that time, my mother, my sister and I were alone in the château with a small staff,' resumed our hostess in Le Salon Rouge. 'I was seventeen, and my father, Dr Lochon, was working on the Côte d'Azur helping refugees and the Resistance. In those days, all the neighbouring farms belonged to us and we called on the farmers and the villagers to help us move our personal possessions. We loaded everything onto their carts and drove the short distance down the road to the Château de Gandels.

'The Germans gave us strict orders not to come back to our old home, so none of us knew much about life in the château after we had left. Jules carried on living next door, and he told us there were twenty or thirty soldiers stationed here, but he had no idea what they did or where they went. Most of them slept in tents in the park, but we were more worried about the ones inside.'

More recently I have come across oral and documented memories of other villagers. The troops at Garrevaques belonged to the eleventh panzer division, a unit that had fought for two-and-a-half years on the Eastern Front and was nearly wiped out in early 1944 at the Battle of the Korsun-Cherkassy Pocket. The demoralised survivors were sent to south-west France and the division was rebuilt, mainly with reserve troops, and those stationed at Garrevaques included several Poles who had been conscripted into the German army. During their stay, some of the officers fell into the habit of visiting Monsieur Guiraud's *boulangerie* to listen in secret to the BBC from London, but their presence was not without military purpose. They were in the Lauragais to control the local population, and before long something would have to be done about the Corps Franc de la Montagne Noire because being the occupier was turning into a deadly occupation.

If you take the mountain road from either Dourgne or Sorèze, you will find yourself on a twisty nine-kilometre climb which will set any cyclist's heart racing. The two roads meet at the top and then the tarmac descends a couple of kilometres into the village of Arfons where the walls of the houses are protected from the harsh winter weather by slates the size of tombstones. The main

CFMN camps lay in a triangle between Arfons, Fontbruno seven kilometres to the north-east, and La Galaube six kilometres to the south-east. The last of these locations lies a few paces from the spot where the Rigole de la Montagne draws its water from the Alzeau. These are the same forests through which Pierre-Paul Riquet tramped with his surveyors and navvies, and these are the roads where many a German soldier met his end.

I too am a frequent traveller through this area, on foot or by bicycle. Even today there are few dwellings, minimal agriculture and virtually no traffic. I rarely meet a soul, except during the hunting season, and that reminds me of an encounter I had one autumn morning during a lonely bicycle ride along the narrow lane between Arfons and La Galaube. I rounded a corner and began to speed down the gentle slope of a long straight. A man stepped into the road ahead of me and waved a hand to slow me down. He was dressed in military fatigues and he held a rifle. Irrational perhaps, but my stomach tightened and I felt a moment of sympathy for the German soldiers who travelled these same roads. I applied my brakes and spotted more armed men lying in the ditch. Reassuringly all their guns were pointing away from me and into the forest.

'We're waiting for a wild boar.' The man's voice was low. 'Be careful and please keep quiet.'

'D'accord!' I pedalled off and wondered how much noise he expected a lone cyclist to make. Or maybe he thought I would have cried out in alarm if I had spotted his motionless squad at the last minute. But what about the boar? The poor animal wouldn't even suspect the hunters were there until the first bullet ripped into its flesh. This was an ambush, and it was going to be as one-sided as many of those sprung by the CFMN.

The men in the mountains rarely had to carry out their missions on foot or by bicycle. They acquired a fleet of vehicles – either stolen, requisitioned or brought in by new recruits – and they included motorcycles, cars, vans, lorries, and even a dustcart. This turned them into a highly-mobile fighting force.

The day after the D-Day landings, the CFMN drove south and blew up the railway line from Toulouse to Carcassonne. On 9 June they killed six German soldiers in an ambush near Saissac. On 12 June they killed another fifty during a two-hour battle near Les Martyrs on the road from Carcassonne to Mazamet. On quieter days, they waited in ambush but no enemy vehicles came into sight. The CFMN suffered no casualties in these early actions, but despite capturing a few munitions they urgently needed more armaments to sustain their activities. Eventually their requests were answered, and at 13.30 on 24 June they heard the following message repeated five times on the BBC from London: '*The hermits are no longer alone.*' Presumably this meant nothing to the German officers huddled around the radio in Monsieur Guiraud's *boulangerie* at Garrevaques, but Roger Mompezat and his men understood it. At 21.00, the same message was repeated seven times and Mompezat's men exploded with joy: seven planeloads of equipment were on their way!

That night, several tonnes of weapons were dropped by parachute onto the Pic de Nore, and two more planes came back the following night. The delivery included heavy machine guns, submachine guns, rifles, grenades and explosives. Mompezat's only regret was that there were no mortars.

On 29 June, the CFMN used its new arsenal to attack a group of thirty German soldiers who were collecting firewood near Saissac. After a deadly exchange of fire, the Germans escaped, leaving behind eight dead, three prisoners, four lorries and numerous weapons. The CFMN mourned two dead and tended the minor wounds of two others.

The next day, Mompezat received an unexpected visitor: Monsieur Jalabert ran the gold mine at Salsigne, hidden in the mountains above Lastours, and some of his miners wanted to join the Resistance. Over the next few days, Mompezat welcomed eighty new recruits who had been born in North Africa. The Corps Franc de la Montagne Noire was now a truly cosmopolitan outfit: around half of them were locals from what is now Occitanie, but other contingents came from Alsace, Paris (mainly fugitive Jews), Georgia, Poland, Spain, Algeria, Morocco and Tunisia.

50

AMONG THE *MAQUISARDS*

Before my French was good enough for me to delve into the wealth of literature written by people who experienced the German occupation first-hand, my image of the French Resistance was largely formed by the television series *'Allo! Allo!'*: most of its members were young women dressed in berets and long beige coats, or were men disguised as onion sellers; idiotic British airmen hid in the wardrobe or hen coop; and the essential link with London was provided by a clandestine radio set hidden under an invalid's bed. In contrast, the Corps Franc de la Montagne Noire was a paramilitary, men-only group trained and run on military lines. Mompezat believed putting his men in uniform would instil discipline, so in early May he had sent a vehicle to Toulouse to steal a lorryload of uniforms. After that, his men were always dressed as soldiers during their operations, never in disguise. Admittedly most of them wore berets, but never beige coats. As for the other comedy clichés, the stories of Richardson and Pagels are perhaps stranger than the televised fiction.

At two-thirty in the morning on D-Day, Roger Pagels took off in his P51 Mustang from Suffolk, England and headed south with the rest of his squadron. Their mission was to patrol central France and intercept any German aircraft that tried to fly north and attack the Allies on the landing beaches of Normandy. At five-forty-five Pagels felt something hit his fuselage. His plane still responded to the controls, but the engine temperature began to climb and Pagels doubted it would get him home. Instead, he headed south, intending to land as close as possible to Spain and escape over the Pyrenees with the help of the Resistance before the Germans could catch him. With the first light of day he saw that the terrain below his damaged plane was too mountainous to risk a crash-landing, so he jumped.[50]

That same morning, Robert Jalbaud was working in his onion field near Villemagne on the southern slopes of the Montagne Noire. He saw a parachute in the sky and rushed towards the landing spot to help the man dangling beneath it. The onion farmer took the fallen pilot into the mountains and hid him in a foresters' cabin while he made contact with the Resistance, and three days later Pagels took up residence with the CFMN near Fontbruno in a village called Laprade. He was desperate to talk about his adventure, but no one spoke any English, and the only French Pagels knew was the word for 'door' because that was where he was born: La Porte, Indiana.

Richardson was the man with the radio. His real name was Henri Marcel Despaigne, but he preferred 'Harry' to 'Henri', and he was even fonder of his code name, Major Richardson. He was born in London to a French father and Belgian mother, and his fluent French soon earned him a posting to the Special Operations Executive. He had been working with the Resistance since June

---

50 Pagels knew his plan would work because three weeks before D-Day, another pilot from his squadron had returned safely to England in this way. It had taken him two months, slow by his standards, but Chuck Yeager had taken time out to teach the Resistance how to make bombs. Three years later he became the first man to break the sound barrier.

1942, and his was a nomadic existence: he and his radio never stayed in the same place for long because the Germans were trying to track him down using ground-based and airborne detection equipment. They had also put a price on his head. Richardson had been a part of the Corps Franc de la Montagne Noire since its inception, and he was itching to meet Pagels, but it was not until 13 June that he came to Laprade. Mompezat relates their first encounter.

'This meeting in a French forest between an English soldier and an American soldier could not have been more moving. Pagels turned pale, then bright red, and he started to talk without stopping and ignoring any interruptions, as if he were in a hurry to get out all the words which since several days he had been unable to speak. As he spoke one could sense an almost physical relief take hold of him; his face, full of nervous tension at first, gradually relaxed, and his eyes filled with joy and his mouth broke into a smile.'[51]

From that day on, Roger Pagels dropped his idea of escaping to Spain and instead became an active member of the CFMN. Unlike his fictional counterparts, there was nothing comical about his stay in France. Over the next three months he would be bombed by the Luftwaffe and participate in some of the most violent combats with the enemy.

France's national holiday is 14 July, Bastille Day, and it had been erased from the official calendar since the capitulation of 1940. For Roger Mompezat, it represented, '*the victory of the young French Republic over the European coalition; it was the desire of man to break free from servitude*',[52] and for him this symbolism seemed

51 Translated from: Mompezat, Roger. *Le Corps Franc de la Montagne Noire Journal de Marche (Avril – Septembre 1944).* 4th edition. Castres: Les Anciens du Corps Franc de la Montagne Noire, 1994 (pages 52-53).

52 Translated from: Mompezat, Roger (page 89).

as pertinent in 1944 as it had been in 1789. After his string of successful attacks and the recent airdrop, Mompezat vowed that 14 July 1944 would not pass unnoticed. He planned to boost the morale of his men, show his compatriots that France still had an army despite the occupation, and demonstrate to the Germans just how powerful the Resistance had become. The best place for this display of strength, he decided, was Revel.

On the morning of 14 July, Mompezat and a handful of men occupied the police stations, and outside the *mairie* they flew the *tricolore* from the flagpole by the war memorial. The comings and goings of these men in unfamiliar uniforms alerted the townsfolk that something unexpected was about to happen. By the time a convoy of twenty lorries rolled into town, an excited crowd had gathered. Four hundred soldiers formed into columns behind their standards and marched through the streets towards the *mairie*, and the message was passed from house to house: 'The French soldiers are here!' The garden of the *mairie* was too small to hold everyone and the spectators spilled out into the neighbouring streets. Mompezat recalls that at the end of the ceremony everyone sang '*La Marseillaise*', and the women cried and the men were overcome with emotion.

The crowd followed the men of the Resistance back towards their vehicles and begged them to stay for lunch, and Mompezat remembers how, '*the bronzed faces of our volunteers bore the traces of the kisses they had received from their young admirers*'.[53] He also observed that Pagels was one of the favourite targets for those lipstick lips. But it was too dangerous to linger, too dangerous for the Resistance and too dangerous for the people of Revel. The uniformed men climbed back into their lorries and trundled up the road to Dourgne where they repeated the ceremony. After that, they returned to their camps in the Montagne Noire and at two o'clock they tucked into a celebratory lunch of French fries,

53 Translated from: Mompezat, Roger (page 93).

chicken and rabbit. The day had been so well-planned that on 12 July a team had made the 150-kilometre round trip to Gaillac, running the risk of being stopped by German patrols, for the sole purpose of purchasing a generous supply of sparkling wine. At the end of the meal, the members of the Corps Franc de la Montagne Noire toasted their success in style and enjoyed a show put on by some of their more artistic members.

51
Dawn Attack

Despite their military triumphs and the symbolic statement of Bastille Day, a sense of unease had taken hold of the CFMN commanders. Instead of small cells of Resistance fighters who could carry out guerrilla actions and then melt away into the countryside, they had created an army with permanent camps and an unquenchable appetite for weapons, ammunition, food, drink and tobacco. There was enough wild game in the mountains to provide target practice and meat, but other staples such as potatoes, flour and oil were all rationed and therefore had to be raided from shops and depots on the plain. But not everything was stolen. The sparkling wine for the 14 July dinner was paid for in cash, and so were purchases of many other non-rationed goods, and the men received a small monthly salary which covered modest personal expenditure. Most of this money came from London, and the rest from bank loans granted to the CFMN thanks to the professional contacts of Mompezat and a wealthy CFMN member. Larger items were acquired in other ways. For example, on 8 June the CFMN requisitioned two cows in Saint-Amans-Soult. One – belonging to the farmer – was paid for with a numbered IOU which was reimbursed by the new government after the Liberation; the other – belonging to the boss of the local pro-Nazi militia – was taken with the help of a quick burst from a submachine gun. Petrol was another problem: it was essential to their operations, but the only way to acquire sufficient quantities was to capture or steal it.

An even more serious drawback of such a large group was its vulnerability to attack, particularly from the air. On several occasions Mompezat's men had watched reconnaissance planes flying over the Montagne Noire, and there was no doubt the Germans knew the precise location of all the Resistance camps. The enemy would not continue to ignore the CFMN indefinitely, not after the deadly ambushes of recent weeks and the provocation of Bastille Day. And indeed, alarming messages began to arrive the day after the parade in Revel. How did they reach Mompezat? With the help of a girl on a bicycle.

Some young women did more than merely kiss the heroes of the Resistance. Some, such as Adrienne Albert, played an active and dangerous role. Her family ran the Café Albert in Laprade where Mompezat, Richardson, Pagels and other CFMN leaders used to congregate in the kitchen to enjoy grandma's cooking and listen out for messages on the radio from London. It was perhaps inevitable that one day they would ask her to be a messenger. She accepted, and from then on she made a weekly journey, using combinations of bicycle, lorry and bus, to Castres and Carcassonne where she delivered letters to CFMN agents and brought back their messages.

On 15 July, one of these intelligence reports warned of impending airstrikes. Two days later, another agent announced the aerial bombardment would be supported by a powerful infantry contingent and armoured vehicles. On 18 July, agents in Toulouse and Carcassonne repeated the same warnings.

But nothing happened, so on the night of 19 July Mompezat reduced the state of alert and allowed his men a full night's rest. He authorised them to sleep inside their buildings, but to remain fully dressed and ready for action.

I have seen a photograph of the camp at La Galaube taken before the events of 20 July. It shows a cluster of wooden buildings with windows, doors and chimneys standing in a large clearing in the forest. Neither this camp nor the others had been built by the Resistance. In June 1940, the French authorities found themselves with around 100,000 twenty-year-olds on their hands who had been overlooked by the terms of the armistice. These young men had been called up, but defeat had come before they could be incorporated into the army. The minister of war decided to divide them into groups of 2,000 under the control of the military and send them off into the depths of the countryside to live a life that has been described as a cross between a soldier and a Boy Scout. Their first job was to build their own accommodation – usually from wood – and then they were tasked with carrying out public works such as road building and forestry. The CFMN took over several of these *chantiers de jeunesse* at the start of June 1944, and they made frequent raids on the organisation's depot at Labruguière, a few kilometres down the mountain from Fontbruno, to steal everything from shoes and bedding to surgical instruments and medical supplies.

These ready-made camps in the mountains came with one main disadvantage: they made easy targets from the air. Mompezat's journal entry for the 20 July starts like this: '*06.45. It was scarcely daylight. The men were rubbing their eyes before getting up. A noise in the sky grew louder and then became deafening. Eight aircraft, six Junkers 88s and two reconnaissance planes, flew over La Galaube. In the tight valleys of the Montagne Noire the roar of their engines was terrifying. The planes were at around 200 metres and there was no doubt about their identity or the intentions.*'[54]

54 Translated from: Mompezat, Roger (page 96).

Pagels was at La Galaube, the first camp to be hit, and throughout the morning the German aircraft bombed and strafed the three largest camps. La Galaube lost most of its vehicles, and four men were killed, but the camps at Riedgé and Plo del May were emptied of personnel and most of their equipment before the first bombs fell.

Between missions, the Junkers returned to their base to load more bombs. The CFMN fired back as best they could, and Mompezat claims his men either shot down or disabled three of the bombers because they emitted smoke and flames and only three aircraft returned for the last raid.

By this time, German ground troops were destroying what was left of La Galaube. The CFMN launched a counter-attack but they were facing around a thousand heavily-armed men supported by armoured cars and half-tracks, so they withdrew. Towards midday, Mompezat received reports that eighty German vehicles were rolling along the road from La Galaube to Arfons, the same road where I met my hunters. Towards midday, they were on the outskirts of Les Escudiès where they were held up for several hours in a fierce firefight until the CFMN fighters began to run out of ammunition.

Around four o'clock, two civilians demanded to speak to Mompezat in his command post near Laprade. They had spotted fifty more German lorries approaching from the south near Fontiers-Cabardès. Mompezat estimated he was now facing 1,500 German troops who had already blocked his escape routes to the west, south and east. Many of his own men were by now exhausted and the CFMN was at risk of being surrounded and wiped out.

In his journal, Mompezat observes, '*The Corps Franc had been given a precise mission to carry out guerrilla action against the enemy, but not an order to hold a fixed position at all costs*'.[55] He ordered a retreat to the Pic de Nore before it was too late, while he still

55 Translated from: Mompezat, Roger (page 118).

had most of his vehicles and material, while he still had nearly all his fighters. They had fought the enemy for twelve hours and had lost only four men, all in the first air raid on La Galaube. By Mompezat's calculation, as well as the three downed bombers, his enemies had lost two half-tracks, two armoured cars and around a hundred men.

The first CFMN vehicles left Fontbruno at five-thirty and headed down the northern slopes of the Montagne Noire to Aiguefonde, and then followed the twisty road that skirts around the foot of the mountain. When they reached Mazamet, cheering crowds lined the streets and shouted, *'Long live the maquis! Long live the Montagne Noire!'* Mompezat had feared he would find the route blocked by the town's German garrison, but inexplicably there was no sign of them. The convoy headed up the valley towards Pradelles-Cabardès and found temporary safety near the summit of the Montagne Noire.

Over the next few days, Mompezat and his lieutenants gathered intelligence and considered what to do next. The news was alarming in the extreme: German tanks had arrived in Labruguière on the north side of the mountain, more tanks were gathering in Castres, large numbers of troops had been seen around Montolieu in the south, and the Germans had established a new headquarters at Saint-Ferréol. The enemy was encircling the Montagne Noire in preparation for a decisive assault aimed at destroying the CFMN, and even if the Resistance fought off the armed attacks, they would quickly run out of food now they were surrounded. Finding three meals a day for 800 active young soldiers had been a logistical challenge at the best of times.

Mompezat still hesitated. One option was to take refuge in the Monts de Lacaune to the north, but they were so remote it would be impractical to carry out any further attacks on the enemy. On 24 July, representatives arrived from several nearby villages and begged the CFMN not to stay in the Montagne Noire. They feared brutal reprisals against their populations, and this argument proved decisive.

Reluctantly the CFMN decided to disperse. Mompezat went back to Toulouse, Pagels and Richardson hid in a shelter they had built in the forest above Mazamet, and the fortunate few who had nothing to fear from the Gestapo went home. The rest of the men split into groups of fifty or sixty and scattered themselves around the Tarn and the neighbouring departments.

The Germans maintained a heavy presence in and around the Montagne Noire and sought to track down the fugitives. During the next three weeks, a dozen members of the CFMN were killed – three times the death toll suffered on 20 July. Others were arrested and some were interrogated in a temporary prison in Revel.

On 12 August Mompezat called his commanders together for a meeting in the Café Albert at Laprade. Their short period of hiding was over and the CFMN was about to reform. In three days' time, events elsewhere would force the Germans to evacuate all of south-west France.

52

Homecoming

On 19 August, members of an unidentified Resistance group machine-gunned a German vehicle and killed two of its occupants on the road between Garrevaques and Revel. The wreck was towed back to the Château de Garrevaques, and Sergeant Büchner and Lance-Corporal Gatuska were buried in the park. The villagers feared reprisals, but by now the Germans had more pressing business to occupy them. On 15 August the Allies had begun landing 50,000 troops on the coast near Marseilles. Over the next few days, all German units in south-west France received orders to march east and re-group in the Rhône Valley. The occupiers were about to leave Garrevaques, and now is the time to rejoin Madame Barande in Le Salon Rouge for the story of her homecoming.

'Late in the afternoon [on 19 August], Jules was wandering around in the grounds between his home and the château when a German soldier stopped him. "Tomorrow, there will no longer be anyone living in the château." That was all the man said. During the evening, Jules mulled over the soldier's words. Did it mean the Germans were about to depart? Would *madame* and her children be able to return to their home?

'He was woken at five in the morning by the noise of engines. Voices shouted orders he could not understand. He tiptoed outside and watched them drive out of the grounds. He realised that the previous day the Germans had parked their vehicles in the dried-up moat. Safely hidden from Allied aircraft by the trees of the park, they had loaded all their equipment ready for a dawn departure. As soon as the noise of the engines faded away, Jules crept into the château to check everyone had gone and to see what damage had been done. He started his inspection downstairs in our kitchen, which the Germans had transformed into a workshop. He opened the door to the big pantry cupboard, which I shall show you later, and recoiled in horror. He knew about explosives from the Great War and he could see that the mine in the cupboard was set to explode in less than an hour!

'He ran out of the building and sprinted towards the *gendarmerie*. Minutes later he was back with the gendarmes. There were now forty-seven minutes left on the timer. While one of the men started to defuse the bomb in the kitchen, the others searched the rest of the château. They discovered a dozen more mines, all wired together, enough to bring down the whole building.'

Madame Barande paused for effect, and I had time to wonder if this was what they meant by working against the clock. It also crossed my mind that the departing Germans may have mined the château to avenge the two comrades they had just buried in its park.

'Shortly before six they had disarmed all the explosives. Jules had saved the château.'

There were gasps from the audience and someone started to clap. Madame Barande graciously acknowledged the applause and then she continued, because this was neither the end of her château nor the end of her story.

'What else did we find when we returned to our home? Luckily for us, the damage was not too severe. The soldiers had stolen all the mattresses and bedding, apparently to provide extra protection inside their armoured vehicles. They had carried our billiard table down from the first floor and left it under the old oak tree in the park. All our crockery lay smashed in a heap on the floor. And they had left us two copies of *"Mein Kampf"*, which I still have. By this stage of the war perhaps even they had lost faith in the words of their Führer.

'As well as turning our kitchen into a workshop, the soldiers had swapped things around on this floor as well. The room where we are sitting became their office. Through the doors behind me is my dining room, but they turned that into their kitchen. And if you look through the doors to my right, you will see portraits of my ancestors hanging on the walls. We call it Le Salon des Ancêtres and the Germans used it as their dining room. They had taken down the valuable old mirror that hangs above the fireplace and replaced it with a picture of Adolf Hitler, but my family portraits remained on the walls to keep an eye on him.'

Madame Barande rose from her seat and we followed suit. We inspected the grey wallpaper of Le Salon Rouge, and the portraits in Le Salon des Ancêtres, and then she led us down the worn steps of a spiral staircase in one of the towers. She opened the door to a walk-in cupboard in her kitchen, and I peered inside at the place where Jules had discovered the first mine.

Two days after the Allied landings of 15 August, the CFMN reassembled, not in the Montagne Noire but further east in the department of the Hérault near the village of Agoudet. A few kilometres to their south lay the town of Saint-Pons-de-Thomières where five roads meet in the valley of the Jaur.

On 20 August, the commander of the 4,000-strong garrison at Castres was persuaded to surrender without firing a shot[56], but most of the other German troops in south-west France obeyed orders and headed east to combat the Allies in Provence. Mompezat was sure some of these retreating columns would pass through Saint-Pons.

For the Germans, it was a chaotic and perilous retreat. Allied aircraft controlled the skies, and every Resistance group along the way was itching to attack them. Even former collaborators were out to save their skins by claiming a German scalp or two. Columns ranging from a couple of hundred to six thousand men criss-crossed the countryside, often seeking minor roads through the forests and mountains where they would be less visible from the air and where they had more chance of finding cover if they were attacked.

The column that passed closest to Garrevaques came from Montauban. Caught by a storm on 21 August, the troops stopped for the night at Verfeil, and the next day they marched south-east across the Lauragais through Lanta and Caraman, and by early afternoon they reached the village of Le Vaux on the Revel-Toulouse road. In the words of a report by the gendarmes of Saint-Félix-Lauragais, '*a German column of around 3,000 men... composed principally of Georgians and Mongols traversed part of the commune of Le Vaux causing panic along its route*'.

Compared with the exactions committed elsewhere by other columns, Le Vaux got off lightly: a young man was shot dead while he was tending his cows, and a doctor was wounded by several

56 A large proportion of the 'German' troops occupying south-west France were prisoners-of-war who had been captured on the Eastern front. Nearly all the garrison of Castres came from areas such as the Caucasus, Georgia, Kyrgyzstan, Mongolia and Turkestan. When they heard about the Allied landings in Provence, these men grew restless and the seventy German officers barely prevented a mutiny. Doubting his ability to control his men, the commandant was persuaded to surrender after a long night of negotiations with the Resistance.

bullets. When the soldiers had finished pillaging the houses and farms, they continued on their way towards Carcassonne with the help of twenty stolen bicycles, and two horses and a pair of mules complete with their carts. The column was destroyed somewhere on the southern slopes of the Montagne Noire.

Did the troops from Garrevaques join this column, or had they already tagged onto one of the many other columns traversing the countryside a few kilometres further north? All I can say for certain is this: at least one of the soldiers stationed at the Château de Garrevaques made it home safely, as Madame Barande would discover a quarter of a century later.

The first column to cross the CFMN's field of fire came from an unexpected direction: Narbonne, which lies to the south of Saint-Pons. Late in the afternoon of 20 July, this column was ambushed by Mompezat and his men, and early the next morning the survivors surrendered. Later the same day the CFMN attacked another column; this one came driving along the road from Mazamet and it was much stronger. Mompezat's men withdrew at dusk, and six thousand enemy troops pillaged Saint-Pons during the night and continued their journey east the next day.

On 22 August, a column of 400 men with artillery marched through the CFMN's old haunts in the Montagne Noire and descended into Mazamet. After a two hour fight with local Resistance fighters, they surrendered.

The next day, the Corps France de la Montagne Noire fought its last and bloodiest battle in the mountains to the north of Saint-Pons. An anti-aircraft battalion with nearly 2,000 men and 150 vehicles had left Toulouse on 20 August. They were attacked on the Pont Vieux in the centre of Albi, but the column forced a passage, joined up with troops from elsewhere and continued into the mountains. Twenty kilometres after Lacaune they were brought to a standstill by a broken bridge in a hamlet called Pont de la Mouline. While they tried to repair the crossing, Mompezat and 120 of his men launched an attack. The fighting lasted for several hours, but eventually the CFMN was forced to retreat carrying nine dead. Mompezat was among the fifteen injured; Pagels was unharmed. After that, they lay in wait for another week but no more columns appeared.

By now, all the towns in south-west France had been liberated, and in the middle of September the Corps Franc de la Montagne Noire broke up. Some of its younger members joined the French Forces of the Interior and fought in Alsace and Germany until the end of the conflict. Pagels and Richardson caught a plane back to England and carried on with the war. Before long, Roger Mompezat began transforming his journal into a book. It was published in 1945 and the proceeds helped fund the construction of a memorial at Fontbruno, built by eight German prisoners-of-war.

This monument lost in the forest provided me with my first introduction to the story of the Resistance in my part of France. Thirteen members of the Corps Franc de la Montagne Noire lie buried in an underground crypt, and a fourteenth tomb awaits Louis Fourcade who was last seen alive in a temporary prison in Revel on 6 August 1944. Above the fallen fighters stands a concrete signpost as tall as Riquet's obelisk at Naurouze, and its fingers direct the traveller towards the places where the men of the Resistance fought their battles. At the base of the obelisk, a bronze plaque shows the bust of Mompezat, and twelve slabs of granite record the names of all the CFMN fighters killed in action. Mompezat himself is buried in Terre-Cabade, the giant cemetery where I lost myself when I was researching the Battle of Toulouse.

If one day you choose to wander along the roads and paths between Arfons, Fontbruno, La Galaube and Laprade, you may not be as lucky as Jean-Paul Calvet who, in the 1980s, discovered three parachute containers which Mompezat and his men had failed to locate, but you will find numerous other memorials to the Corps Franc de la Montagne Noire. Granite steles mark the locations of the main camps, and plaques like the one on a corner near Les Escudiès commemorate specific feats of arms. In the tiny cemetery of Laprade, three CFMN leaders lie next to one another: Henri Sévenet, who was decapitated by shrapnel in the bombing raid on La Galaube, and two others who died more peacefully after the war but requested to be buried with their fallen comrade. In the village itself, what was once the Café Albert is easy to identify: 'Chez Leon Hotel Café Tabacs' is marked in white lettering above the front door, but today neither the Alberts nor the Leons are in business and the building is a private home.

Should you be tempted to hunt down these memorials, I shall add a word of warning for those of a nervous disposition: armed men patrol these forests looking for wild boar between the second Sunday of September and the end of January.

During the years that followed my visit to the Château de Garrevaques and its terrifying kitchen cupboard, my wife and I became acquainted with three more generations of Madame Barande's family. We met at mutual friends, or we dined or listened to concerts in Le Pavillon du Château, the beautifully restored building next door which had once housed servants, horses, carriages, Count Henri's distillery and, of course, Jules and Sidonie at the time of the German occupation. On these occasions, the stories of the château were always on my mind. My eyes would be drawn across the dried-up moat and I would spot fragments of a tower or a turret peeping through the trees like pieces in an unfinished jigsaw puzzle.

By the time I begin work on this chapter, I find that my memories of Madame Barande's tales are similarly fragmented.

Sadly, she died in 2013, and when I try to picture her sitting in Le Salon Rouge I see only her eyes. They jog my memory about something else she told me, something that happened long after the war. I telephone her daughter, Marie-Christine, and ask if I can pay her a visit to refresh my memory.

A few days later, I make myself comfortable once again in Le Salon Rouge. Marie-Christine disappears to make tea, and her husband, Claude, shows me bits and pieces he has found over the years in the moat: ammunition clips, parts of a submachine gun and other less identifiable military objects. Outside, the November evening is dark; inside, the lighting is subdued. Our voices sound unnaturally loud and they break an eerie silence.

Marie-Christine returns with a teapot. She pours me a cup and we run through the story of the château from the beginning and I note down a few points I had forgotten or misunderstood. By the time I start my second cup of tea, we arrive at the point where Jules and the gendarmes have finished defusing the mines.

Life returned to normal surprisingly quickly once the Germans had left. The family returned to its ancestral home, the young Marguerite-Andrée Lochon became Madame Barande, and before long Marie-Christine was born.

'When I was old enough to run around in the grounds of the château my grandmother used to tell me never to play in one particular corner of the garden. A pair of iron crosses marked the graves of two German soldiers. When I was twelve or thirteen, the German army came and took them away.'

These, I realise, were the graves of Sergeant Büchner and Lance-Corporal Gatuska. Between 1958 and 1961, nearly 20,000 German soldiers were disinterred all across southern France and reburied together in the cemetery at Dagneux near Lyon. Most of them were killed after the Allied landings of August 1944.

'Twenty-five years after the war, *maman* was offering bed-and-breakfast in the château. She also provided dinner, and one particular evening some of her guests were German. They were very polite, charming even, but there was one man who made her uncomfortable. They were all standing here in Le Salon Rouge enjoying an aperitif before dinner when this particular man started talking about Auvezines. "Isn't that the village up the road where the Cathars massacred the crusaders?" He knew far too much and she began to suspect he had been here before. And then, when *maman* announced dinner he marched straight into Le Salon des Ancêtres where the portrait of Hitler had watched over the German troops while they took their meals. "That's not my dining room," said *maman*. The man laughed, but if he was one of the officers billeted here in the war, why didn't he say so?

'After dinner she telephoned me and I could tell she was uneasy. "Do you want me to come over?" I asked. "Yes, I would prefer it if you were here to do breakfast." At that time I was living in Toulouse with Claude and our children, but I drove over right away and stayed the night. At breakfast, the gentleman asked me if I was the daughter. He was very polite. Later, he was standing on the front steps ready to leave and he addressed me again "Won't we be seeing your mother this morning?" "No, she is resting; she is tired after last night." He gazed far beyond the trees of the park. "Please will you tell her she still has the pretty blue eyes of her youth." '

I put down my tea and suppress a shiver. I remember with perfect clarity how Madame Barande had sat here in Le Salon Rouge and widened her eyes to show us that, even in her eighties, they still shone with a startling blue.

During winter months I make a weekly pilgrimage to Auvezines. Shortly after the village church comes into view, I turn into the lane that leads to Philippe's farm. I come in search of a large bale of hay for our hungry horses, but one day in 1944 some less-welcome visitors called in on Philippe's grandfather. They were carrying out an extraordinary mission.

It was towards the end of June and the harvest was in full swing. Joseph Séménou and his family were eating lunch. Two vehicles clattered into the farmyard making even more noise than I do with my empty trailer. A German officer jumped out.

'Come with us!'

Joseph was the mayor of Montgey, so official visits to his farm were not uncommon, but understandably each time the military took him away his family wondered if he would come back alive. What if the Resistance had made another attack? What if the Germans were rounding up hostages?

Later that afternoon Joseph returned with an astonishing tale. The Germans had not driven him far: they had stopped in the centre of Auvezines. In the presence of a colonel, he had been ordered to participate in a solemn ceremony of remembrance for some of their compatriots who had died in an ambush. But they were not stormtroopers slain by the Resistance in 1944. They were the six thousand pilgrim-crusaders slaughtered by the Cathars in 1211.

Whenever I come to buy another bale of hay, I wonder how Joseph Séménou's visitors learned about the massacre at Montgey. The stele erected by Abbé Crozes says nothing about the nationality of the victims, and I doubt the village elders would have shared their folk memories willingly. But the Germans obviously got the story from somewhere, and so did Madame Barande's revenant. Perhaps a scholarly officer had read *'The Song of the Crusade'*, or the works of Pierre des Vaux-de-Cernay and Guillaume de Puylaurens.

Joseph Séménou's tale has brought me back to the time and place where I started this journey through the Lauragais, a sort of historical homecoming that manages to be both welcoming and unsettling at one and the same time. The past, I realise, has caught up with the present, and this book is nearing the end.

I have heard seasoned authors describe a sense of relief, or even a dopamine moment, when they write those final two words. Maybe it is different with novels, because already I feel a sense of loss, all thirteen shades of the Colbert Blues rolled into one, the feeling you have when you board the plane at the end of a visit to an enchanted land. But no, I reassure myself, this adventure is not over. In the Lauragais, the past does not disappear: it merely hibernates until someone wakes it up.

If you want to discover the future all you have to do is wait, but if you want to rediscover the past you need perseverance, dedication, imagination, instinct, an obsession with detail and preferably a large dose of luck. I know plenty of people like that in the Lauragais. They are hard at work in their clubs and associations, in municipal and private archives, searching through thousands of documents on the internet, digging up archaeological sites (hopefully with permission), washing the soil from fragments of excavated pottery, analysing the colour of the paint on their shutters, poring over ancient texts in Occitan and Latin, or generally nosing around. They do so because they are passionate about their heritage and they are convinced there is much more to discover in the Lauragais. I am sure they are right, but there is no need for me to sit idly by and wait for them to unearth some new treasure. In this book, I have rarely strayed south of the Canal du Midi and I have barely touched on the centuries before anyone called this land the Lauragais.

There is much more to explore, and much more to write.

THE END

EPILOGUE

'What a coincidence you should contact me now!' says Jean-Louis Enjalbert. 'I've been meaning to get in touch with you for weeks.'

'Pourquoi?' I ask. Why would the president of the Puylaurens centre for archaeology want to speak to me? I would be surprised if he even knew of my existence before I sent him an email yesterday.

'I've discovered that towards the end of the tenth century there was a motte and bailey castle in your field. We'd like to take a look at it.'

I'm sure my heart has stopped. I always assumed the only castle in my village was the *château d'eau*. I beam at my new best friend. I almost want to kiss him.

'That's why I suggested meeting on our premises instead of answering your questions by email.'

I offer a silent prayer of thanks to Madame Colombié. Touching her cannonball has truly brought me good luck. It was she who gave me the president's email address and told me to contact him about another matter.

'I can also give you some useful reference points to help you understand the history of this area. It's a colossal task you've set yourself, trying to cover everything from palaeolithic times to the present day.'

I am in a daze. With one hand I reach for my notebook while the other fumbles with the on-off switch on my voice recorder. I need to know more about this castle right now, but Jean-Louis does not pause for breath and he is determined to start with the Stone Age. While he talks, he hands me an impressive volume the size and weight of a paving slab. I flick through its 700 pages, and an endless succession of photographs and drawings pass me by in a blur, most of them illustrating the vast number of polished stone axes that prehistoric man has left behind in the department of the Tarn.

'You see what I mean? You'll be writing an enormous book.'

I endeavour to explain that my own work will be less academic and more succinct, and that I may even sidestep the palaeolithic entirely, but Jean-Louis is unstoppable. I feel myself foundering beneath a mountain of stone axes. The door of the workshop opens and a lady walks in. The fresh air clears my head, and Jean-Louis introduces me to his vice-president, Marthe Boyer. We shake hands and exchange a few pleasantries, and then she begins to wash fragments of pottery discovered during a recent excavation. She tells me they will be deposited in one of the huge arrays of plastic boxes stacked on the floor-to-ceiling racks in the archive room next door. The boxes, Jean-Louis assures me, are stuffed full of pieces of pottery, sections of carved stone, bits of rusty metal and a miscellany of other artefacts. Would I like to see them?

My eyes dart around the room in search of an escape route. In the floor near Marthe's feet I spot a pane of glass over a black hole.

'What's down there?'

'It's a well,' says Marthe. 'Normally it's illuminated but the bulb has broken.'

'We always wondered why the linoleum in the corner was damp,' says Jean-Louis, easily diverted. 'Now we know the water is only a metre or so from the surface. We discovered the well and an eighteenth-century clay pot when we decided to tile the floor.'

I cannot restrain a smile. How appropriate for a bunch of archaeologists to discover something beneath their own feet! I tell Jean-Louis about the much deeper well in the other president's *cave*, and we discuss the height of the water table in Puylaurens and how this is one of the factors that has attracted man to settle here since the dawn of human history.

I nudge our conversation towards the original reason for my visit. I am trying to obtain a copy of a document Madame Colombié showed me. It describes two sites, one on top of the other, uncovered during the construction of the Puylaurens bypass in 2006. One was a Gallic settlement from before the birth of Christ, and the other was a cemetery used between the eighth and eleventh centuries. A study of the skeletons found in the 400 tombs confirmed what historians already knew: these people lived through far more agreeable times than their descendants who suffered all the horrors of the Four Horseman of the Apocalypse. Their bones and teeth showed no signs of famine or widespread disease, and although there were a few fractured bones, these were consistent with the hazards of everyday life rather than the ravages of war.

Jean-Louis finds his copy of the booklet and tells me it is out of print. I study the photographs of the graves and my thoughts flit back to the start of our conversation. How could I allow myself to be diverted from what may be my biggest scoop? Never mind the other half of the Lauragais; I haven't finished with the bit on my own doorstep.

'These tombs must date from the same period as the château in my field.'

'More or less,' says Jean-Louis. 'Towards the end of the tenth century various minor lords installed themselves in the countryside all around Puylaurens. They built motte and bailey castles, usually of wood. There's a good depiction of one in the Bayeux Tapestry.'

He shuffles through a pile of papers and finds an image taken from the famous Norman embroidery (technically speaking, pedants will tell you, it is not a tapestry). A flight of steps leads up what looks like an artificial mound, or motte, and a wooden palisade encircles a simple tower at the top. This type of castle had only one tower, and I make a mental note to use this in evidence next time I find myself debating the meaning of the word 'château'.

'We know of a dozen sites like this around Puylaurens,' says Marthe. 'I've just finished surveying one by the road to Péchaudier.'

'The local topography meant most of them could be built on natural mounds,' adds Jean-Louis. 'Like the one in your field.'

My head starts to spin again. I nearly drop my voice recorder. I am falling into another adventure almost as *rocambolesque* as the Château de Montgey. Can there really be the remains of a thousand-year-old castle in my own field?

'So what should I do?' I ask. 'Start digging?'

'No, you mustn't do that, you'll disturb the site! We cannot do anything without authorisation from the Regional Director of Cultural Affairs. It's not like in England where anyone can wander around with a metal detector and start excavating the past.'

I take another look at the illustration from the Bayeux Tapestry. I remember reading that its blue threads were dyed with *pastel*, but the tapestry is too old for the colour to have come from the Lauragais. I decipher the word 'REDNES' embroidered around the palisade (now the city of Rennes), and a couple of animals confront each other on the lower slopes of the motte. I look more closely and decide a dog is baiting a bear. They make me think of the horses in my own field and suddenly my excitement begins to unravel. I have missed something, a catastrophic and insurmountable problem that should have been blindingly obvious from the start.

'I live at the bottom of the hill! Surely the château would have been on top of Montlong!'

Marthe stops washing her pottery and there is a moment of silence. Jean-Louis stares at me and his expression is as horrified as my own.

'You don't live at the top?'

'No!'

'When I read your email and saw the name of your house, I was sure the top of Montlong must belong to you.'

We consult a map and I tell him I know all three owners of the area where 'my château', as I am determined to call it, once stood. I offer to make the introductions and I console myself with the thought that, although the site may not be in my own field, I can see it from my kitchen window.

'I still don't understand why you think there used to be a château up there' I say. 'I've often walked over Montlong and I haven't noticed a thing.'

'A few months ago I started some research on another château for the Department of Cultural Affairs. I came across what we call a *reconnaissance féodale* for Montlong. That was where a minor lord swore an oath of loyalty to a more powerful noble. At first, I thought the act referred to a Montlong near Semalens, but when I translated the documents the facts didn't match up. Then I realised it must be the one above your village.'

I picture the view from my kitchen sink. The land rises steeply, and at the highest point the soil is meagre and sections of bare rock hide among ragged bushes of broom. In spring and summer their bright yellow flowers glow in the light of the setting sun. The panorama from the top is just as stunning as those from Puylaurens, Montgey, Saint-Félix, or any of the other promontories of the Lauragais. It was an obvious place to build a château.

'There probably won't be much there,' says Jean-Louis. 'These tiny châteaux disappeared quickly as soon as stronger lords exerted their power, but it will be interesting to carry out a study. We may be able to date the site from fragments of pottery, and if it's as rocky as you say, some of it may have been built of stone. That was often the case in the north of the Tarn.'

'You mean there may be the foundations of a stone keep, like at the Castlar de Durfort?'

'Exactly! But it will take a year or so to obtain permission to start work.'

A year or so? I tell myself I shall have to be patient, but in the meantime other vegetation in our garden risks meeting the same fate as our *pastel* plants. It is already difficult enough to concentrate when I sit on our lawnmower, distracted as I am by our views of Montgey and Auvezines, Roquefort and Revel, the Montagne Noire and the Pyrenees. Now my eyes will be glued to the top of Montlong as well.

We continue chatting about the history of Puylaurens and its surroundings, and I even risk a visit to the archive room. Eventually, I thank Jean-Louis and Marthe for their help and step out into the street. My mind continues to be absorbed by the past, but my instinct guides me back up the hill to Les Ravelins where I have left my car.

I lean on the railings and look south. It feels as if ten years have slipped by since I stood on this spot and filled my mouth with Medieval Cobblestone and dreamed of writing this book. Back then, I told myself if you scratch below the surface, the soil of the Lauragais is steeped in history and soaked in blood. But I never expected to find a thousand-year-old castle on my own doorstep.

Colin Duncan Taylor, The Lauragais, 2018.

A Note From the Author

Thank you for reading '*Lauragais: Steeped in History, Soaked in Blood*'. If you are among those who do not already know the Lauragais, perhaps it will encourage you to jump on the next plane to Carcassonne or Toulouse. In the meantime, if you would like to take a brief audiovisual tour of the Lauragais, or let me know what you thought of my book, please visit my website:

www.colinduncantaylor.com

Lauragais Timeline

118 BCE	The Romans build the Via Aquitania through the Lauragais to connect Narbonne and Bordeaux.
407 CE	Toulouse besieged by the Vandals.
418	The Visigoths make Toulouse their capital.
507	Clovis, king of the Francs, defeats the Visigoths at Vouillé and Toulouse loses its importance.
721	The Moors march through the Lauragais and besiege Toulouse.
c.1150	First recorded mention of the name 'Lauragais'.
c.1160	First recorded use of the term 'Cathar'.
1135-65	Birth of Raimon de Miraval.
1209	Start of the Albigensian Crusade (July). Fall of Carcassonne (August). Simon de Montfort appointed military leader of the crusade (August).
1211	Surrender of Cabaret and destruction of Miraval (March). Battle of Montgey (April). Siege of Lavaur (May).
1213	Raimon de Miraval writes his last composition. Battle of Muret.
1216-29	Death of Raimon de Miraval.
1218	Death of Simon de Montfort
1222	Raymond VI succeeded by his son Raymond VII as Count of Toulouse. Founding of the first bastide (now Cordes-sur-Ciel).
1224	End of the first part of the Albigensian Crusade.
1226	Louis VIII relaunches the Albigensian Crusade.
1229	Founding of the Inquisition in Toulouse.
1244	Cathar martyrs throw themselves in the flames at Montségur.

1302-05	Dante classifies European languages by their word for 'yes'.
1323	Founding of the Academy of the Floral Games in Toulouse.
1337	Start of the Hundred Years' War.
1342	Founding of Revel.
1348	The Black Death reaches its peak in the Lauragais.
1355	The *chevauchée* of the Black Prince through the Lauragais.
1356	Battle of Poitiers and capture of Jean le Bon.
c.1370	Castrum de Roquefort occupied by one of *les grandes compagnies*.
1381	Gaston Phoebus wins the Battle of Montègut-Lauragais.
1416	Destruction of the Castrum de Roquefort.
1453	End of the Hundred Years' War.
1463	The great fire of Toulouse.
1460-1560	The golden age of *pastel*.
1504	Work starts on the Hôtel de Bernuy in Toulouse.
1517	Martin Luther publishes his disputation on the power of indulgences.
1519	Catherine de Medici becomes Countess of the Lauragais.
1539	Edict of Villers-Cotterêts imposes the use of French for official business throughout the kingdom.
1555	Work starts on the Hôtel d'Assézat in Toulouse.
1556	Jean de Bernuy killed by a bull.
1562	Start of the Wars of Religion. Protestants try to take over Toulouse but are forced to flee.
1563	End of the first War of Religion.
1567	Start of the second War of Religion.

1568	End of the second War of Religion (March). Puylaurens besieged by 6,000 Catholic troops (April). Start of the third War of Religion (August).
1570	End of the third War of Religion.
1572	Saint Bartholomew's Day massacre in Paris.
1572-77	Fourth, fifth and sixth Wars of Religion.
1579	Start of the seventh War of Religion.
1580	Siege of Sorèze Château de Garrevaques captured by the Protestants. End of the seventh War of Religion.
1584	The Protestant Henri de Navarre becomes heir to the throne of France.
1585	Henri de Navarre visits Puylaurens. Start of the eighth War of Religion (and the War of the Three Henrys).
1591	The Catholic League calls in Spanish troops to occupy the Lauragais.
1594	Henri de Navarre crowned Henri IV of France.
1598	Edict of Nantes signals the official end of the Wars of Religion.
1610	Henri IV assassinated and religious tensions resurge.
1621	Protestant rebellion in the Lauragais.
1622	Caraman and Cuq-Toulza captured by the Catholics.
1623	The ramparts of Puylaurens are demolished on the orders of Louis XIII.
1659	Louis XIV decrees the transfer of the Protestant academy of Montauban to Puylaurens.
1662	Pierre-Paul Riquet puts forward his plans for building the Canal du Midi.
1666	Louis XIV approves construction of the Canal du Midi.
1667	Work starts on the Canal du Midi and its supply network.
1669	Colbert introduces regulations covering all the colours used by the textile industry.

1680	Death of Pierre-Paul Riquet.
1682	Official opening of the Canal du Midi.
1685	Four infantry companies demolish the temple of Puylaurens (October). Louis XIV revokes the Edict of Nantes (October). Vauban begins his programme of improvement works for the Canal du Midi (December).
1787	Thomas Jefferson travels the length of the Canal du Midi.
1790	Château de Garrevaques destroyed by revolutionaries.
1794	Abbé Grégoire presents his paper calling for the elimination of all regional dialects and languages including Occitan.
1814	Napoleon's first abdication. Battle of Toulouse.
1827	Official opening of Riquet's memorial at Naurouze.
1942	German occupation of Vichy France, including the Lauragais.
1944	Creation of the Corps Franc de la Montagne Noire (CFMN) (April). D-Day landings (June). Air and ground attacks on CFMN bases (July). Allied landings in Provence and withdrawal of German troops from south-west France (August). Disbandment of the CFMN (September).
1958-61	Reburial of 20,000 German war dead at Dagneux military cemetery, including those buried at Garrevaques.
1990s	Rebirth of *pastel* dyeing and the development of a new extraction process.

Bibliography

It would be impractical to list all the documents and websites I have consulted while researching this book. The main published sources I used are noted below, arranged by section. Most of them exist only in French, and I am guilty of all translations from French to English except those taken from Richard Barber's book, *'The Life and Campaigns of the Black Prince'*. Other sources included: information obtained during my meetings and interviews with various people, principally those I thank in the 'Acknowledgements' section; unpublished notes and documents provided to me by local historians; my own notes taken during conferences and talks given by local historians; the Museum of the Canal du Midi at Saint-Ferréol and the Museum of Protestantism at Ferrières.

Those Murderous Cathars

Bouyssou, Pierre. *Histoire de Montgey: Tome 1, Le Temps des Roquefort.* Biarritz: Atlantica, 2009.

Puylaurens, Guillaume de. *Chronique de Maître Guillaume de Puylaurens sur la Guerre des Albigeois (1202-1272).* Translated into French by Charles Lagarde. Béziers : Bénézech-Roch, 1864. Retrieved online from Google Books.

Roquebert, Michel. *Histoire des Cathares.* Paris: Editions Perrin, 1999.

Roquebert, Michel. *Simon de Montfort.* Rev. ed. Paris: Editions

Perrin, 2010.

Serrus, Georges. *The Land of the Cathars*. Portet-sur-Garonne: Editions Loubatières, 1994.

Vaux-de-Cernay, Pierre des. *Histoire de l'hérésie des Albigeois et de la sainte guerre contre eux (de l'an 1203 à l'an 1218).* Translated into French by François Guizot. Paris: J-L-J Brière Libraire, 1824. Retrieved online from: gallica.bnf.fr.

On the Trail of a Troubadour

Chabbert, Raymond. *Lire & écrire l'Occitan*. Valence d'Albigeois: Vent Terral, 2005.

Grégoire, Henri. *Rapport sur la nécessité et les moyens d'anéantir le patois, et d'universaliser l'usage de la langue française*. Paris : Convention Nationale, 1794. Retrieved online from : fr.wikisource.org.

Meyer, Paul (editor). *La Chanson de la Croisade Contre les Albigeois commencé par Guillaume de Tudèle et continué par un poète anonyme. Tome Second.* Paris : Librairie Renouard, 1879. Retrieved online from: gallica.bnf.fr.

Nelli, René. *Raimon de Miraval : Du jeu subtil à l'amour fou.* Lagrasse: Editions Verdier, 1979.

Roquebert, Michel. *Simon de Montfort*. Rev. ed. Paris: Editions Perrin, 2010.

Thomas, James (editor). *Grains of Gold: An Anthology of Occitan Literature.* London: Francis Boutle Publishers, 2015.

Of Bastides and Adulterers

Batignes, René, Albin Bousquet, Jean-Paul Calvet, Francis Costes, Jean-Pierre Gaubert, Michele Guigou, Yumiko Mikuriya, Francis Pujol and Bernard Velay. *Le Beffroi de Revel : pôle économique ouvert au marché depuis des siècles.* Revel: Société d'Histoire de Revel Saint-Ferréol, 2015.

Calvet, Jean-Paul. *Les Remparts et la Présence Militaire dans la bastide de Revel.* Les Cahiers de l'Histoire de Revel, No. 16, janvier 2011.

Doumerc, Gustave. *Histoire de Revel en Lauragais.* Albi: Ateliers Professional de l'OSJ, 1976.

A Hundred Years of Misery

Albarel, Jacques. *Roquefort Les Cammazes.* Brassac : Frererie de Ferrières, 1983.

Barber, Richard. *The Life and Campaigns of the Black Prince from contemporary letters, diaries and chronicles, including Chandos Herald's 'Life of the Black Prince'.* Rev. ed. Woodbridge: The Boydell Press, 1986.

Becker, William (editor). *Durfort Musée du Cuivre.* Revel: Collection Lauragais-Patrimoine, 2011.

Buchon, Jean-Alexandre (editor). *Les Chroniques de Sire Jean Froissart, Tome Premier.* Paris: A Desrez, 1835. Retrieved online from Google Books.

Clos, Jean-Antoine. *Notice historique sur Sorèze et ses environs.* Rev. ed. 1845. Reprint. Nîmes: Editions Lacour, 2003.

Doumerc, Gustave. *Histoire de Revel en Lauragais.* Albi: Ateliers Professional de l'OSJ, 1976.

Vidaillet, Frédéric and Bernard Pousthomis. *Une Maison du castrum de Durfort (Tarn): le batiment 9.* Archéologie du Midi Médiéval Supplément, 1996.

In Search of *Pastel*

Banessy, Sandrina. *Le pastel en pays d'oc.* Labège: Tourisme Médias Editions, 2002.

Brumont, Francis. *La commercialisation du pastel toulousain (1350-1600).* Annales du Midi: revue archéologique, historique et philologique de la France méridionale, Année 1994, Volume 106 Numéro 205. Retrieved online from: persée.fr.

Brumont, Francis. *Pierre Assézat, un marchand de son siècle.* Article published in *L'hôtel Assézat*, edited by Louis Peyrusse and Bruno Tollon. Toulouse: Association des Amis de l'hôtel Assézat, 2002.

Brumont, Francis. *Politique, religion et affaires: Pierre Assézat (vers 1515-1581).* Annales de Bretagne et des Pays de l'Ouest, tome 112, n° 4, 2005.

Casado Alonso, Hilario. *Finance et commerce international au milieu du XVIeme siècle : la compagnie des Bernuy.* Annales du Midi, Année 1991, Volume 103, numéro 195. Retrieved online from: persée.fr.

Caster, Gilles. *Les Routes de Cocagne.* Toulouse: Editions Privat, 1998.

Giobert, Giovanni Antonio. *Traité sur le Pastel et l'Extraction de son Indigo.* Paris: Imprimerie Impériale, 1813. Retrieved online from: gallica.bnf.fr.

Thibaudeau, Antoine Clair. *Le consulat et l'empire, ou histoire de la France et de Napoléon Bonaparte, de 1799 à 1815, Volume VII.* Paris: Jules Renouard Libraire, 1835. Retrieved online from Google Books.

Youngs Jnr, Frederic A. *The Proclamations of the Tudor Queens.* Cambridge: Cambridge University Press, 1976. Retrieved online from Google Books.

A Question of Religion

Alayrac, Edmond. *Puylaurens d'Hier: Regards sur le Passé.* Albi: Imprimerie Coopérative du Sud-Ouest, 1991.

Clos, Jean-Antoine. *Notice historique sur Sorèze et ses environs.* Rev. ed. 1845. Reprint. Nîmes: Editions Lacour, 2003.

Doumerc, Gustave. *Histoire de Revel en Lauragais.* Albi: Ateliers Professional de l'OSJ, 1976.

Laux, Christian. *D'où vient donc Marianne ?* Annales historiques de la Révolution française, Année 1983, Volume 254, Numéro 1.

Pradel, Charles (editor). *Journal de Faurin sur les guerres de Castres.* 1878. Reprint. Nîmes: Editions Lacour, 2002.

Pradel, Charles. *Notes Historiques sur la Ville de Puylaurens.* 1907. Reprint & rev. ed. Puylaurens: Centre Archéologique du Puylaurentais, 2012.

Pradel, Charles (editor). *Mémoires de Jacques Gaches sur Les Guerres de Religion à Castres et dans le Languedoc 1555-1610.* Paris: Librairie Sandoz et Fischbacher, 1879. Retrieved online from: https// archive.org.

Richard, Bernard. (2014) *Marianne, représentation féminine de la République en France.* Retrieved online from: bernard-richard-histoire.com.

From the Bottom of a Lake

Adgé, Michel. *Les premiers états du barrage de Saint-Ferréol.* Les Cahiers de l'Histoire de Revel, No. 7, 2001.

Ariès, Lucien. *Les pierres de Naurouze, de la légende à l'histoire.* Couleurs Lauragais, Numéro 112, mai 2009.

Béa, Adeline, Jérôme Bonhôte, Emilie Collet, Claire Fournier, Axelle Raynaud, Patrick Roques, Sonia Servant and Samuel Vannier. *Aux Sources du Canal du Midi.* Second edition, Toulouse: Conseil Régional Midi-Pyrenées, 2013.

Chatillon, Alain. *Rapport de mission : une ambition légitime pour le canal du Midi et le canal des Deux Mers.* Report produced by Senator Chatillon for Prime Minister Fillon, February 2012.

Clos, Jean-Antoine. *Notice historique sur Sorèze et ses environs.* Rev. ed. 1845. Reprint. Nîmes: Editions Lacour, 2003.

Crevon, Gérard. *La rigole de la montagne (Canal du Midi) : un traçage difficile.* Les Cahiers de l'Histoire de Revel, No. 18, 2013.

Doumerc, Gustave. *Histoire de Revel en Lauragais.* Albi: Ateliers Professional de l'OSJ, 1976.

Jefferson, Thomas. *Notes of a Tour into the Southern Parts of France, &c., 3 March–10 June 1787.* Retrieved from: Founders Online, National Archives, last modified April 12, 2018, http://founders.archives.gov/documents/Jefferson/01-11-02-0389. [Original source: The Papers of Thomas Jefferson, vol. 11, 1 January–6 August 1787, ed. Julian P. Boyd. Princeton: Princeton University Press, 1955, pp. 415–464.]

Jefferson, Thomas. *From Thomas Jefferson to William Short, 27 March 1787.* Retrieved from: Founders Online, National Archives, last modified April 12, 2018, http://founders.archives.gov/documents/Jefferson/01-11-02-0242. [Original source: The Papers of Thomas Jefferson, vol. 11, 1 January–6 August 1787, ed. Julian P. Boyd. Princeton: Princeton University Press, 1955, pp. 246–248.]

Jefferson, Thomas. *From Thomas Jefferson to Martha Jefferson, 21 May 1787.* Retrieved from: Founders Online, National Archives, last modified April 12, 2018, http://founders.archives.gov/documents/Jefferson/01-11-02-0350. [Original source: The Papers of Thomas Jefferson, vol. 11, 1 January–6 August 1787, ed. Julian P. Boyd. Princeton: Princeton University Press, 1955, pp. 369–370.]

McGrath Morris, James and Persephone Weene (editors). *Thomas Jefferson's European Travel Diaries: Jefferson's own account of his journeys through the countryside and wine regions of the Continent, 1787-1788.* Ithaca, New York: Isidore Stephanus Sons Publishing, 1987.

The English Cemetery

Beamish, North Ludlow. *History of the King's German Legion Volume II.* London: Thomas and William Boone, 1837. Retrieved online from Google Books.

Frexinos, Jacques. Toulouse: *Histoire panoramique des origines à la*

*Révolution.*Supplément hors abonnement à *l'Auta*. Toulouse : Les Toulousains de Toulouse et Amis du Vieux Toulouse, 2017.

Geschwind, Henri and François de Gélis. *La Bataille de Toulouse (10 avril 1814) d'après les documents les plus récents.* 1914. Reprint. Cresse: Editions des Régionalismes, 2015.

Gurwood, John. *The Dispatches of Field Marshal the Duke of Wellington during his various campaigns in India, Denmark, Portugal, Spain, The Low Countries, and France. Volume the Seventh.* London: William Clowes and Sons, 1845. Retrieved online from Google Books.

Hélie, Georges (editor, translator). *Journal de Lieutenant Woodberry: Campagnes de Portugal et d'Espagne, de France, de Belgique et de France (1813-1815).* Paris: Librairie Plon, 1896. Retrieved online from: https://archive.org..

Lapène, Edouard. *Evènements Militaires devant Toulouse en 1814.* Paris: Chez Ridan, 1822. Retrieved online from Google Books.

Lapène, Edouard. *Campagne de 1813 et de 1814 sur l'Ebre, les Pyrénées et la Garonne.* Paris: Chez Ridan, 1823. Retrieved online from Google Books.

Montbel, Guy de. *1787-1861, Souvenirs du comte de Montbel.* Paris: Plon-Nourrit, 1913. Retrieved online from : gallica.bnf.fr.

Odol, Jean. *La Bataille de Toulouse et l'Occupation Anglaise d'Ayguesvives.* Unpublished typescript provided to me by the author, dated 1978.

Oman, Charles. *A History of the Peninsular War, Volume VII.* Oxford: The Clarendon Press, 1930. Retrieved online from: https//archive.org.

Rousselet De Mortarieu, Yvan. *La rencontre de Ste Colombe.* Bulletin de l'Association De Recherches Baziégeoise: Racines, Environnement, Tome 25, 2014.

Vidal de Lablache, Joseph. *L'évacuation de l'Espagne et l'invasion dans le Midi (juin 1813-avril 1814). Tome II.* Paris: Berger-Levrault, 1913. Retrieved online from gallica.bnf.fr.

A Deadly Occupation

Archives Départementales du Tarn, Albi. *Soldats allemands tués et enterrés dans le département.* Dossier 506 W 230.

Archives Départementales du Tarn, Albi. *Combats de la Libération.* Dossier 506 W 285.

Damnés, René. *La véritable histoire de la colonne allemande qui traversa notre Lauragais les 21 et 22 août 1944.* Les Cahiers de l'Histoire de Revel, No. 18, 2012.

Jullia, Roger. *Témoignage d'enfant sur la guerre de 1939-1945 à Saint-Ferréol.* Les Cahiers de l'Histoire de Revel, No. 19, 2010.

Mompezat, Roger. *Le Corps Franc de la Montagne Noire Journal de Marche (Avril – Septembre 1944).* 4th edition. Castres: Les Anciens du Corps Franc de la Montagne Noire, 1994.

Périlhou, Sylvie. *Le Corps Franc de la Montagne Noire.* Revel: Société d'Histoire de Revel Saint-Ferréol, 2014.

Séménou, Léo. *Garrevaques et Gandels en Pays Lauragais.* Toulouse: Impression Corep de Toulouse, 2007.

ACKNOWLEDGEMENTS

The people who helped me discover and research the stories in this book are not professional historians, but they are all passionate about the past and many were born here. Most of them have devoted years of their lives to the history of the Lauragais, and without their hard work I could not have written this book.

First, *in memoriam*: both Lucette Colombié and Claude Combes sadly passed away before publication. Thank you, Lucette, for allowing me to borrow all those notes you made over many decades about the history of Puylaurens. Thank you, Claude, for helping me with the history of the Château de Garrevaques, and for a birthday party I shall never forget.

Second, I would like to thank the following people (in alphabetical order) who also helped me with my research, sometimes unknowingly: Laurent Alibert, Bruno Berthoumieux, Gilles Berthoumieux, Jean-Pierre Bonnet, Pierre Bouyssou, Sophie Bouyssou, Marthe Boyer, Francis Brumont, Pierre-Alain Buvry, Jean-Paul Calvet, Marie-Christine Combes, Jean-Louis Enjalbert, Jean Fabre de Massaguel, Jean-Louis Fragasso, Denise Lambert, Anny Lapeyre, Marie-Laure Mézières, Yvan Rousselet De Mortarieu, David Santandreu, Jean-Pierre Suzzoni.

Third, I would like to thank my wife, Donna, and my father, Alan, for providing invaluable comments on my manuscript. I also owe a debt of gratitude to Sam Jordison at The Writers' Workshop for his editorial advice, and to all the team at Matador Books for helping bring my project to fruition.

Finally, I would like to thank two organisations. The Revel branch of Accueil des Villes Françaises (AVF) is an association that aims to help newcomers of any nationality to settle in a new town. It was through AVF that I first met people like Jean-Paul Calvet and the owners of the châteaux at Montgey and Garrevaques; it was with AVF that I first visited places such as the Tour de Roquefort and the English Cemetery at Saint-Félix. Second, the Société d'Histoire de Revel Saint-Ferréol: its long list of publications and extensive website provided the starting point for much of my desk-based research, and these resources helped me enormously when it came to identifying and tracking down the original texts and source documents that allowed me to complete this project.